SERENDIPITY ROAD

SERENDIPITY ROAD

CATHERINE DEVRYE

McArthur & Company
Toronto

First published in Canada in 2007 by
McArthur & Company
322 King St. West, Suite 402
Toronto, ON
M5V 1J2
www.mcarthur-co.com

Library and Archives Canada Cataloguing in Publication

DeVrye, Catherine   Serendipity Road : a memoir /
Catherine DeVrye.

First published 2005 under title Who says I can"t?
ISBN 978-1-55278-645-1

1. DeVrye, Catherine. 2. Businesswomen—Australia—Biography.
3. Women executives—Australia—Biography. 4. Adoptees—Canada—
Biography. 5. Motivational speakers—Biography. I. Title.
HC602.5.D49A3 2007   338.092   C2007-902013-5

Printed in Canada by Webcom

The publisher would like to acknowledge the financial support of
the Government of Canada through the Book Publishing Industry
Development Program (BPIDP) and the Canada Council for
our publishing activities. The publisher further wishes to
acknowledge the financial support of the Ontario Arts Council
for our publishing program.

10 9 8 7 6 5 4 3 2 1

CONTENTS

For Mum, Dad and Granddad . . . and anyone
who has adopted a child, a country or an optimistic outlook

PRELUDE

What a good thing it would be to be liberated from any filial complex or be an orphan.   — Miles Franklin

 By the time I was twenty-two, I had been orphaned twice. Admittedly, somewhat melodramatic, this statement is technically true.

It feels a little strange to now write about events in my life that even close friends were previously unaware of. I suppose I never told anyone because I wanted neither their sympathy nor their curiosity. Or maybe I was simply afraid that the facts would make me seem even more different than I already felt.

In March 1994, I was invited to tell my story at an International Women's Day function in Melbourne. I struggled nervously to prepare my speech, and shared my life's journey as best I could. I was staggered by the response. Many commented that I'd changed their life that day. That certainly was not my intention.

Those are amazing circumstances and coincidences. You ought to write a book.

How often had friends said likewise? But, for the life of me, I couldn't comprehend why anyone would be interested to read about my life.

Then again, the comments of others had prompted me to pen best-selling business books. So I now offer my personal story and hope it may help others clear hurdles of aloneness, identity and grief far faster, and more elegantly, than I did. It's by far the toughest thesis I've tackled. But if sharing my sojourn of loss and renewal might lighten someone else's load, then maybe it's time to tie together the loose threads of narrative previously confined to the private pages of the diary that I've kept almost every night since I was sixteen.

This story isn't just about me. It's about all of us, because trauma strikes each of us sooner or later. In my case, it happened to be sooner – and if I'd known about some of the setbacks in advance, I'd have said I couldn't cope. But what I have learnt is that we *do* cope.

I was just an ordinary person, forced to face extraordinary circumstances relatively early in life. Only a minority learn from other people's mistakes. The majority of us are those "other" people. Often, we are so paralyzed by events that we can see no light at the end of the tunnel – or fear it's a train coming the other way. Blinded to any potential opportunities, our self-confidence disappears in the shadows of sorrow and self-pity.

Although we can't always control events in our lives, we can always control how we *react* to those events. It is our choice alone whether we adopt a positive or negative attitude in the face of adversity – to be victims or victors of those potholes in the road. If we approach bleak situations with a lightness of heart and spirit, stumbling blocks can become stepping stones.

If you've ever felt alone, that no-one understands or you don't quite fit in, be assured that you're not on your own.

Others share similar inner insecurities and fears. In unearthing the life-affirming aspects of seemingly despairing situations, we become empowered to take personal responsibility for our lives.

This book is written from the heart. Admittedly, the heart was sometimes on the sleeve in early drafts, when I shed enough tears to be convinced of a market for waterproof computer keyboards!

Everything isn't always as rosy as it might appear on the surface. It's been tough to write my story and perhaps I've dug up emotional artifacts best left buried in the archives of time. Maybe I'll look back with regret on these words because my views and values will surely change over the next twenty years, just as they have over the course of my life so far. That's the risk I take.

Conceived before the advent of the pill, I came into the world as an illegitimate baby, surrounded by shame in that era. Maybe it wasn't exactly what one would call a great start in the game of life but I'm grateful that it made me a player. My birth mother gave me the chance of a lifetime in a lifetime of chance. Luck was with me from the start and life has since offered more success and joy than I ever dreamed possible. It's there for us all so that's why I'm now happy to tell anyone who's interested. But there was a time when I wouldn't have told anyone at all . . .

1

SEARCHING

 **Tokyo, 28 May 1986**
Name? Address? Blood type?
I answered their questions as best I could. I was ill plus sick and tired of communicating via interpreters. My answers had been impatient and automatic until I heard:

Next of kin?

I gazed up at the concerned faces of these Japanese nurses. *Next of kin?* Something tore inside me. "None," I replied, fighting back tears because all I wanted was my mother. I wanted to feel her arms around me. I wanted to hear her say that everything would be all right. But that was impossible. She couldn't comfort me now. Even less than I could her when I'd helplessly watched her release her hold on life thirteen years before, only a year after my father had also died of cancer in hospital rooms not dissimilar to this one – but on the other side of the world. Now as I lay between starched white sheets, it felt as if their deaths had happened only yesterday.

No next of kin. The medicos scrawled on their clipboard notes, or perhaps simply ticked a box. The clinical questioning continued. "Any hereditary diseases?" the interpreter asked.

I looked into the dark eyes of these people crowded around my bed – kind strangers whose fathers may have fought against my own during World War II. I bit my lower lip and again hesitated to answer. They had a right to ask. They needed some clues to work out what was wrong with me. A heavy silence lingered in the sterile hospital air as my mind swam and I managed to whisper, "I don't know."

They looked at each other, surprise registering on their faces. "What do you mean, *you don't know?*"

"I was . . . I was . . . adopted."

The shame of that stigma, especially in Japan. I never thought I'd have to tell anyone again. There was never any need to.

They sucked air between their teeth, as is custom. Then silence again. Something else was written down.

The origin of my illness remained a mystery. The medicos left and I sobbed quietly into my pillow. I felt vulnerable and disconnected from anything familiar in a strange country. It was not exactly what one would expect of a so-called tough IBM executive but I couldn't have cared less. At that moment in the Japanese hospital, I was alone as I had been in the beginning. Except I don't remember the beginning – who does? We can only rely on other people's memories of those early days.

Yet I do remember 1973, as if it were yesterday – sitting in a bank vault, looking down at an assortment of my parents' legal documents – those neatly typed certificates, proof of their existences. I needed my mother's birth certificate before I could obtain her death certificate to arrange her funeral. In the safety deposit box, I found a document on Department of Public Welfare letterhead, dated 26 February 1951. Another doctor had once written the following comments, as matter-of-factly as a registration certificate for a car:

- Born – September 29, 1950 at Calgary General Hospital
- Weight at birth – 7 pounds 5 ounces

- Current weight – 13 pounds 4 ounces [rather underweight for a five-month-old baby]
- Current height – 25 inches
- Heart, eyes, ears, nose, blood count, abdomen and genitals – normal
- Adenoids and mentality – apparently normal

The baby described was me. How dare they describe my now Mensa-rated intelligence as only "apparently" normal – although at that moment, I was a mental basket case.

I already knew that my folks had been subjected to a rigorous adoption process when they requested a child of "similar looks and religious background" because they were physically unable to have children. They'd married late and had almost resigned themselves to the notion that they were too old to meet the strict adoption requirements. My mother's own mother was firmly opposed to the idea of adoption so, because Mum and Dad didn't want negative reactions from anybody else, they kept their plans to themselves.

Still, they were desperate to love a child.

It wasn't "want" a child. It wasn't "need" a child. The request was to *love* a child, according to the yellowed form in my hands.

Perhaps by 1951, they had given up all hope of that ever happening.

Perhaps it was a normal day, like any other. My soon-to-be father was going about his business, my soon-to-be mother attending to hers. Or perhaps they were having a cup of tea and a piece of homemade cake when the telephone rang. Perhaps my dad-to-be sipped his tea and muttered, "There's the phone, Marg," and she sighed and went to answer. Dad seldom did so because of his heavy Dutch accent.

Perhaps whoever took the call was stunned into silence, which made the other immediately think, oh no, who's died? Or perhaps the call culminated in a shriek of joy, of celebration, excitement? Whatever scenario took place on that March day would change all of our lives forever and my new Mum and Dad were totally unprepared for my arrival.

The call was to say they were to pick up their long-awaited baby the very next day. I arrived with nothing more than a diaper, a worn, plain white woollen sweater, and a good set of lungs.

That was, basically, all I knew of my beginnings. As I lay in that Japanese hospital, alone, and alienated from anything remotely familiar to me, I felt a little too sorry for myself. Perhaps it was because of the sickness? The questions? The confrontation with stark reality?

What *was* my medical history?

In the past I'd not wanted to know anything about my biological parents; the thought had hardly crossed my mind. But I wanted to know now, if for no other reason than to obtain details of my genetic background in order to find out if whatever disease I was suffering from was hereditary.

There was nothing to lose. I wanted no emotional connection whatsoever with my next of kin – I simply wanted information. Would this want become a need? Would I become obsessed with the search? I didn't think so. Searching out my biological past required the logical mindset that I applied at work, if not always in my personal life. I'd adhere to my adopted mother's calm philosophy of *whatever will be, will be*. My usual pragmatic approach was to first evaluate the information at hand and from that determine a plan of action to achieve the desired result.

I eventually recovered from the illness, which turned out to be a bizarre viral infection. But the desire to trace my origins lingered, like a side effect of the medication. I didn't have much information, apart from what my name had once been. Bachman. My past likely lay buried in a bureaucratic jungle so I'd have no alternative but to use my initiative. It had taken me this far.

I decided, in time, to write to every Bachman listed in the telephone directories of the Canadian Consulate in Tokyo. For most of my adolescence I desperately wanted an ordinary name. It might have helped with peer acceptance. It was so tiresome to have to spell my name aloud. DeVrye isn't common (it rhymes with rye bread or rye whiskey – whichever you prefer!). I was occasionally called "Devine" – which sounded good – but more often "Deprived" – which did not. Anyway, DeVrye derived from a spelling mistake on my father's immigration forms. Now, for the first time in my life, I saw the value of a name that was not run-of-the-mill, not a Smith or a Brown. Had I been born one of these, my search may have been doomed before it even began. Even so, Bachman was more common than I'd guessed. According to the phone books, there were over three hundred Bachmans living in Canada at the time. Each was destined to receive a personalized letter. Whether the number was three hundred or three thousand, I had to do what I had to do.

Strategically, I sensed that the timing of my letter would be crucial. In my heart, I was certain there was a woman some-where who would always remember the birth date of the baby she'd given up. So, in September 1987, a few weeks before my thirty-seventh birthday, I wrote from Tokyo:

TO: ALL BACHMANS
Hello,
I was born Marilyn Darlene Bachman on September 29, 1950

at Calgary General Hospital and am writing to all families of the same name in Canada; in hopes of discovering my origins.

Shortly after birth, I was adopted by wonderful parents and had the good fortune of their love and care until their untimely deaths in the early '70s. At that time, I moved to Australia and currently enjoy a wonderful life. I am grateful to both sets of parents for providing that opportunity.

However, I am now 37 years old and would like to locate my birth parents if they share that interest. I do not want to cause any disruption to their existing lives. I am uncertain of circumstances surrounding my adoption and do not even know if Bachman was my mother or father's name. However, assuming I was a child born out of wedlock, I am grateful to the mother who chose not to have an abortion and would like to thank her.

I am conscious that my mother or father may be dead or not the least bit interested in re-establishing a relationship after all these years. But, *if* you or anyone you know would like to make contact with me, I visit Calgary regularly. I can be reached at the addresses below in Australia or Tokyo – or via Parent Finders or the Alberta Department of Social Services, which allows people to make anonymous inquiries.

I am sorry to have troubled you but am sure you will understand my situation even if there is no personal connection.

Thank you
Catherine DeVrye

I waited. I waited some more. During those first two weeks, twenty-four hours took forty-eight to pass. I soon realized that the response was going to be underwhelming. Over a dozen letters were returned to sender almost immediately. Some had *deceased* scrawled across the envelope. My heart sank as I carefully crossed each name off my master mailing list.

Within two weeks, another letter arrived. This handwriting was shaky, but at least it was from a Bachman. I looked at the letter. It seemed to stare at me as if it had eyes of its own. Nausea rose. I hesitantly reached for it a few times, needing to tear it open and devour its contents, but equally terrified of what it might reveal.

A thousand questions battled for supremacy like dodgem cars in my head. A succession of "what ifs" were swallowing me whole.

What on earth have I done? I thought, all courage dissipating. But then I thought of my father's words: *Any job worth doing is worth doing well, cowboy. Remember that.*

Okay. I'd started this and I had to see it through, all the way. I opened the letter.

Dear Marilyn,

Marilyn? Why Marilyn? Didn't I sign it Catherine DeVrye? I'd been called Cathy, Cath or Cate but never Marilyn. My mouth went dry. I read on.

Raise no hopes but I may give you a lead. When I was about 8 years old, we had a visitor from Swift Current, Saskatchewan, of Bachman stock. Swift Current is a whistle-stop town and Calgary, not too far away, would be an ideal place to send a young girl to holiday and presto – you. We wish.

If I may digress…I know my background but still went to visit my mother's birthplace in Germany. Most delightful of all, I visited the room where she was born and looked out the window from which, as she said, she could pick cherries from a nearby tree.

I may sound sentimental but my heart and hopes go out to you. You must and surely will be successful. Hopefully, I have

played a little part in your success, even if it is just to encourage you to go on.
Gerhardt (Garry) Bachmann

I put the letter down and sighed, touched to receive a letter from a total stranger who took the time to care. I was surprised that it came from a sixty-six-year-old male because for some inexplicable reason, I didn't expect replies from men.

A few days later, he sent another note to apologize for addressing me as "Marilyn."

I'm worried that it may have raised your hopes and nearly had a heart attack when I realized my mistake.

I immediately reassured him. His thoughtfulness was appreciated. It was nice to know that somebody – somewhere, anywhere – cared.

More replies arrived and each envelope came with expectations. Each also delivered its unique disappointment. Most wrote that they weren't related but wished me well in my search. Only a few were less caring in tone but I didn't mind. At least they'd taken time to categorically deny that I had anything to do with their family. It further narrowed possibilities from my master list but I was no closer than before to finding my roots.

2

GRANDDAD

 In quiet, reflective times – of which there seemed precious few these days– I wondered what my grandfather would have thought of this search. Once upon a time, I had more time; in that time when I thought the world was perfect and everything would be okay if Granddad said so.

Would he have understood today? Probably. He seemed to understand me more than anyone I'd ever known. He knew my origins long before I was aware of them and it made no difference to his love. But now – if he'd still been alive – would he think this search was some kind of betrayal? Such questions can never be answered.

As far as I can remember (and thankfully I can't recall the first few months) I had a carefree childhood, growing up in Calgary, Canada, in the stable era of the long-serving Social Credit government that had been in power all my life. Not that I knew much about politics then. I was just a kid who sucked her thumb contentedly. Mum was convinced this habit was linked to some early emotional disturbance, but the only concerns I had were everyday ones. Like why our pipes froze on a cold winter's day. How would the snow-plough man get to work in a blizzard? What made those Northern Lights blaze in the sky? Would I find the nickel buried in the Christmas pudding and birthday angel food cake without having the foil wrap grate upon my teeth?

I'm sure that when my first day of school finally came, Mum walked me to the gate with much relief. Someone else could now be barraged with the continual succession of:

But why?

Yeah, but . . . why?

"Sit down and be quiet for a while. You've got ants in your pants."

Today, we're so keen to affix labels; I may be diagnosed as hyperactive, as surely would Anne of Green Gables, orphan heroine of classic Canadian children's fiction. Like everyone else, I carved my initials in the old wooden desks with their wrought-iron legs. A school report card states: "Catherine would be an excellent student if she didn't move around so much and followed instructions."

My grandfather was the only person who never seemed to tire of my endless questions and energy throughout what I remember as a totally conventional, normal childhood, as bland as my grandmother's oatmeal. My mother's parents lived with us in our white stucco duplex, two doors down from where they first settled on McLeod Trail after emigrating from Scotland. Named after the first Royal Canadian Mounted Police Officer in Calgary, it was a once-proud street. That was, according to my grandmother, before the Italians moved in and painted everything pink and green – and it was renamed Spiller Road.

I was an only child – perhaps one was enough for my parents. I never needed a babysitter. I had Granddad instead. He'd retired the year I arrived in the family, so he had plenty of time to be my best friend, confidant and mentor. He was like a big brother with wrinkles and without rivalry.

We grow up. We grow old. Granddad saw me grow up but I never saw him grow old. He was always the same and we didn't care what colour people painted their houses! He was the only one who thought it was perfectly normal for me to swap my dolls for my cousin's dump trucks. Mum had a fit. She was trying hard to turn me into a lady. Granddad liked me just the way I was and cherished me unconditionally. It mustn't always have been easy to do so!

I sometimes wonder what their conversations must have been like: *Marg, let the lassie be. If she wants to wear a cowboy outfit for the Stampede, let her. It's only once a year, what harm can it do?*

The rest of the time I was dressed in florals and frills. My poor mother so wanted a little lady. She got a tomboy and would-be cowgirl instead. To me, the week of the Calgary Stampede was more exciting than Christmas – at least in my hometown, where this rodeo carnival was billed "the greatest outdoor show on earth." Cowboys and Indians, tepees and chuck wagons camped on the main street where everyone joined in square dancing and flipping flapjacks. Was this hankering for the outdoors an atavistic trait, apparent even then? My mother may have thought so.

Although I occasionally had nightmares of Indians galloping over the hill to take me away, I was usually a little girl safe and secure in a family's love, each day dancing with the promise of potential. Back then, I never had a thought about tomorrow or what it might bring, even though I was often in trouble for daydreaming. I was a child, living each day as it found me – and it often found me reading *The Little Engine Who Could, Lassie Come Home* and *Black Beauty*. Each Christmas, *Oor Willie* comic books arrived in parcels from "the old country" of Scotland but I was more interested in Nancy Drew novels than the mysteries of past or future life. I was somewhat precocious but always polite because Mum maintained that manners were even more important than cleaning my room. When naughty, I always had my grandfather as backup and mostly he was on my side. I say mostly because he was the only human being who could reason with me when all attempts of parents and teachers alike failed.

In winter, Granddad and I made snowmen and shovelled snowdrifts long past the age it was healthy for his heart. His warm words would melt a glacier. In summer, he watched me play softball in my team's baggy, green-and-gold uniform, which always seemed too big every season, regardless of Mum's assurance that I'd grow into it.

Every Saturday night as we listened to the radio broadcast of "Hockey Night in Canada," he'd shine his best pair of lace-up black boots in readiness for a Presbyterian sermon the next morning. And every evening, his grandfather clock chimed at precisely eight o'clock when the Canadian Broadcasting Corporation brought the world news into our home.

In the days before I poured out my thoughts in my diary, he was my confessor. I can still see us sitting together on the well-worn, deep-burgundy sofa; he in his tartan shirt, woollen trousers, braces and wire-rimmed glasses. His floppy peaked cap and sweater hang on a huge curly hook near the back door while the suit and tie hang in the closet, awaiting Sunday. A big brass plate depicting Edinburgh Castle is positioned over the mantelpiece and overlooks a beige high-backed chair with carved wooden arms. No-one else ever sits on it because it was Gran's.

"Granddad?"

He looks at me over the top of his glasses – that look I'll carry with me to the grave. There will never be another man quite like my grandfather.

"Granddad, why did you leave Scotland?"

"You and your questions . . . So your Mum's not told you then?"

I shrugged. Whether she had or hadn't wasn't the point. It was a question I was asking him. I think he knew that, too.

He sighed and said, "You know about Dr. David Livingstone, aye?"

I nodded. Of course I knew. Who didn't know about the Scottish explorer of Africa? What did David Livingstone have to do with Granddad emigrating to Canada?

"Well, it was in 1907, a long time ago now. I went to the Old Monkland School at Coatdyke and back in those days you got a book."

I looked at him, my face quizzical. What did getting a book have to do with moving to Canada?

"The one I received was a first edition biography. It was about Livingstone."

Granddad rose, took the book from the cabinet and handed it to me. I'd seen it a thousand times but never recognized its importance. A fancy, yellowed bookplate written in faded ink on the flyleaf read, *Presented as first class prize to David Smart, 1907.*

He sat down again. "The only thing I had in common with Dr. Livingstone was the name, David. But oh, I treasured that book. Was about all I ever got from school. I never had the chances like you. A good education'll see you a long, long way, lass. Study hard. Learn something new every day, even if it's about yourself."

Yeah, yeah, get to the point, I urged silently, conveying the message by my squirming.

"I'd not the education, lass. Only work I could get was in the mine, you see. It was hard and dirty but it was work all the same. Then they closed it down. There was no work on the farm, either. Wasn't big enough to support us all. And I was a married man by then, too. I'd got myself a wife and wee bairn . . . Oh aye, I had my Catherine . . ."

A shadow crossed his face as he spoke the name of my grandmother and he looked at my namesake's chair as if wishing she were there to help him tell the story. Until then I never realized my granddad could be lonely and missing her.

He sighed again, as if waking from a reverie. "Aye, well, there was no work to be found anywhere. Your mother, Marg, she was but a wee bairn in arms. There was no future in Scotland for any of us."

Again all went silent as he remembered. "Now your gran, she didn't want to leave her bonnie Scotland, but she came along all the same. She'd no choice and I'd no choice. What could I do? As the liner sailed down the Clyde, we both knew then we were really leaving."

There was quiet for a while, broken only by the ticking of the clock. In his mind, my grandfather was remembering. Recalling how his young wife cried into her baby's curly brown hair and whispered, *Lassie, you'll never ken how bonnie Mossywood farm is. Oor Scotland you'll never ken...*

"And that's why we came here, Cath. Even though the sailin' was rough, I had some hope in m'heart and a few pounds in m'pocket. It was the biggest gamble of m'life. I left home with a wife, a wee lassie, a pocket watch and a book. This book. I thought if the good Dr. Livingstone could go off into the unknown like that, and do some good while he were at it, then by gosh, so could David Smart. As Glasgow passed us by, I saw tears in your grandma's eyes and made her a promise as we stood together on the deck, watching oor Scotland fade into the distance.

And I'm a man of my word at that when I told her she'd be seeing it again."

For a moment I thought I saw tears in his eyes. "You never broke your promise."

"Aye. Aye. A promise made. A promise kept. But it'd all changed, lass. Scotland was…" His voice faded away. "And your grandma, well, you know about that already. Her mind and all…We dinna need to talk about it."

He didn't say any more. It was late and he was tired. He reached for his Bible, read out a passage, kissed me goodnight and went off to bed, leaving me alone with my thoughts. Mostly, I thought how much I loved that old man. How brave he'd been to walk away from all he'd ever known, with so very little except a dream and hope for a better life in a new country. He did it for the love of his family and although love was a word never spoken out loud, I felt it buried deep beneath his stoic Scottish brogue – and was proud to be a part of that family, never once imagining there could be any other.

Their ship sailed into the sanctuary of the St. Lawrence and the small family disembarked in Montreal. Unhappy with the alien French influence in that city, my grandfather soon doubted his decision to emigrate. Still, there was no other option, at least for the time being. Yet we always have more choices than we imagine.

Two years later, he moved west, choosing a city named after a town in Scotland. In Gaelic, Calgary means "clear, running water" and in that city the family soon blossomed. Three more girls and, finally, a boy, Jack. But Jack wasn't well. He contacted diphtheria when he was five years old and died of heart failure just after his twenty-first birthday. When Jack died, a part of David Smart died as well. He felt as if he'd lost his best friend and that the void would never be filled. Neither this tragedy nor the stillborn daughter before my mother's birth would ever be spoken of.

Working twelve hours a day as a fitter and turner at Bell and Morris machinery works, my grandfather was able to buy a house on the edge of Scotchman's Hill. A few years later, horses moved the two-storey house, propped on wheels, to the bottom of the hill, as soil erosion had made the bank unstable. At whatever cost, David Smart was determined to have a solid foundation for his family. This was now home. Their home.

It would, in time, become my home, too.

With views to the Rocky Mountains, Scotchman's Hill was not named in honour of the early settlers but because of the vantage point over the world-famous Calgary Stampede grounds. Those too thrifty to pay admission could witness some rodeo events from the top of the hill. Where the Scots gained this reputation for thriftiness, I'll never know. Our kitchen griddle always sizzled with scones and shortbread prepared for endless bake sales at St. Andrew's Presbyterian Church, all destined to raise money for missionaries in some Godforsaken part of the globe. Perceptions – and the names of many of those countries – have changed since the days I leafed through *The World Book Encyclopaedia* that a travelling salesman had sold my folks.

At the ripe old age of six, I desperately wanted to be a missionary. It was the only way I knew of that could take a person around the world. And that's where I wanted to go, or at least I wanted to migrate south, like the Canadian geese in autumn, to escape the dark, cold winter mornings. Alas, there was one annoying hiccup to this "missionary" objective: I wasn't so sure about God, especially since I'd been kicked out of the Sunday school choir because I couldn't carry a tune, only to be reinstated on the proviso that I imitated a goldfish and didn't let a solitary sound exit my open lips. That, amongst other church-related rules, seemed pretty unreasonable to me but I didn't tell a soul about my disbelief, especially since my father was an elder in the church and Mum president of the Missionary Society. My Prairie Presbyterian upbringing precluded such blasphemy. In spite of a perfect attendance record at Sunday school and prayers before every meal, I didn't share that innate faith with the rest of the family. Perhaps I questioned too much for everybody's comfort.

> Why did God let my uncle die? Why does he let good people get sick? Why doesn't he make bad people sick so they can't hurt anyone anymore?

I believed in everything else my grandfather believed in and more importantly, I believed in him. God was an entirely different matter. God wasn't nearly as real or important as Granddad in my world.

Granddad would take me with him on long walks to sit on the fence at the stockyards where he'd simply meet up with his cronies for their regular "yarn." And because of his stories, I longed for a Scottish collie just like the one he'd once had.

For some unfathomable reason I wanted a horse even more than a collie and at every opportunity, I'd sneak away, across the Elbow River, to the Stampede grounds where, like a bad smell, I'd hang around the corral and pester the cowboys. Uh-oh, here comes that kid again…The horsy odours of straw, manure and leather tack were irresistible. I was too naïve to consider the spurs of cruelty to broncs or bulls. All I ever wanted was to be near a horse; to brush it, pat it, walk it.

Once, I sat on Roy Rogers' horse. Well, the stable hand said it was Trigger and the saddle certainly seemed fancy enough…I idolized the Cisco Kid and Diablo; the Lone Ranger and Silver; and of course, Gene Autry and Champion, the Wonder Horse. Gene Autry and I were born on the same day many years removed. Maybe I was the equivalent of a cowboy groupie when I was still too young to be impressed by rock stars and other celebrities? Even chatting to Cary Grant, hanging around the corral one day, I had no idea who he was until a friend's mother appeared and gasped in awe of this Hollywood legend, who quickly disappeared into a nearby barn.

Exactly where I got this love of rodeo would remain a mystery for many years.

Every Christmas, I asked Santa for a horse but Santa never heard me. Maybe he didn't have his hearing aid turned on. One year I received a budgie. A *budgie*? Someone's wires got crossed here! A budgie ain't a horse! For a child, it seemed the ultimate definition of disappointment. Promising someone the world . . . and giving them a dog-eared atlas instead!

Granddad never made a promise he couldn't keep and that was why he never promised me a horse. But many years earlier, as he sailed down the Clyde towards a new life in a new country, he had told my grandmother that she would again see the lush hills of the Highlands. Nearly half a century later, with a minimum wage of only 75 cents per hour in 1950, some assiduous Scottish saving had been required for this homeward journey the year I was born. It was a melancholy visit that served only to confirm his notion that he had indeed made the right decision to leave all those years ago.

My grandmother's mind didn't quite make the return trip across the Atlantic. She could only talk about the brothers and sisters she once knew, and remembered only the past in Scotland. She was totally senile and had forgotten her family in Canada by the time the ship again touched the North American coast. The rest of her life was spent in and out of a psychiatric institution. When she finally died, I couldn't understand why everyone else in the family was so upset yet called it "a blessing." I only cried because my mother cried, and my mother never cried.

Gran died of Alzheimer's disease. It was a shameful subject at the time.

So too was adoption.

My parents kept their application a secret. They'd both married late. Dad was a Dutch immigrant who'd been raised in an orphanage and wanted to give another child a better chance at life. And my mother? She simply wanted a child to love.

They got me.

Now, so many years after my parents' deaths, I was searching for my biological origins and wondered if forces beyond my control would hinder such a discovery. Granddad probably would have told me that worry was as daft as shovelling the path *before* it started to snow. Still, the deep recesses of my mind drifted to the "what ifs." What if I hadn't been given up? What kind of life would I have led?

3

SECRETS

The life I led was far easier than it had been for my parents, who both lived through the Depression but never suffered from that dreadful illness so commonly diagnosed today. If Mum ever felt sorry for herself, she never let on. She was always busy helping others.

A stenographer at Metals Limited, she became a full-time housewife and homebody and through necessity had her own version of recycling long before environmental consciousness. An old dress was reincarnated as an apron or multiple potholders. Socks were darned and never discarded. Nor were jars that could be used for jam at bake sales. Seemingly happiest in the kitchen, she was adept at home economics. Sunday's roast became Monday's mince and any leftovers were transformed into tantalizing casseroles. Mum was a nurturer by nature while I only wanted to explore the great outdoors. It was a recipe for mother–daughter conflict and I sadly remember few shared hobbies or passions, apart from roasting marshmallows and popcorn over an open flame, and seeing *The Sound of Music* together.

But I will never forget the moment, frozen forever in time, when I first discovered I'd been adopted. I was drying the dishes and arguing with Mum again. Heaven knows what the argument was about but it escalated into the usual, full-scale battlefield – teenage know-it-all, filled to overflowing with rampaging hormones, versus Mother: She Who Must Be Obeyed.

It began no differently, really, to any other fight, but this time no-one was declared victor. I retreated to my usual strategic bargaining position, the only toilet in the house. The standard ploy was to lock myself in and negotiate until my parents promised not to punish me. Not this time though. That childish tactic never occurred again. My self-centred teenage world crumbled around my ears when my mother screamed: *I should send you back to the Salvation Army where you came from!*

I remember the silence. I first gasped, and then held my breath. My chest and stomach tightened. A certain numbness welled inside. What'd she say? What'd she mean? I wasn't her daughter? What was going on here?

A hundred questions simmered but I was rendered speechless.

Then I heard Mum crying, for only the second time in my life, and I emerged from behind the locked door. There was fear in her eyes. Fear, I suppose, of how I'd react because now I knew the truth and she could no longer deny me that realization. We stared at each other for what seemed a long time but was probably only seconds. I desperately wanted her to hug me like she had when I was little but we weren't a hugging sort of family. It would be trite to say that emotions were swept under the carpet but in our home, *nothing* was swept under the carpet, as my mother vacuumed every day and kept her feelings bottled as tightly as the raspberry preserves.

"What do you mean? The Salvation Army?" What was happening? People said I was so much like my father . . . what did she mean?

"Cath," she said, voice shaking. "We have to talk."

She did most of the talking. I listened, truly listened – probably for the first time in years. She told me how she and Dad were unable to have children of their own. They hadn't told me about my adoption because they wanted me to be like everyone else. Peer acceptance was important back then but I'd still never quite fitted in – at least, not in my own mind. That was undoubtedly a good thing. My folks worried I would fall in with the wrong crowd, which was the right crowd as far as I was concerned. Other kids seemed to have more fun and less discipline. As a teenager I resented but later came to appreciate my parents' principles. I'd been naïve in my junior high class, where girls were pregnant and boys were in court. Apart from a dare to blow up a balloon in class (which was actually a condom) and steal a pack of cigarettes I was the goody-goody, even winning a citizenship award, sponsored by the police department, for school patrol crossing . . .

"But why didn't you tell me, Mum?"

"Cath, we were frightened you mightn't love us if you knew we weren't your real parents."

What can you say to that? How many years had she lived with that fear? Fifteen?

Tears filled my eyes. I told her I would always love her, that no-one, and nothing could ever steal that love away.

"Would you like us to help you find them?"

I shook my head. There was nothing I wanted to know about my biological parents because they weren't really my parents. I didn't say it to make Mum feel better. I said it because it was true.

She led me into their bedroom and opened the old cedar hope chest. In it was a carefully folded and very faded woollen baby jacket. It was all I had when I came to them as a five-month-old infant (and is today worn by my child-hood teddy bear as a reminder of my past). She then opened the bottom dresser drawer and said, "This is where you slept. We weren't expecting you so soon. And didn't have nine months to get ready. But you always were full of surprises." Wasn't that the truth! Finally, we both laughed and she reapplied her powder and lipstick. Mum never wore any other make-up or nail polish and no perfume lingers on the perimeter of my memory. Maybe that's because my earliest recollection of childhood is being bedridden with bronchitis, while she rubbed my chest with the heady eucalypt scent of Vicks. As I sipped homemade chicken noodle soup or hot lemon and honey, she'd place a cool washcloth on my brow, tuck me in and stay until I fell asleep; leaving the door only slightly ajar to allow the steam from the vaporizer to ease my coughing through the night.

Although she surely "wore the pants" in our family, I never saw her in anything but a dress. I never saw my mother in trousers, nor my father in anything else! Dad must have had legs but I never even glimpsed his bare feet, not even in the garden where he planted yellow tulips from his native land, white lilies-of-the-valley, purple hyacinths and coaxed pink and white peonies the size of cheerleader pompoms to hide the cracks in the stucco. Strange really, that I never saw him anything but fully dressed. Also odd that we never discussed my adoption.

I'd like to say I never gave adoption another thought but insecurities settled in. I couldn't help thinking that my grandfather wouldn't love me as much as his other grand-children – after all, I wasn't flesh and blood. Even though he was my best friend and I spoke with him every night before bed, I couldn't broach the subject with him. I was too afraid of his answer. Still, I had to know. Did he love me as much as the others?

Courage rose. I knew I'd first told Mum that I wouldn't mention it again, but this was important. If anyone knew the truth, it was Mum. After all, Granddad was her father.

"Mum?"

She turned and looked at me, a silent "what?" lingering in her eyes. It was almost a wary expression – as if she never knew what I might ask next.

"Does, um . . . Does Granddad love me even though I'm adopted?"

A warm smile crossed her face. "He's always known, Cath."

The sense of relief at my own stupidity was overwhelming. Being adopted didn't matter anymore to me if it had never mattered to Granddad. I had a life to live!

Nothing really changed, except perhaps my relationship with my mother. We didn't fight quite so fiercely after that day of discovery. Unfortunately, I still took her for granted as if it were an offspring's right to do so.

4

DETOUR TO DREAMS

I will never leave thee nor forsake thee.

A young girl takes such promises literally and seldom thinks of mortality or the finality of death. Suddenly it confronted me when Granddad died before I could say goodbye. I didn't think he'd die – certainly not then. He'd only been in hospital for a few days with mild pneumonia and had never been hospitalized a day in his life. I guess no illness is mild when you're over eighty.

I'd been at a slumber party at my best friend Val's place. We'd become firm friends at Western Canada High School, where neither of us knew anyone else in our class. The next morning, I visited the hospital to see Granddad on my way home and walked in full of teenage optimism. "Could you please tell me what room David Smart is in?"

The nurse tried to find his name. "There's no David Smart here."

"Yes, there is. He's my grandfather and has pneumonia."

"Sorry. There's no David Smart here."

Someone else came along. Voices were muffled. I caught the occasional sidelong glance. A nurse stepped out of the huddle and beckoned me to follow her to the end of the corridor.

"I'm sorry but Mr. Smart passed away a couple of hours ago . . ."

I didn't hear what else she said. I fled down the fire escape of the hospital; I sat, shivered and sobbed in the stairwell, thinking I may as well die, too. So much for Christmas. So much for promises. All I had left were memories and the old dog-eared Bible he had given me when I was eight years old. In the flyleaf he'd written, *I will never leave thee nor forsake thee* . . . But he *had* left me. Granddad was dead. I'd never see him again. I thought I'd never love anyone or anything as much as I loved him and now he was gone. I was sixteen and my life was over, too. Nothing would ever be the same again.

The tears I thought would never end eventually dried. Mum would be worrying by now. It was dark and it was cold like someone had left a huge deep freeze open forever. I knew I had to go home. Maybe it was teenage selfishness, but it never occurred to me that she would be hurting, too. Her own father was dead and she would never see him again, but that thought never crossed my mind.

If only I had my time over . . . But we don't have that luxury. All we ever have is hindsight. And hindsight, if nothing else, helps us to learn the most important lesson of all: how we could have loved better if only we'd thought to at the time.

I missed my grandfather terribly. I had no-one to talk to now. So I talked to myself – not out loud but scribbling in a notebook the thoughts I once might have shared with Granddad. I missed his calm intelligence – his cool head and warm heart. Most of all I missed his wisdom and that certain look which reflected back at me whenever I looked into his eyes. When I was feeling a little out of sorts, he'd always say, "Cath, a smile is a frown turned upside down."

Then, one day he wasn't there to remind me anymore. That's the first time I felt sorrow and loss because most of all, Granddad taught me how to think, how to question and how to dream – especially in an imperfect world.

About a year after his death, I was selected to attend World Expo 67 in Montreal as part of a multicultural program to enhance relationships between native Canadians and other nationalities. I was the token Dutch girl who felt distinctly more Scottish. And although I can't recall any Sioux or Blackfoot girls on the trip, I became friends with a Chinese and a Jewish girl, as we vicariously explored other worlds amid the Expo displays of faraway cultures. I struggled with schoolgirl French (it wasn't yet Canada's second official language and more people spoke Ukrainian in Calgary). Still, I loved Montreal. My folks had bought me a leather-bound diary before I left but knowing that I couldn't discuss this eye-opening visit with Granddad dampened any homecoming enthusiasm. I had to make do with imagining how proud he would have been.

By then, I'd caught that incurable work ethic from both my father and grandfather. I'd had a job delivering flyers since I was thirteen. As well, I babysat, waitressed and washed dishes at a prestigious golf club, where my father was chef. Now I had a permanent part-time job to add to the casual ones. Two nights a week and all day Saturday I dispensed hotdogs and doughnuts at the Woodwards department store snack bar. Granddad would have been proud of me for that as well.

I became vice president of Western Canada High student council and for my first public speaking experience roller-skated on to the stage dressed as the Flying Nun. Heaven knows what he would have thought of that! Student council responsibilities included planning our 1968 graduation prom. But I was dateless and even though Val and I talked on the phone for hours, I wasn't sure if she understood what being dateless felt like, as she'd had a boyfriend before her family moved to the West from Eastern Ontario.

Guys never took a second look at me. I went to dances with my best friend from primary school, Lorraine, who'd become a teen fashion queen at the same department store, Woodwards. She sold sling-backs in the shoe department, while I shuffled around in white, food-stained Oxfords and a matronly uniform in the snack bar. At dances, I felt the guys flipped a coin. The winner asked Lorraine and by default, his friend asked me. I was never a very good dancer and nicknamed Clubfoot Catherine by one such loser!

I wanted desperately to be like Lorraine and fit in during junior high school but in our neighbourhood it wasn't cool to excel at school, so from being a straight A student, I'd intentionally gone out of my way to get lower grades and higher peer acceptance. I even managed to get expelled briefly a couple of times for what would be considered minor demeanours by today's standards.

Years later, in this new high school class, it seemed more socially acceptable to get good grades. As for boys, I still always managed to trip up in anything but sporting situations.

I was taller than most of them, but not quite tall enough or fast enough to be a star on the basketball team and was furious that I wasn't allowed to play gridiron football just because I was a girl! I was as good as Billy, who made the team. Son of Bill the barber, he was both the brother I longed for and the "boy next door" – except he lived across the street. In those days, I'd never heard of sexual discrimination and knew no avenue of redress, so pummelled the old metal locker in frustration until it was dented and my hands were bruised and bleeding, with childish outrage: "It's not fair. It's just not fair."

I felt somewhat accepted when I was invited to join a sorority. It was a teenage rite of belonging and how I longed to belong. But the activities seemed silly and I couldn't even pretend to enjoy myself. Even when included, I still felt excluded. I couldn't afford expensive clothes like the popular girls wore. I wanted to be shorter, so I slouched.

Although a self-centred teen, I remember the juxtaposition of being concerned about social justice and wanting to change the world. We weren't even old enough to vote but were swept away by Trudeaumania and the social reforms he promised as Canada's new prime minister. The slaying of Martin Luther King enraged us to write letters to the editor. We participated in Walks Against Want and blood donor drives, and constantly challenged the status quo. While questioning the norms of adults, we created our own, sometimes inconsistent worldview, never giving a second thought to wearing sealskin boots in those days. They were warm and practical and part and parcel of teenage status symbols in 1960s Canada.

Mum never allowed me in the house with the big bearskin coat I bought from a second-hand shop for ten dollars and she never understood why I'd buy new jeans and then scrub the kitchen linoleum with them to make them look "old." She must have thought we were as weird as we thought adults were.

And through it all, I'd have grown cobwebs had I sat waiting for the phone to ring, for a boy to ask me out on a date. All I had was my diary and my mother's repetitively annoying assurance: *There's lots of fish in the sea. Things always work out for the best.*

Tell that to a teenager who thought she was a permanent wallflower, and had the dreaded final year exams to contend with. Granddad would have understood all these things that I did not. Study seemed so meaningless.

> I sit by the storm window in the kitchen. My head leans heavily in my hand, my elbow rests on the laminated tabletop. I gaze blindly at the glass but see nothing for a while until I notice a fly. It's caught between the panes of glass. Strange. Why is the double-glazed storm window on in the middle of summer anyway? It's only needed in winter . . . I should be studying, not daydreaming. But the fly struggles. Poor thing. It's trapped – like I feel. Suddenly the life of an insect seems important. I don't want to kill it. Any other time I'd reach for the swatter and not even think. Now, I want to set it free. I go down to the basement and find a screwdriver. Soon, the outside glass is off and that fly is free. All it takes is a plan, a little effort, determination and sometimes, a little help – from where you least expect it. So what if I should have been studying history. This is the present.

Turned out, Mum was right. After breezing through final exams (and having a gorgeous guy on the basketball team eventually invite me to the prom) I received a partial scholarship to university to study physical education. Until then, when it came to studies, mediocrity had been my motto. Although I passed my exams, a true education had passed me by. Well, that would no longer be the case. With a scholarship, a student loan and part-time jobs, I was on my way to a lifelong love affair with learning (including lessons I never intended to study!).

At the University of Calgary I finally found my niche but not until the first few months were wasted playing bridge for money in the student union. I always was a bit of a gambler and usually won but decided that a safer long-term bet would be to buckle down and study hard. Here, on campus, students and staff alike actually respected intelligence and academic excellence. I didn't have to hide away anymore. So much for our previous school principal's prophecy at Ramsay Elementary School: *You kids will never be anything because your parents aren't. Or you wouldn't live in this neighbourhood.*

How to kill ambition before it's really born.

I had told Mrs. Allan, the wonderful mother of my friend, Lorraine, the fashion queen, what he'd said to us at assembly. We'd always go to her place after school. Her mother was more tolerant of our music and teenagers in general because Lorraine had three older brothers who I adored.

"Don't worry, Catherine. It's not where you live but how you live that's important."

Others may choose to believe that principal's words, but I never would, thanks to Mrs. Allan.

His statement angered me. I'll show *him*, I thought.

At university I could be who I wanted to be. Finally. I even played powder-puff football – gridiron for girls – and represented the university in basketball, volleyball and field hockey, before being selected for a couple of international volleyball matches. But I lacked the skill necessary to be a champion: just being a part of a team was important enough for me. I loved to compete and win but even if we lost that was okay too, as long as I knew in my heart that I'd played my best. What else could be expected? I was plotting my course daily and loving each moment of being alive and studying to be a physical education teacher. After all, I thought that secretaries, nurses and teachers were the highest professions a girl could aspire to. I admired my aunts who were all stenographers but being office-bound held no appeal. Auntie Helen was a "spinster," a dreadful label, but the absence of children gave her the freedom to travel. She was a role model long before I'd heard the term. Likewise, my mother's cousin in Scotland, "Auntie" Janet was a nursing sister who sent postcards from exotic places; but the blood and guts of nursing held less appeal than the far-flung destinations.

So I chose teaching, not because of a love of children but through a process of elimination.

Then it hit, without warning. The course of my life has always taken detours. Hasn't everyone's? Perhaps they are simply unordered wake-up calls. Tall and gangly, I was never good at gymnastics. Maybe I wasn't aware of my own limitations. Maybe I'm still not, but little is ever achieved without some kind of effort.

I'm struggling with a gymnastics routine. It seems easy to others and I'm cheesed off that I can't master it. Hands blistered and bleeding, I won't give in and attempt cheerleader-like splits on the balance beam. My leg slips off the narrow polished wooden bar and a sound, like a sheet tearing, rips through the gym. But it's not a sheet. It's my ligament. So much for my dream of becoming a phys ed teacher, is my one thought. What will I do now? In slow motion, my entire life crumbles as my body hits the gymnasium floor.

I quit university. What else could I do? Simple deferment never occurred to me. If I couldn't play by the rules, I suffered the consequences. I applied for a secretarial job, admitting in the interview that I couldn't type or operate a switchboard. I actually even got the job – the interviewer appreciated my honesty. But the easygoing dean of physical education convinced me to stay at university.

Rather than continuing with physically demanding courses, I switched to psychology and sociology and surprised myself with more of an aptitude for sports administration. I vowed never to quit because of a minor setback ever again. Just take one of those little detours to dreams – the first of many.

Around the same time, I bought my first car, a Chevy Corvair – a purchase that scared my mother half to death, not just because it was considered a deathtrap by early consumer advocate Ralph Nader. We'd never owned a car and had been dependent on my aunt for weekly trips to the co-op grocery store five miles away. My cousin and I always raised our eyebrows when Mum repeatedly commented, "I remember when this was nothing but bald prairie." She also amused us by telling my aunt that I'd bought a Corvette, but as far as I was concerned, the old green Corvair was hotter than any sports car. It symbolized new-found freedom, even if I'd pull into a service station and joke, "Fill up the oil and check the gas."

It was certainly no joking matter when I had to take my old cat, Smoky, for her first and last drive. I'd had her since I was about eight, after my folks realized that my constant pestering for a pony or collie needed a more substantial response than that damn budgie. Well, Smoky still wasn't a dog or horse but to an only child, she was a close second. The kitten became my constant companion. I pretended she was a dog, took her for walks and taught her how to fetch. Unlike a horse, she was always welcome to curl up under the bedcovers and, in later years, on my lap when I studied. I'd sometimes talk to her, as I had to my grandfather. I'd thought I was over his death, but not so, as my diary confirmed.

> Life goes on after the death of those close to us. We can never replicate that same love, nor would we want to. Nor should we. But voids can be filled — not easily like a cavity in a decayed tooth. Yet, we can slowly rediscover emotional affection and attachment of different dimensions.

Who wrote that? It's hard to believe it was in my diary because although Smoky had signified that rediscovery of emotional affection and I still missed my grandfather, I recall no lingering heaviness of heart in youth.

There were happy tears because I was bridesmaid for my school-friend Lorraine and also for my widowed Auntie Kay. She married a wonderful man who I'm proud to call my Uncle Frank and friend. I wondered if the same happiness I saw shining from her eyes on her wedding day would one day shine from mine. After being dumped by the basketball player who took me to the prom, I felt males might only be valuable as sporting buddies, although a linebacker on the football team rekindled my interest in the dating game.

By the end of my bachelor's degree, I was president of the Women's Intramural Sports Association and had excellent marks, many friends and found another loving pet in the form of a pure white homeless puppy named Blitz.

I was also the first person in our family to complete a university education, but with part-time jobs as varied as slinging hotdogs in the snack bar, shovelling dirt to build a bike path and working as a lifeguard and rental agent at a luxury apartment complex, I had no time to attend the graduation ceremony.

I do not wish you joy without a sorrow
Nor endless day without the healing dark.
Nor brilliant sun without the restful shadow
Nor tides that never turn against your barque.
I wish you love and faith and strength and wisdom
Goods, gold enough to help some needy one.
I wish you songs but also blessed silence
And, God's sweet peace when every day is done.

The above was written on the graduation card that my parents gave me. They had just celebrated their twenty-fifth wedding anniversary when I carefully placed their precious card in my diary and packed the precarious Corvair. My yellow alpaca sweater was itchy and so were my feet as I sped along the aptly named Going to the Sun Highway in Glacier National Park. Over the high mountain passes, I headed south of the border to start a Master of Science degree at the University of Montana in Missoula – thanks to a combined basketball and academic scholarship.

5

MUCH EDUCATION, LITTLE WISDOM

On 29 August 1971, I shared a room for the first time in my life. My roommate had previously trained to be a nun. Helen's spiritually inspired tolerance and forgiveness must have been the key to successful co-habitation because, at first, all we really had in common was the bare light in the middle of the small rectangular dormitory room – and the fact that each of us was an only child. She was religious. I wasn't. I was an athlete. She wasn't. She studied a lot. I studied when I had to. I partied and she didn't.

But here in Missoula, my old childhood curiosity reawakened like a hungry grizzly bear in springtime. I loved the questioning, the learning and the freedom. Some of my eternally unanswerable questions were no longer met with stony gazes, but actually encouraged.

Life couldn't be better. That feeling should have been an omen.

You never learn to live until it's time to die. Had Aristotle been trying to tell me something that previous week in philosophy class? Was it a subconscious preparation for the news that was to come? Those ancient words take on new meaning when someone you love has so little time left.

My dad had worked long, hard hours all of his life to provide for us and he'd only just retired. He should have been able to enjoy, now.

Enjoy . . . it's such a little word.

And so is pain – easy to say but enduring its reality is another matter.

Your father's got cancer, Cath. Your father is going to die soon. You'd better get yourself back to Scotchman's Hill, ASAP.

On that 500-mile drive home, I realized life was not an endless highway. No speed limit applied in Montana and my foot was flat to the floor as fear followed me, damn near tailgated me, down the open road.

I walked into the hospital room to see him lying there with tubes protruding. It took all of my strength to put one foot in front of the other and it took all of his to smile. It was feeble, hardly a smile at all. But he tried, his nicotine-stained teeth clenched tight with agony when he murmured, "Catherine. I'm so happy. So happy to see you again."

He cried then. I'd never seen my father cry before. He'd always been the one to dry my tears.

Perhaps all he needed was to see me at that moment in time. But he must have known I'd come home.

There is no word or phrase in any known language that can adequately explain the agony of cancer. Nor are there words to describe the feeling when you sit by the bedside of someone you love – someone who is suffering. Even suffering yourself doesn't suffice.

What do you say to someone you love when you know they are going to die, and they know they are going to die? That soon, you'll never see each other again? What do you say? So much wells up inside and rarely does anything of great importance ever emerge, so you stick to the basics. After all, isn't that what family is for? The basics? You talk softly of nothing that really matters in the greater scheme of things. Family is just . . . well . . . there. Foolishly, you once believed that these people you love will always be there.

Suddenly, you need to say, thank you for all you've done for me, Dad. Thanks for giving me a chance by adopting me. What would I have been – no, what would I be, without you? But no words come, so you pull up the chair that's still warm from your mother's constant presence in that hospital room and you sit, mostly quiet, hoping your presence alone is enough to get the message through. Or maybe you reach out to hold a hand that you know will not be there to hold in the near future. With courage rising, you take it, say nothing, and hope to God – if indeed there is a God – that you can hold on; that he can hold on – as long as possible. Or hope that the pain will pass as soon as possible. And although you want to say, "Thank you, Dad. Do you know how much I love you?" nothing comes out the way your heart wants it to. It all stays locked up inside because you fear what freeing it may do. He'll think you're being silly for showing such emotion. Hadn't he always said to keep a stiff upper lip? He'd been strong for us and now you need to be strong for him and Mum. After all, our family was never a touchy-feely one and it was easy to forget that love declared itself in the unspoken words and unselfish deeds of a parent. You don't want to change the status quo. Yet you want to change everything. He's dying. This is not some dream from which you know you will eventually wake.

Because by now, the medication is working and your father is asleep again, and you know that when he's asleep he can't feel any pain, so why wake him to more agony? You walk out of the hospital, a well of words filling and filling but remaining unsaid. You go on home to the house you lived in as a child, where you took so much for granted.

Death was on our doorstep and Mum was in the kitchen, making some tea. I slumped at the table, the same place I'd sat, fidgety, as a curious little girl. Dad's chair was empty. He'd never sit there again. I looked around. Nothing had changed. Not even the smells. Baking for the church. Ajax cleaner. That view from the kitchen window was a constant. Yet, everything had changed. I remembered that summer day when I was supposed to be studying and saw the fly, trapped. That was many seasons ago. No longer a child, I felt trapped by despair and the tears that wouldn't fall.

I was a young woman now, though still my mother's little girl. Maybe that's why we always fought, because I needed more than the view from this kitchen window while she was content with what was; neither of us understanding the other.

A huge part of Mum's life was slowly dying in a hospital bed, and there was nothing, absolutely nothing, that she could do to stop it happening. Already the void was looming but I could not comprehend the magnitude of it because I was not her. I could only see it in her eyes and even that from a distance, because she was trying to be strong for me, as I was for her. I sensed she needed me and it was time to give something back so I announced: "I want to defer my studies, Mum. I'll stay home and help you."

"Help me?"

She turned around so quickly that she nearly dropped the teacup. With abject horror in her eyes, she stared as if I'd just stepped off a UFO. "What?" she asked.

For a moment, I thought Mum, this strong woman, was going to crack into a thousand tiny pieces. But she didn't. Most of all, I admired her quiet strength. At that moment, I wished I could steal some of it from her. Something, anything to ease the helplessness I felt.

"Oh, no, Cath. No."

She wouldn't hear of it. "Nonsense. Absolutely not. Dad and I want you to have chances we never had and he'd be horrified to hear you say that. Don't you dare mention it to him and I don't want to hear another word about it."

But I wanted to be there and help. Then, when I saw such pain in her eyes I knew. How could I help someone who herself had given up hope? I hadn't thought of that. As in my teenage years, all I'd thought of was myself and maybe I needed her more than she needed me. But I was older now and surely wisdom had thrown a lifeline. I insisted on staying. "But Mum . . ."

"But nothing, Catherine!" I knew she was serious when she called me Catherine.

"No. You can't give up your studies. Don't you know how proud we are of you? Of all you've done?" Her hand shook as she poured another cup of tea. I watched it shake but didn't offer to take the teapot because I knew my hand would tremble worse than hers.

Proud of me? Hadn't they once said there was no point in girls going to university? Proud of all I've done? What? What had I done to be proud of? I'd been nothing but a self-centred teenager.

Maybe that was the trouble with our family. We weren't demonstrative. We never said those things that needed to be said. Like, *I love you*. Or, *thank you*. Or, *my world would be empty without you in it*.

We sipped hot tea and talked. Mum never complained nor took sugar in her tea. She always cared for others and claimed a chat over a cup of tea could cure all the ills of the world.

Not now. Even a thousand teapots wouldn't help Dad. But, as usual, Mum's advice to me made sense. It hurt – but it made sense.

It was the week of my twenty-first birthday but there would be no celebration as we went back to the hospital. Perhaps I would never see my father alive again. So I held his hand, held back the tears and left the hospital room with his final word echoing in my head.

Smile.

I tried to smile over the next three months as I made the 500-mile journey home whenever I could. He never spoke again.

Returning to the dorm, my roommate, Helen, gave me a Desiderata poster; undoubtedly hoping the first line would register: *Go placidly amidst the noise and haste and remember what peace there may be in silence.*

By then, I'd discovered the opposite sex could be enjoyed for more reasons than simply playing sport. Hormones started hopping when I dated a football player who rodeo-ed in the off-season. I was coaching basketball and my competitive spirit extended to beer-guzzling competitions at the local pizza place on Wednesday nights. I'm ashamed to admit that this was a sport I readily excelled at because Canadian beer was more potent than American brews.

Sometimes my friend Ellie and I went straight from the bar to a breakfast of greasy bacon and eggs at the Stockman's Grill before fronting up for 8 a.m. classes. Helen never judged and we became very close, in spite of our outward differences. Other friends were party pals and fellow adventurers on whitewater rafting trips down the Blackfoot River.

It wasn't long before I was heading back up the highway to Canada as Dad had lapsed into a coma. He died on 15 December 1971.

My entire being was anaesthetized as I looked down at his body for the last time. It was 18 December, my grandfather's birthday. There was a dreadful, impenetrable silence in our house. Time stood still on tiptoes and Mum sank into the rose brocaded sofa in quiet despair. Both had seen better times.

While we were readying his personal items for the Salvation Army to collect, Mum found a letter Dad had written when I was seven and a half. My dad, the Dutch immigrant who was raised in an orphanage and gave a child just like himself a chance, had written:

Yellowknife, Monday March 17, 1958
Hello Cowboy ... dearest Sweetheart,

Thank you very much for the lovely letter you wrote to me and nice report you send in a previous letter. Mummy and I are awfully happy at that and are very proud of you. Mummy also wrote what a good cowboy you have been lately and I hope you try your best and keep that up. Mummy needs all the help she can get from you.

I have no troubles right now but am very worried about Mummy and Grandad and Grandma, which does not make it very pleasant the work here so far away. Besides, I miss you all terrible. But I think I will have to stay here a little while longer to earn enough money to keep us all. So, keep your chin up even if it is hard sometimes to be a good cowboy, as I depent an awful lot on you.

I hope soon Mummy and Grandad and Grandma will all be better again and we'll have no more troubles and have lots of funn together. And now sweetheart, my letter is allmost full and it is time for me to get to work. Give my love to all and a big kiss to Mummy from me ...

I couldn't remember receiving this letter, written in broken, misspelt English. As my heart broke, I wondered how much else I had forgotten.

Driving back to Montana, I dared not look in the rear-vision mirror. Dad would have wanted me to drive into the future looking forward. Only the reflection of hindsight showed me just how much I loved my father. I'd never told him, but I always hoped that he knew.

The year I lost my father was the year I gained my Master of Science degree. Hardly a fair trade, was it? So much education and still so little wisdom about what was truly important.

6

MOTHER'S DAY

 While living away from home for the first time, I surprised myself by usually applying the same high standard of self-discipline that my parents had once enforced. I say "usually" because there were, admittedly, those all-night parties after football games.

Near the end of term, Dr. Wally Schwank, the dean of the physical education school, wrote a fantastic letter of reference for me. Then, placing it in a drawer, he added in a stern voice that I'd better live up to it. I'd run out of time to procrastinate on my thesis. I no longer danced until dawn. I typed. I retyped. When this exercise in mental gymnastics was nearly complete, Mum rang.

"Cath? I have to go into hospital . . ."

I was back at the wheel of my Corvair again, on my way home, driving with the window down and singing at the top of my lungs to stay awake. I'd just attended my first rock concert, with then little-known Australian, Helen Reddy, as the backup artist for Johnny Rivers, performing on campus. Her punchy lyrics helped, for a while.

"I am strong. I am invincible. I am woman." Love that song but feel anything but invincible. Kept singing Anne Murray, Neil

Diamond, John Denver . . . "Rocky Mountain High" as I headed
over another pass. But spirits stayed low as I pulled up to home
more in tune with Gordon Lightfoot's lyrics: "My eyes were red,
my hopes were dead – and the drizzle turned to snow."

Even with clear skies, I needed windscreen wipers for
my eyeballs. A sudden weather change on the other side of
the pass saw me drive back to Montana through a blizzard
but I never told Mum that I skidded on ice and spun into a
snowdrift near Joni Mitchell's hometown of Nanton. Just
like in the song, they'd "paved paradise and put up a parking lot" and it's true that we don't know what we've got till
it's gone.

Doctors found nothing wrong with Mum. She'd taken
ill soon after Dad died, and now the medicos suspected her
illness was psychosomatic. I guess I did, too, but the so-called
generation gap became less of a chasm and our relationship
strengthened with each visit. Her health did not.
Unfortunately, my mother *was* ill. Again, the revelation
came via hindsight.

Barely a year after my father's passing, she was rushed to
hospital again with suspected myeloma, cancer of the bone
marrow for which there was no known cure. Was it related
to the malignant melanoma, the most deadly form of skin
cancer, that she'd had removed years earlier? I was about ten
at the time and had been sent to stay with my Auntie Pat in
Kimberly, British Columbia. No-one told me about Mum
being in hospital until I came home and I never knew the reason. Now, I was almost as bewildered. Myeloma or
melanoma? She seemed resigned to whatever it was and
reluctant, or embarrassed, to ask the doctors questions or
give me answers. Or had she lost the will to live without Dad?

By now I had graduated and had been offered a lectureship at a university in New Jersey, but instead I settled for one at Grande Prairie College, only a few hundred miles away from home. Home was wherever Mum lived so it seemed there was nothing grand about Grande Prairie (apart from the people)! To label the college at the time an "educationally challenging" environment would have been an understatement. Only slightly older than most students, I found that the young men on the ice hockey team were not impressed that I didn't dish out the same generous grades as their previous lecturer, who had also been their coach. In spite of the myth that physical education is all brawn and no brain, I had to work diligently for my degree and therefore so would they; but I found myself skating on thin ice when one jock physically threatened me. I much preferred coaching volleyball and the thrill of leading a team from last place to first in the provincial competition – even though I felt I was often well and truly out of my league.

I visited Mum regularly and we talked on the phone as she was now out of hospital and in remission. But when she needed me the most, I wasn't there.

I can still hear her asking me not to go. I ignored her plea and attended a conference for the American Association of Health, Physical Education and Recreation. I'd only be gone less than a week and the doctor said she could last a few months or a few years. Yes, she was lonely, but I had my own life to live. Hadn't she said that herself after Dad died?

I called repeatedly from a payphone in Florida but there was no answer. Finally I spoke to my cousin who confirmed my worst fear. I returned to Calgary immediately. By 30 April 1973, I was sitting by her hospital bed, reliving scenes that had once played in the miserable past. I shouldn't have gone. I should have arrived sooner. I would have, too, were it not for flash floods in St. Louis that grounded the plane on its stopover from Miami; then a freak blizzard delayed me on a mountain pass in Montana. The rental car wasn't equipped with snow chains and skidded to a grinding halt on the side of the road, with fuel fast running out in sub-zero temperatures. Rescued by a passing truck driver, I arrived at the hospital over 48 hours after leaving Florida – an emotional wreck from a head-on crash with reality – to see Mum looking so much like Dad as she lay there, amid the organized tangle of plastic tubing. My mother was dying.

The doctor gave her three or four more days to live. The despair and helplessness were inexplicable, but worse, far worse was the guilt that still sometimes clouds my life. She'd asked me not to go and now I was paying the ultimate price. My mother didn't even know who I was.

I slept by her bed on a fold-up lounge.

She awoke on the first of May. I looked at the time. It was 6 p.m. She knew me for a moment, and even tried to talk but I couldn't understand a word she struggled to say. I hummed her favourite hymns, hoping they would comfort her. What tiny amount of faith I had – or worse, thought I had – cracked beyond repair. I asked my diary those questions that only people in pain can ask, or expect answers to:

Is it a prerequisite of death to be stripped of all dignity? Hooked to life support? Interminable suffering? Why do good, decent humans die this way, while madman Idi Amin is alive and murdering his own people in Uganda?

There was no answer.

An artificial flower hung from the intravenous pole. Everything was artificial. I wanted to tear those tubes out.

But I couldn't. The most I could do was be there, whether my mother knew it or not.

Mum died on 7 May at 3:54 in the afternoon.

I looked at her for a long, long time. I touched her face. Her hands. But she wasn't there anymore. It was just an empty shell.

I folded up the lounge and left. I called the doctor to say thanks for his futile attempts to save her life and then went for a walk with Blitz and my Auntie Kay before returning to my empty childhood house. It was home no more. My family life was over.

A stranger, someone I'd met on the plane coming home, sent me a postcard. Only he knew why I was impatient, anxious to get home when the flight was delayed by floods, and racked with guilt for going away in the first place. So I wrote back to this Bernie O'Neill and told him *everything*. It was easier to do. Much easier than the next task of having to go through the list of relatives and friends in my mother's address book. I had to tell them that Marg had died. People said she was at peace now. There was no more pain. If I'd any strong conviction in an afterlife, I'd have known that Mum and Dad were together again, but I had no such faith. All I had left was myself – and had never been so alone in my life.

Mum once told me of Dad's final words to her.

We two are one.

And they were.

I guess I cried myself to sleep but apart from what I'd scrawled in my diary, it was all a blur.

Next day, I went to the funeral home. It didn't look like my mother there in that casket. Didn't look like her at all. The undertaker told me in professionally acquired, soft, serene tones that he'd need her birth certificate before he could proceed any further.

I went down to the Bank of Montreal, opposite the Hudson's Bay Company, to the safety deposit box, where all the family's legal papers were kept.

Sorting through a pile of unfamiliar documents, I came across an "Adoption Order in the District Court of Southern Alberta." It was signed by a Judge M.J. Edwards, in the presence of Marion W. Bath, Dougald McLean and Charles B. Hill. I knew who Marion and Dougald were – another honorary aunt and uncle – but who was Charles B. Hill? To this day, I have never found out.

The blue-uniformed gentleman who'd shown me in and unlocked the box stood a little way off, his arms folded as I sat, as if in a prison, reading all about my adoption. My biological parents.

Mum had once offered to tell me about them, but I hadn't wanted to know. And, as she only asked once, I suspect she really didn't want to tell me.

I still didn't want to know but I read on, regardless, as if in a trance – as if this whole scene was unreal and I'd wake up and things would be back to normal again. I should have known that they never would be – and probably never were – not since I came into the world at 4:10 p.m. on 29 September 1950 in Calgary General Hospital, according to the carefully folded documents, yellow with age. My biological mother was five feet, four and a half inches tall, and weighed 116 pounds. Blue eyes, brown hair, and fair complexion, she was described as good-looking, with a pleasing personality. The family was musically inclined.

My biological father was five feet eleven, 178 pounds.

What relevance to anything was height and weight?

Occupations. Education. Number and ages of siblings.

No known serious illnesses in either family, but concerning these two individuals, these human beings, there wasn't a thing.

And then I saw the piece of paper that meant much more to me. It was the application form for adoption. Mum was forty and Dad was fifty and I read how much they desperately wanted to adopt and love a child.

For the twenty-one years since I arrived, life had been one constant surprise for them both. They never knew what I'd be up to next. Or in what physical state I'd be when I dragged myself home. They were stuck with an adventurer, a constant questioner, when they were at an age where they really should have been taking life easier.

Now they were both gone. I'd watched each of them die in much the same way. That was the moment when the truth hit like a tidal wave. I started crying. I thought I was crying quietly. Not so. "Is everything all right?" the man in blue asked. Another stranger who, for a moment in time, cared a little.

"Yes, thank you. Everything's fine," I politely lied.

I left with my mother's birth certificate in hand and the knowledge that my name at birth had been Marilyn Darlene Bachman. But I walked away knowing that I was Catherine Fredrika DeVrye, and always would be.

I didn't cry at the funeral. I was too nauseous and barely remember the service, but it was one of those dreary, impersonal, religious ones about Jesus saving souls rather than a celebration of a life well lived. It hurt to later learn that some neighbours thought I was heartless. They could think what they liked because they would anyway and were not to know that the inside of my mouth and tongue were raw and bleeding where I'd bitten the flesh to curb the tears. All of my life, Mum had scolded me about my conduct. This time, I intended to get it right. Apart from Dad's, the only funeral I'd ever seen was John F. Kennedy's, so I acted the way I thought Mum would be proud of – trying to emulate Jackie K – and showed no emotion. Maybe I should have. Maybe if I'd grieved openly, sadness, loss and guilt wouldn't have followed me faithfully through the next countless number of years.

No sooner had the spring hyacinths pushed through the wintry ground of her garden, than I'd picked them to place on her coffin and felt part of my own life shut down with a padlock of sorrow. Busy buffers pity, so I tidied the house meticulously for the wake. She'd have hated anyone to see it unkempt. Even my grade three teacher and the mailman came to the funeral.

Mum died two days before Mother's Day and I cringed at the marketing hype that surrounded that day. Perpetual bombardments of *Remember Your Mum on Mother's Day* made me want to scream an addition: *And every other day!*

I wanted, so badly, to believe her words: *Things always work out for the best, dear.* How could they now? Would the pain ever end?

The ache that started in my heart and worked its way up into a crashing headache didn't ease at all when the tears, but never the pain, finally welled out – only when no-one was around. Returning to the empty house was the worst part because there were times that I forgot my parents weren't there anymore. And would catch myself starting to talk to them. In all the times Mum had patched up my childhood wounds, she never mentioned that broken bones mended faster than broken hearts. When I left the hospital, I remember being offered medication and counselling. But

I stoically refused both because in our family, psychologists were only for crazy people – or people from California!

In those days, so-called normal people just got on with their lives and left me to get on with mine. But I needed to know how. Instead of flowers, a university friend, Barb, thoughtfully sent me the latest Carole King album that included the track "You've Got a Friend." I'd need friends because there was just my dog Blitz and me. Although my Auntie Kay, Uncle Frank and favourite cousin Dale were supportive, the loss wasn't anything we talked about a lot, so my only therapy was crying myself to sleep – quite effective in many ways. As Mum used to say, *Just sleep on it.*

I went back to Grande Prairie and tried to pick up the pieces. My boyfriend had become engaged to another woman in my absence. Great timing when I needed a shoulder to cry on. I should have been devastated, I suppose, but losing him to another wasn't in the same league as losing my mother. I was still too numb to feel much of anything so simply threw away the ring he'd given me.

Loneliness is as personal as pain; only the affected can truly feel it. There had been times when I envied the bond between my parents although I never fully recognized it until after Dad died, because they were never physically demonstrative of affection. I thought true love was only the romantic, sexy kind – not the deeper feeling of mutual respect and genuine caring for the wellbeing of the other. It seemed to be a love I could only ever hope to have.

Then I met Tim Park on a blind date. We shared three fantastic weeks, including long walks and longer discussions about the meaning of life. I was surprised at the instant intimacy of our relationship. Although I found him incredibly sexy, a bit of a Robert Redford lookalike in my eyes, the attraction was far more than that. In hindsight, it was a bond born of shared grief as much as shared interest. His younger brother had recently committed suicide and we confided to each other our innermost thoughts. Well, almost everything.

The couple who introduced us had adopted a baby but even then, I still didn't tell anyone that I had been adopted. Why? I'm not sure. Possibly I felt it might have been a betrayal of my parents who raised me. They never saw a need to tell anyone so why should I? It was nobody's business. After all, Mum's own sister, my Auntie Kay, didn't know of plans to adopt until, on one of their regular Friday visits to pick up the farm-fresh eggs that the Doukhobor sect religiously delivered to our door, my two-year-old cousin, who'd run in ahead for chocolate chip cookies, rushed right back out to tell his mother, "Auntie Marg has a baby in a drawer!"

As well as sharing the grief of losing loved ones, Tim and I still managed to share laughter. I'd almost forgotten what it was like and Tim was a good escape. But all escapes are short-lived and no-one can run forever. The fun only lasted three weeks. If he'd asked, I'd have probably stayed. He didn't ask.

> My mind more black and clouded than a Prairie sky before a thunderstorm. All this growing up is getting me down. If choices are but stepping stones along the river of life, why haven't I drowned yet?

Even my best friend Val was on the other side of the world. She and her husband, Rod, who I'd once dated, had gone to Melbourne on a teaching exchange. We had been a terrible twosome for many years, apart from my time at graduate school, and I missed her dreadfully. In days prior to email, her letter of reply eventually found its way into my hands at the time I needed it the most. I was both grieving and hiding in pretence.

Dear Cath,
Words are pretty meaningless at a time like this aren't they? I'm sorry everything had to happen to you all in such a short space of time. You must be pretty lost ... There are lots of jobs here and I'm sure Peter Reichenbach would help ... You could get a small flat for $16–$20 per week in South Yarra and would earn about $6000 per year. It would help you start again – if you'd let it. Or at least get away for a while ...

Get away for a while. She'd enclosed a phone number so I called her immediately and it was so good to hear her voice again. Before I'd hung up the receiver, I decided to go to Australia. Everyone thought I was crazy to turn my back on a job I had worked so hard to attain, but my employer refused to give me compassionate leave. Even though frightened and confused, I knew that something had to be done. And soon. I either made the break, or broke.

Peter Reichenbach, the Australian rugby coach at the University of Calgary, informed me that there was a teacher shortage in Australia and the government would pay my airfare and allow me to work tax-free for two years. I'd just seen the film *On the Beach* and had heard what its star Ava Gardner had said about Melbourne: it was the perfect location to film the end of the earth! I had no intention of staying and couldn't make a commitment I wouldn't honour. I was too much like my grandfather in that way. I booked my own flight to

Melbourne, via university summer school in Hawaii (and countless stops in between) and then wrote job applications for what I thought would be a three-month working holiday. I didn't want to stay Down Under forever.

Peter said it would be easy to obtain a permanent resident visa, which would allow me to work. But nothing, not even a piece of official paper, seemed permanent in my life. I was still too frightened of what the future held or even if I had one.

I went home to Scotchman's Hill and cleaned out the house for my cousin to move into. I cleared the basement pantry of all the food supplies Mum had squirreled away, just in case. Just in case of what, Mum? War? Famine? What, exactly, do we *need* all this food for? There are only three of us in this house . . . *were* only two of us, since Granddad and Dad died.

I came across old cardboard boxes of photos. Sadly, there were none of all of us together, because one of the adults was always pointing the camera. Few photos were labelled and I had no idea who many of those pictured were or why they were worth saving.

I also unearthed a collection of primitive paintings and pottery that I'd brought home from school over the years, which Mum had put in the basement for "safekeeping." A card in another tattered brown box read: *Catherine, we hope all your dreams come true.*

I almost heard their voices as I read the words. Well, one of my dream-wishes was being granted very soon as I readied for my travels. But what I wanted the most was the impossible dream – for Mum, Dad and Granddad to be there with me. Right then. All three of them. I wanted everything to be just like it used to be.

I was alone in an empty house that had once been my home.

I was leaving it, hoping for a new life, at least for the next three months.

I continued packing and clearing items for the church. More wares for the missionary sales, no doubt. Baking and knitting that would no longer be displayed on the trestle tables in the church hall. And I thought, as I sat on her bed, her half-complete knitting in hand, of how I'd once wanted to be a missionary and travel the world.

Lacking much faith of any sort, especially in myself, all I had was a one-way airfare to Australia. I'd forfeited my ticket to security – a tenured university lecturing position. But what would have become of me had I stayed? Wasn't I about to do something I'd dreamed of as a child? My parents left the planet without seeing much of it geographically. Alone, aged twenty-two, with no safety net of family, I was now about to attempt my own version of exploration.

I couldn't alter the circumstances that had changed my life forever. But I could change my attitude. There was no point looking backward because nothing could change the situation.

I could only change my perspective. And, temporarily changing my geography might assist in that process.

I was taking the biggest risk of my life to date. There *had* to be a reason, I rationalized, for my parents' deaths, but I had no idea what it could possibly be. In the self-absorption of my grief I thought their passing must have freed me from the constraints of ordinary family responsibility to embark upon the extraordinary. I would do something important with my life – maybe discover a cure for cancer, selectively ignoring the fact that I'd failed high school physics. If not curing cancer, then I'd achieve something equally magnanimous like negotiating world peace. I had no idea what I'd do but for the next three months, I'd do it in Australia.

In short, I had no idea at all what to do! But I did know

that responsibility for my own life rested squarely on my shoulders, those same ones Mum always nagged me to straighten when I hunched as a gawky teenager. Now they carried guilt along with my backpack. I sewed a maple leaf flag on the backpack and carefully stitched jewellery, a hair dryer and other assorted sundries into the lining of my red suede jacket, strictly observing the forty-pound luggage limit. If there'd been airport security in those days I'd have triggered every alarm in the place as I waddled my way through. I didn't know I could pay for excess baggage and had carefully weighed my backpack on the bathroom scales, and then made my contingency plans!

Securely stashed in my underwear was $300 – all I had until I could find a job, which had not yet been confirmed.

Before I said goodbye to Canada, the only sea I'd seen was from the Nanaimo ferry in Vancouver while securely holding Mum's hand. On my flight to Australia, as the group of green Hawaiian Islands appeared across the expanse of Pacific blue, I remembered I no longer had a hand to hold. Instead I grasped at the positive thoughts within Richard Bach's parable of *Jonathan Livingstone Seagull*, the first so-called self-help book I'd ever read. The gull in the tale flew alongside the mechanical metal bird, cawing:

> If you think you can, you're probably right. And, if you think you can't, you're also probably right.

I'd been pushed out of the nest by events beyond my control and had no choice but to frantically flap my wings and learn to fly as best I could to avoid a nosedive into despair. On this initial flight of unwanted freedom, my first stop was Hawaii.

7

SHE'LL BE RIGHT, MATE

 My résumé testified to a sound education. An official gold-edged degree was neatly framed, but the degree of inner fear and sadness knew no such borders. I enrolled in both Golf and Communications at the University of Hawaii Summer School because the dorm was the cheapest accommodation in this Pacific paradise. I explored the possibility of rekindling the spark of a relationship with a gridiron player from my Montana days who now lived in Honolulu. Maybe that would make me happy?

I was once paranoid about Mum reading my diary. Now I wanted to share everything with her. If only I could have . . .

You're young. You're free. You're acting it, too. Then someone will say, concern in their eyes: "Don't your parents miss you?" They died. Oh, I'm terribly sorry. Was it an accident? No, it was cancer. An awkward, heavy silence ensues.

Such questioning occurred only two or three times, but it was far too often for my comfort. I vowed never to mention my parents again. Sympathy would not be a crutch once I reached Australia. No way. I felt sorry enough for myself without having others feel it too. So, subsequently whenever anyone asked if I missed my family or they missed me, I'd simply reply: *It's not an issue*. And quickly change the conversation.

Maybe these well-meaning people imagined all kinds of childhood horrors. Denial was my defence against sorrow – and not a very effective one, as the pain was buried so deep inside that it became invisible to others.

The old boyfriend led a lifestyle that may have temporarily appealed to my sense of youthful adventure and newfound freedom but when guns were brandished at parties, I knew this wasn't my sort of long-term lifestyle. I loved Hawaii but still hated myself for not being home for Mum and the void inside simply deepened. I felt no better on the beautiful beaches of Hawaii than I had on the land-locked prairie of Calgary and hoped Australia would cure whatever it was that ailed me as I headed farther west and south to the much bigger island Down Under.

Good things are worth waiting for, Catherine. My mother's words echoed in my head as the unending flight continued. In those days, with stops in Fiji, Tahiti and New Zealand, it took nearly two days to reach the land of kangaroos, koalas, sandy beaches, bronzed surfers and endless sunshine. I couldn't wait to get off the stinking plane. On 29 August 1973, I walked out of the arrivals hall at Tullamarine Airport, Melbourne, wearing white bell-bottomed pants and a hot-pink floral bare-midriff Hawaiian shirt. A freezing southerly gust straight from the Antarctic greeted me, along with Val and Rod holding a bunch of daffodils.

Enduring the interminable flight had been worth it. Mum was right again. A good thing was waiting for me. Val. Val was here . . .

But it was so *cold*. Where were the bronzed Aussies? How could you get a tan without any sun? Where could I buy a sweater? (Or jumper, as Australians called it.) What a dismal place this was.

Expectations again. Nothing is ever how you imagine it will be. Strangely, Val and I never really spoke about grief. We were both too uncomfortable with this thing called death – so we just ignored it. But at least she was there and she explained where I should go to apply for a job the next day.

The Education Department supervisor asked, "Do you mind going to Broadmeadows High?"

Sounded good to me. It conjured images of lush, green English pastures spreading as far as the eye could see. "No objection. Should I?"

"Of course not."

Maybe I didn't quite recognize that *here's a sucker look* in the supervisor's eye when he added, "You can start next week," conveniently omitting that Broadmeadows was the roughest school in Australia.

Fine. I had a job and next needed to find a place to live, as it was time to move on from the living-room floor of Val and Rod's South Yarra flat. An accommodation agency sent me on wild goose chases to places with outside toilets, no phones, screaming kids and even to a brothel! No thanks.

I felt ready to give up when I knocked on the door of 25 Margaret Street, Oak Park. Margaret. My mother's name. It seemed a good omen. There was a welcome mat underfoot and a dog barked from inside. A big dog. My hopes rose. I thought of Blitz and wondered how she was.

Frank Jansen opened the door. At first, all I saw were his laughing blue eyes and for an instant there was something almost magical that reminded me of my grandfather, until Frank opened his mouth and broke the spell. In a broad Australian accent, he said, "Gidday. You must be Cath. Get yourself inside." He stood aside as I walked into the warm, homely lounge room. "This is Betty, me wife. She won't talk yet. Not while her show's on telly." So I sat and waited for

Aussie entertainment icon Graham Kennedy to end his hour – a photo of this talk-show host was propped on the mantel. I wondered with an inner smile exactly what I'd stepped into here, and then I felt the wet nose nuzzling my hand. The dog I'd heard barking was a golden labrador and it was love at first sight.

I moved into Frank and Betty Jansen's home the next day and immediately took my place within their family of two. They were childless and I had no parents so it seemed a good fit.

My life in Australia truly began from the moment I knocked on that door. Frank, past president of the Flemington Bowls Club, was a "have-a-chat bloke" by nature, provided Betty let him get a word in, of course. No-one I've met, then or since, could compare to Frank, as he regaled me with tales of Oz. "Shut up, fat!" Betty would screech. "You'd talk under wet cement!"

He'd ignore her. "Pass the Uncle Ned along the Aesop's Fable, would ya, love?" he'd say, and I'd look for whatever possibly could be the Uncle Ned on whatever might be the Aesop's Fable. In his rhyming slang, he simply wanted me to pass the bread along the table. Betty threw a lamb chop at him instead. It took me a while to get used to it, as I'd never heard an angry word pass between my own parents. Fate surely brought me into the Jansen household so I could better appreciate the harmony in my childhood home.

At their fiftieth wedding anniversary, Frank proclaimed: "Righto then. Shoosh up now! Hoi!"

The gathering in the backyard quieted.

"Now, a lot of you think Betty and I fight a lot but the truth is we've only had one blue in our lives."

The group was aghast and pin-drop quiet.

"It started the day we got married and hasn't bloody well stopped!"

Roars of laughter ensued.

Betty never wanted a party. "Who'd want to be reminded of being bloody married to him for fifty miserable years?" Yet they adored each other.

Once I dated a divorcee and Betty answered the door with a screech: "Cath! Your second-hand man's here!" I never saw him again. But it didn't matter. I was one of the family by then, according to Frank. His pearls of wisdom included, "Look, love, we're here for a good time, not a long time. Right?"

Right. Whatever you say, Frank.

Life was either bonza, beaut or fan-bloody-tastic and *Bob's your uncle* meant fine. No worries mate, she'll be right.

Maybe. But as far as I was concerned, this was not the land of perpetual sunshine and bronzed surfers. I was cold and miserable most of the time. "But you mustn't mind the cold, being Canadian."

"Why do you think I left? Am I as silly as I look?" (No need to answer that last question.) I'd recount stories from Calgary of emerging from an indoor swimming pool with wet hair which, if not thoroughly dried before we left the sports complex, would freeze and snap off. It got so cold your nostrils burned.

Still, we had always enjoyed the ever-present comfort of central heating. Now hanging my behind over an open fireplace in Australia was not my idea of how to keep warm. By the time my ski jacket and mitts arrived by sea mail from Canada, a 42°Celsius Melbourne summer was upon us when it was about that much below zero back home.

And who could get used to the names of meal times? Frank helped as much as he could. "Look, luv," he'd say, voice deep and serious, underscoring subtle humour. "Over here, tea is dinner. Supper's a late-night snack. Breakfast is brekkie. Lunch is still lunch." Now when are you going to get it? Frank's bright, teasing eyes would ask. Surely, you're not *that* thick? Didn't you say you had a degree in somethin' or other?

Frank's education came from the University of Life and some of his gems remain embedded in my psyche. My favourite, now on my business cards, was a pithy one-liner; nine little words that gradually helped me look forward: *Every day above the ground is a good one.*

It took me a long time to recognize the truth in his philosophy. I was still pretending back then – pretending all was fine when inside I was crumbling – although I still had that smile on the outside, remembering my father's last word.

Then there was the job. It was . . . character-building. My first encounter with students at Broadmeadows High was a paradox of uniformity and chaos. Parallel lines of identically clad students gathered at morning assembly on a drizzly wet day. On the field hockey pitch, a horse and a few sheep grazed, oblivious to the heated debate between two teachers before the principal commenced the day's proceedings.

"We're going to sing 'God Save the Queen.'"

"No, we're not. It's not the national anthem."

"No-one knows the words to the national anthem."

"I do."

"That's because you're a Communist."

What have I got myself into here? I wondered that first day. My own education in a so-called underprivileged school was of some benefit in understanding what went on in the grey matter of those kids seated in identical grey uniforms in neat rows before me. It would have been easy to forget that each was an individual. Discipline was virtually non-existent. The principal couldn't understand why I ousted one twelve-year-old from class for telling me to "F . . . off."

"He said it was the first time he said it to you."

Yeah. The first and the last as far as I was concerned. The education system seemed more Victorian than the state. I was barred from teaching Australian Rules football to the 120 girls in one class. The principal worried about the moral implications of females lifting their legs to kick the football, but for some illogical reason, they were allowed to high jump.

"Who do you barrack for, Miss?" I'd never heard the term "barrack" but figured the students wanted to know what team I supported. Knowing little about Aussie Rules football, I thought it was a safe bet to pick the winning team.

"I root for the Tigers," said I, innocently.

The entire class looked at me aghast.

"*All* of them, Miss?"

"Of course!" I thought this raggedy portion of Australian youth were all a little strange in not cheering for the entire team.

One thing Frank *hadn't* told me was that in Australia "root" meant sexual intercourse. I had no idea of the extent of my faux pas until the next morning, when angry mothers phoned to question my morality. Pity those migrants who don't have English as a first language. Frank was equally incensed that I didn't cheer for his beloved Swans so I readily switched allegiances.

How I held my head high in class the following day is anyone's guess.

After that blunder, I was assigned to teach a new subject without texts or curriculum: *Australian Folklore*. Me? They had to be kidding! I hadn't even seen a live kangaroo yet nor heard of legendary outlaw Ned Kelly. Needless to say, I learned fast. At Broadmeadows High, you had to.

I generally enjoyed the enthusiastic youngsters but was an inadequate teacher of curriculum so tried to instill self-esteem instead. Although I'd once lived in a "disadvantaged" neighbourhood, I had been fortunate enough to have many excellent teachers. I still remember their names and was influenced, one way or another, by them all. One enlightened school principal wrote in my autograph book, *Minds are like parachutes – dangerous if not kept open.*

I remembered that because I knew what it was like, buying into self-fulfilling prophecies. Unfortunately, I had little inner pride during my time at Broadmeadows but I tried to help the students when I couldn't help myself. I was homesick for Canada and what made it worse was the stark realization that there was no home to return to.

During those early days Down Under, my diary writing went berserk with random thoughts and poor poetry. Much of the ink was smudged with tears, as I still didn't speak to anyone about my parents' deaths.

Val went to hospital for a minor operation. I broke down while visiting. There were still too many memories of hospital rooms. Other Canadian friends dropped in while she was recovering. They didn't have a telephone and debated the cost of calling their parents from the post office. Could they afford it?

Could they afford not to? I thought but said nothing. Learning comes from personal experience. I could have told them what it was like not having parents anymore but none of them would have really listened. They were too much like me – before, of course.

My experiences at Broadmeadows High made me more fully appreciate my own upbringing. I'd had parents who cared. Many of my students didn't even have that.

I had only planned to stay one term and had not saved enough for my return airfare to Canada, although Val and Rod had now returned. Constantly fighting blinding headaches, which plagued me for months, I was certain I had a brain tumour. The doctors found nothing and said it was psychosomatic. That's what they said about Mum . . .

It was only a severe allergic reaction to wattle and other unfamiliar spring pollens. The pain eased when I travelled, and I took every opportunity to do so.

On 20 October 1973, a friend and I took the night train to attend the opening of the Sydney Opera House by Queen Elizabeth II. "God Save the Queen" was indeed played on that occasion. Although controversy surrounded its construction, I couldn't imagine Sydney without the Opera House. It was hardly an intimate gathering with a million spectators, 2000 boats and 50,000 balloons – and the Botanic Gardens littered with streamers in the midst of a garbage strike. The frequency of industrial action in Australia was no longer a surprise. One radio show interrupted a broadcast to announce: "This station will be going on strike in ten minutes."

And so it did!

In November, another teacher and I flew to Tasmania and hitchhiked from Launceston to Deloraine in a cattle truck. The driver proudly informed us: "I've never been outside Tassie. Don't need to. 'Ava good life here. I'll give yous a tour of Mole Creek. On your right is a tree. On your left, a sheep."

He roared with laughter. Oh, boy, Australia sure is a strange kind of place, I thought – or maybe he was lucky to be happy within his narrow horizons. A country of contrasts – the next person kind enough to give us a lift was the

British cancer researcher, Sir Richard Doll. I so wished he'd achieve his dream of discovering a cure, but still never mentioned a word about my folks.

Just before Christmas, Carole Lien, an old university friend, sent me a telegram that read simply: *Meet me in Nambour on Boxing Day.*

Where on earth was Nambour? Christmas was the only day of the year when I missed snow. Surely those Santas on street corners must swelter, with faces as red as their felt jackets.

The train headed northwest from Brisbane through the Glasshouse Mountains as I sat and chatted with the driver, thinking of my father as we swapped stories of the Canadian Pacific Railway.

Nambour, a country town in southeastern Queensland, was much larger than I expected. "Do you happen to know if there are any Canadians in town?" I asked. The stationmaster seemed singularly uninterested in my question, so I hoisted my backpack and made my way in the blistering afternoon sun to the Commercial Hotel, where I ordered an ice-cold beer and asked the barman the same question.

"Yep. There's a few of 'em here for the rodeo schools. I think that bloke in the corner there's one of 'em. But he might be American. Never can tell the difference."

I tentatively approached the good-looking stranger and reiterated my question. Yes! Canadian! And yes, he also knew Carole Lien. "She's probably down at the showgrounds and I'm heading down there shortly. Where are you from?" he asked.

"Calgary."

"Me too. Whereabouts?"

"Scotchman's Hill."

"Yeah? I used to live there as a kid. Went to Ramsay School for a while."

"Really!"

We were in the same grade three class. In the interim, Alan Hern had become a handsome man. In his tight jeans, boots and Stetson hat, he easily could have starred in his own Western.

We left the hotel and reminisced all the way to the rodeo grounds, where I met up with Carole again. With her was her heartthrob, Malcolm Jones. He was a Canadian champion cowboy, in Australia to teach bronc riding.

Fifteen years would pass before coincidence connected us yet again, but at the time, 1973, my main focus was on having a good time – at least, that's what my diary says.

> The parties were fun at first but became more boring than a dead bull after a while. I've always wanted to be part of the cowboy way of life, but realize I just don't fit in. Not really sure anymore where I do fit in, or if I'll ever fit in. Can't see the point in going to bars or pubs and answering the same dumb questions asked by the same sort of dumb guys who aren't interested in the questions at all . . .

Carole was luckier. She had Malcolm here and her family at home. The only creatures that shared my cheap accommodation were cockroaches and two other solo female travellers.

After the school summer vacation, I returned to the Jansens and Broadmeadows High. Everyone thought it best that I find a suitable man and settle down. It seemed the obvious answer to all, except me. Yes, it would be good to love someone. But I doubted I could endure loss ever again and besides, commitment was not on my agenda. Instead, after finishing another term at Broadmeadows in May, I travelled even more; working as a waitress in Surfers Paradise, a chambermaid in Cairns and rejecting a marriage proposal on a cruise ship by a gorgeous Greek purser who wanted to keep me barefoot and pregnant in Thessalonika. Perhaps I saw more of Australia than most Australians do in a lifetime. I kept moving. When I travelled, and busily bombarded my senses with all manner of sights and sounds, then I wasn't thinking, was I. Thinking of my own loneliness and aimlessness . . . My lack of goals, dreams, ambitions.

> It sometimes felt I was treading water and someone had pulled the plug on the big bath tub of life as I was being sucked in a downward spiral – even if the water did drain counter-clockwise in the Southern Hemisphere. Maybe I'd made a mistake coming to Australia. Whatever I was desperately seeking certainly wasn't here.

I decided to go back to Calgary but still needed more funds for the airfare. So I headed north to a bauxite mine in Weipa, Far North Queensland, where I'd heard the money was better than teaching. Comalco hired me as a relieving computer operator. Ever the physical education teacher, I overprinted the paycheques: *Health is wealth and tax-free!* It wasn't appreciated, or so I thought, until the data-processing manager offered me either a full-time job to train as a programmer in their head office or a referral to IBM.

What? Me? Work full-time with mindless machines? No way, I'm a people person. Besides, I'm just biding my time to earn enough for the airfare home.

In the early 1970s, it was much easier for young people to get work. Life in Weipa was . . . different. "Stubbies" were central to life up there. A stubbie could be either a bottle of beer or a pair of sturdy, cotton, working shorts. In most instances, the beer bellies created by the former hung lazily over the elasticized waistbands of the latter! With ample supplies of both, a group of us would pile in the "ute" (i.e., a jeep) to explore the surrounds, often encountering goannas (huge lizards) as long as the road was wide. Locals kept pet geckos (smaller lizards) on their walls to eat the flies. Less friendly reptiles were the crocs; as a Canadian, it was of interest to me that crocodiles and polar bears are two animal predators that actively hunt humans. This was not a similarity between the outback and tundra frontiers that I found particularly reassuring!

Weipa was a largely featureless town of identical mining company dwellings then. It wasn't uncommon to walk into the wrong house – even when sober. Sobering too was the post-pub aggression between the miners and indigenous peoples. In contrast, a highlight of my stay was the traditional wedding on Thursday Island of a teacher who shared a house with me and two others.

Political correctness, whether racial or sexist, was unheard of. Only a handful of single women inhabited the mining community of two thousand men. One joked it was more of a gold mine than a bauxite one! Many of the blokes were about as suave as a broken beer bottle. Constant wolf whistles, even on the way to work in the morning, made me decidedly uncomfortable. Maybe I didn't want to get too comfortable. After all, I was going back to Canada, wasn't I?

The "universe" had other plans. The time to leave Weipa duly arrived. There was an unseemly delay on the trip back to Melbourne when the plane was stranded in Alice Springs because of flooding in this normally arid region. Local legend has it that if you see the Todd River in flood once, you will return. If you see it in flood twice, you will stay. In a couple of weeks I never expected to see Australia again, let alone the centre of this outback land. How different to that last flight delay from floods, when I desperately wanted to get home to see Mum. This time I was in no particular hurry and fate was quietly at work behind the scenes as I browsed through *The Australian* newspaper. In the classifieds, an ad jumped out for the newly formed Victorian Department of Youth, Sport and Recreation.

"*He* will have a degree. *His* skills should emphasize leadership . . ."

Oh, will *he* really?

I was challenged just by that wording alone to "give it a go."

Nah, couldn't. I was going home to Canada. I was going to start over again, wasn't I?

I did the crossword instead. But the thought kept niggling. I was qualified. I could do it, even though I was a she. . .

I finished the crossword and still the plane hadn't budged an inch on the tarmac. What else to do to alleviate this tedious wait?

I asked the flight attendant for some paper and penned my application on the airline letterhead with my landlord and now friend Frank Jansen's voice echoing in my head: '*Ave a go, ya mug. 'Ave a bloody go.*

When we finally landed in Melbourne, I hand-delivered the application and informed the receptionist that the bureaucracy had exactly two weeks to decide because I was going back to Canada.

I walked out, never expecting to hear a word.

Two weeks to go. No job, with room and board to pay. A temp agency sent me to hand out cigarettes in a tobacconist's shop on Puckle Street, Moonee Ponds, home of theatrical character, Dame Edna Everage. My first day was rendered unproductive because of yet another strike that left the shop cigarette-less. Day two, I burned someone's nose while lighting his cigarette and an underage kid kicked me in the shins because I wouldn't give him a smoke. I'd never forgotten the damage smoking did to Dad. That job lasted three days when the company rep overheard the subversive spiel I'd devised for a job I hated and felt compromised in . . . *Care for an Ardath cigarette, sir? Only 37 cents a pack and guaranteed to give you cancer as fast as any expensive brand . . .*

I removed the silly sash and resigned before I got fired on the spot, feeling much better about myself, too.

Back at Jansens that night, still my Australian base, there was a telegram waiting. I was invited for an interview with the minister for youth, sport and recreation. *Stone the crows!* Frank exclaimed when he dropped me at the train station to head into town for the interview.

The minister asked the standard question – why had I left my last job? I told him, almost showed him the bruise on my shin, too, and the Honourable Brian Dixon, a former Australian Rules football star and staunch anti-smoking campaigner, roared with laughter.

She got the job. Almost certainly due in part to that all-Australian echo in my head – *'Ave a go, ya mug. 'Ave a bloody go!*

My new job wouldn't start for a few weeks yet, so I cashed in my ticket to Canada for a tour of Manila and Hong Kong instead. Why not?

Mesmerized by Hong Kong, my first visit to a non-Western country, I thought of Mum's threats when I was being a brat to send me on a slow boat to China. Little did she realize what a reward that would have been. I would have misbehaved even more had I known!

An old oriental proverb muses that if the parents lead a good life, the child will have good fortune. Perhaps that's why everything had been going my way, even though I still felt undeserving and had managed to erect my own personal Great Wall firmly around any public display of emotion.

8

PUBLIC SERVICE

I started my new job at the Department of Youth, Sport and Recreation in August 1974. Any self-imposed despair lingering on my work horizon soon evaporated. I had the good fortune to work with Bert Keddie, the director-general, and Doug Neville, the deputy.

They were among life's true gentlemen, and living proof that the term "public service" need not be an oxymoron.

It seemed unbelievable that I was actually paid to be involved in sport! Mum was right again. Good things are worth waiting for. As a small team of sports enthusiasts, we had no idea of the stereotyped public service mentality and often worked late in the evenings and on weekends.

Under the leadership of Dixon, Keddie and Neville, a team of eight men and myself helped set much of the blueprint for sport and recreation in Australia because Victoria was the first state to have a department dedicated to such pursuits. We approached our task seriously and rigorously debated policy formulation. At the same time, it was a labour of love, helped by a sense of humour. We often joked about my being the token female but I only occasionally questioned my chances of survival in that mainly macho world of 1970s sport. I knew I was accepted as one of the boys when a colleague with whom I was having a verbal disagreement stormed out of a meeting with the words: "I liked you better when you were a token!"

Although there are some documented diary entries of harassment, I didn't have time to worry about mere sexist setbacks. Camaraderie, commitment and teamwork overshadowed the occasionally calculated, but largely unintentional, discriminatory actions. In hindsight, the sporadic sexism I endured was but a small price to pay for the establishment of lifelong friendships based on mutual respect when my boss Bert Keddie and his wife Greta took me under their wing and fostered a familylike environment in the midst of the public service.

We were all enthusiastic and idealistic. That helped, considering we were in largely uncharted territory when we tackled such issues as safety standards for buildings, bike paths, sports grounds and pools. We developed funding programs for junior coaching programs and seniors' recreation, held inaugural fun runs and helped stage international events. With the sunny idealism of youth on our side, we possessed a certain intellectual arrogance about the legislation and policies we drafted.

Years later, when the department had grown to more than one hundred employees, one of my staff came to me with a recommendation for financial assistance to one of the eighty sporting associations we funded. When I disagreed with his proposed course of action, he pointed out that a precedent had been set in regard to a similar grant.

"Who in their right mind would have made a dumb recommendation like that?" I asked. He suppressed a smirk and pointed to my own scrawled signature on the ageing file as we burst out laughing. Yes, a sense of humour does help. I took my work seriously but never myself.

Self-assured in the office, I was surprisingly shy in social situations and relied on a few drinks to gain that confidence and "Dutch courage" that my father apparently hadn't needed to sustain him when he left his homeland of Holland. Brandy to light the Christmas pudding was the only alcohol in my childhood home and onions were the only thing ever pickled. Unfortunately, I hadn't learned to handle the "firewater" referred to so disparagingly by my parents. Shame was a fortuitous catalyst for change. On 29 October 1974 I had sipped a few too many sherries and was embarrassingly tipsy when I met Prince Charles at a Royal Commonwealth Society dinner. The conversation apparently included such gems as:

"What part of Canada are you from?"

"Good on ya. Most people think I'm American. No wonder you'll be King one day."

"Are you living here for good?"

"For good or for bad, you know what they say."

"Possibly you'll marry an Australian."

"You never know your luck, sport . . ."

By all accounts the next morning, Prince Charles had seemed more amused than my boss, the minister, who had removed me gracefully from the function. It was only the second time in my life I had been rolling drunk and I vowed it would be the last.

The blokes at work bet $5 that I couldn't go a week without a drink. It was double or nothing for a month. Apart from the riches of $10, waking up without a hangover was an unexpected bonus. How did I do it? I'd always been a determined (some would say stubborn) person so when I decided, that was it. I simply quit. It wasn't easy, though, with the peer pressure to be one of the boys at the pub. The only other non-drinker I knew at the time was runner Ron

Clarke, who carried the torch to light the flame at the 1956 Melbourne Olympics.

Although I'd always believed in a healthy body and mind, I discovered an aversion to mirrors. It must have been the "high life." Too much rich food, booze and coffee was taking its toll. I decided to quit the latter two and, apart from a couple of cappuccinos a month, haven't had tea or coffee since. I also totally abstained from alcohol for eight years, which may have been a bit excessive, but probably only compensated for what I had indiscriminately consumed in my days at university and during my first year Down Under.

And so it was that I started on the road back to fitness. I'd take twenty-three flights of stairs to the office, and use bicycles instead of company cars to get from one meeting to another. In stark contrast to the ideals of my job, I'd been overeating, possibly to try to fill the void inside. A diary entry reads:

> Loneliness is like a bad tooth. All it needs is a filling – but overeating is an empty pursuit. A newspaper article links diet to cancer. With my luck, I'll be on my deathbed when researchers announce that whatever dreaded disease I'm dying from, could have been prevented by more chocolate. Anything that tastes so good couldn't possibly be bad for us!

Pretense, camouflage. Call it whatever label may fit. Maybe I'd been in hiding or if I wasn't hiding, was I still running away? I wished that I didn't have to sleep because when I slept I was plagued by nightmares. I'd be back in the hospital rooms, watching my parents die over and over again. Assuming that excessive physical exercise would make the body too exhausted for the mind to bother it with bad dreams, I took up tennis with a vengeance.

It didn't help my nightmares but being with people was a soothing balm. I realize now what my problem was. I wanted what I couldn't have and tortured myself because what I wanted was impossible. I wanted my parents back. I wanted to tell them I was sorry. If I wasn't working so hard that I had no time to think, I was drowning in self-pity, devouring too much of the wrong foods, and then pushing my body to its physical limits. In short, I was a mess on the inside although seemingly bubbly on the outside.

Cyclone Tracy helped change that, and Christmas Day 1974 became a turning point for me. The city of Darwin was flattened on this most special day of the year for many, although for me it was the most dreaded day because it heightened my sense of loss. Now I saw so many others who had lost loved ones. Too many people had lost *everything* on a day that was meant to be a day of giving. Just who did I think I was? There were so many far worse off than me. On New Year's Eve, I worked until dawn on the telethon appeal for the victims.

When you're down, everyone else seems happy. And when you're happy, who stops to think that someone else might be sad?

Somewhere, from the edges, I'd heard: *You have the gift of life. What you do with it is your gift to others.*

I was spurred to start putting something back into a world that had given me so much. My problem was what to give in return. A newspaper ad provided a quick fix. I sponsored a Filipino girl whose favourite subject at school was physical education. Sending money each month to a foster child didn't compare with the commitment my parents made when they adopted me, but eased my conscience a little and each night I'd pray – or maybe it was more of a self-affirmation, in lieu of any strong denominational faith: *Thank you for everything I have. And everything I don't have . . . like famine, disease, hate and persecution . . .*

I wondered why some individuals had so much material wealth and others so little. Still spending most of whatever I earned from my comfortable but modest public service salary, I took a gamble on a "hot" stock-market tip from a man I met in a pub – hardly the wisest wealth creation strategy to pursue. When my next pay arrived, I entered the doors of the Melbourne Stock Exchange. With the suave sophistication normally reserved for dark-suited business tycoons, I informed the uniformed man on the desk that I'd like to invest $100 and showed him the cash just to be sure he'd take me seriously.

"Who's your broker?" he patiently asked.

"What's a broker?"

So much for financial savvy! He pointed to a sign near the lift, which listed an array of companies. My lunch hour was rapidly running out so I walked into the nearest office and made my first investment. It was a penny-dreadful stock, trading for the whopping sum of 1.5 cents. It doubled to 3 cents the following day and my broker must have doubled up with laughter, or agony, as I sold them, waited another 48 hours to buy again at 1.5 and sell at 3. Buoyed by a rush of business confidence, I did this a few times and before my next fortnightly pay, had earned more money on the stock market in a few minutes than I had at work for two weeks. Being a tycoon wasn't so difficult after all – and would allow me to sponsor more children. I knew I'd been lucky and luckily never believed in putting all my eggs in one basket so sold half the penny-dreadful stock to put into a blue chip . . . and as might be anticipated, soon lost every cent on the stock that got me started.

Membership of the Melbourne Junior Chamber of Commerce, where I was later elected first female on the executive, extended my understanding of business.

But, more enlightening was the introduction to a single word in 1975. Serendipity. It was in a book given to me by a university friend, Barb Marbut, whom I haven't seen since but think of often with gratitude, for introducing me to that wondrous word that set me off on a road that eventually headed towards a brighter new direction. In a nutshell, serendipity suggests that good comes from bad, positives from negatives, and opportunities from obstacles. Mum would have probably phrased it as "every cloud has a silver lining" or "blessings in disguise" because I'm quite sure that, like me, she'd never heard of serendipity. Yet, it was the only thing that had made any sense since her death and it was time to face the past.

On my next annual leave, I returned to Canada. Even though it wasn't home anymore, I had friends and relatives to catch up with. And of course Blitz, my dog. She'd been cared for by Val and Rod, who were now living in my parents' house. Once again it echoed with the laughter of children. They had two youngsters and another on the way.

Mum had always knitted sweaters and booties for new babies so I'd done likewise for Val's first daughter. "Cath, I know home economics wasn't your favourite subject at school and appreciate how much love and work you put into this . . . but I think I should tell you that we had a daughter, not a gorilla!" The sleeves stretched to her toes. Knit one. Pearl two.

Val and I would always be friends, regardless of the different choices we'd made. But the physical distance and the changes in my life were marked. The people I once loved, and still do, hadn't changed at all. My tales of a new land and new perspective – all I'd seen and done – were insignificant compared to conversation centred on new curtains, new babies, new cars and hailstorm damage. It wasn't right or wrong. It was just different. I felt I now looked at my Canadian friends' lives through a telescope, not a microscope.

Nothing at all had changed for these people, but everything had for me and it was certainly not a homecoming. Briefly, I wondered whether it would be wise to leave the verve of Australia forever and settle down in my hometown, Calgary. For peace, quiet. That's what these people said I needed, but what did I want to do, really? Did I still want to make a difference in the world? Would I be happy if I tried to fit in here once again? Apart from my aunt and uncle and a few far-flung cousins and friends who all had their own lives to live, there was little in Canada left for me.

I returned to Australia via Europe to attend a sports conference in Holland. Dad was a Dutch orphan who hadn't been given the same chances I had been. He'd wanted to be an architect all his life but it was a dream he never realized and that was, basically, all I knew about him. My own fault – I'd never thought to ask more. Now, I visited the surviving members of his family, with whom he had only reunited in the year of his death. His niece and her husband picked me up from the train station in the tiny town of Heiloo, just outside Amsterdam, and immediately whisked me away to a church function.

The plethora of Droste chocolate, Speculaas biscuits and Leyden cheese made me feel strangely at home. Fuelled by memories from these powerful taste-triggers, I felt comfortable being introduced to people who could not have been kinder. Many didn't speak English but somehow, we managed to communicate. I'd never seen so much kissing and handshaking! In the loft, tucked lovingly in a featherbed, I wished my dad were with me.

I should have known more about my father, his family, and his native country. More than anything, I should have known more about my father, the man. My Dutch relatives helped fill in some gaps . . .

Hendrick DeVrye was born in 1900 in Amersfoort, the youngest child in a family that encouraged all six children in cultural pursuits. He was orphaned at six years of age when his mother died of cancer and his father, unable to cope, ran off.

A family took Dad in and showed him great kindness, which he vowed to repay one day. He worked as a chef's assistant from the age of twelve. Years later, he again met his older sister. She had married a widower who had a daughter from his previous marriage. Pretty, young Annie was Dad's first love but she died of tuberculosis before her twentieth birthday and, just like me, it was through the separation of death that my father's new life truly began. In 1926, Dad emigrated to Canada, heartbroken but still hoping to pursue a career in architecture. There was nothing left for him in Holland, and there weren't many opportunities for untrained architects in Canada during the Depression. In fact, there was little construction work, even for trained professionals. But people still needed to eat and so did my father, and Canadian Pacific Railway needed capable cooks for their coast-to-coast dining cars.

"I vill vork hard," he proclaimed to the foreman in his thick Dutch accent. He had no option. During World War

II he was a mess sergeant in the Royal Canadian Air Force, stationed in Alaska.

Even though my mother did most of the cooking, I always associated my father with food. He not only provided for us as a chef, but our happiest family times were spent around the old walnut dining-room extension table with its carved legs, starched white linen tablecloth and needlepoint seat covers that he had helped my mother handstitch. My father was on his feet all day in commercial kitchens, so it's not surprising that Mum did most of the cooking at home. Meals were plain and simple – meat, potatoes, vegetables and homemade pie. Always preceded by grace and served on fine china, the actual fare must have been quite a contrast from the cordon bleu delicacies Dad once prepared on the train for King George VI on his Coronation Tour of 1937. It wasn't the same as being an architect but it was a good start in his new country, which he saw from the window of the moving kitchen on wheels.

That was before my time, of course. It's hard for me to think of my father as ever being young. And just as hard to remember what we talked about around our table. I don't recall political discussions, intellectual debates, raucous laughter or anything in particular, just pleasant enough times – apart from when I refused to eat liver. It would appear on my breakfast plate with a tirade about starving children in India. "Mail it to them," was my stubborn reply, as I'd smuggle the leftovers into the pocket of my cobbler apron which never quite protected me, as Mum had hoped, from the spills of life.

Dad forever warned me not to talk to strangers. That was like asking the rivers to stop flowing seaward from the Great Divide near Kicking Horse Pass in Western Canada. Although I couldn't articulate it then, strangers have always simply been friends I haven't yet met and still feel that way.

Apart from the occasional Dutch delicacy and the short-lived bloom of spring tulips, my childhood had little connection with the Netherlands, although one photo in the family album shows me dressed up as little Dutch girl for some unknown occasion. Even without the national costume, people always commented on my likeness to my father, both of us having similar complexions and brown hair. They obviously didn't know I'd been adopted. Nor did I back then.

I talked Dad into riding the Wild Mouse with me at the Calgary Stampede amusement park. I'm sure it took ten years off his life but I never even thought about the risk on the roller-coaster, Ferris wheel or dodgem cars. As I got older, I spent all my pocket money not on fast rides but gambling, throwing balls through hoops . . .

Dad and I flew kites in the park.

"Maginty," he would say, using a childhood nickname, whose derivation is a mystery to me, "we cannot change the wind but we can alter the direction we want to go."

I didn't understand a word of it then, but do now.

On dreary, housebound December days, we played cribbage, Monopoly, and mah-jong with old ivory tiles. We also built model planes (loved that smell of glue before I knew the dangers!) and played with the train set he'd erected in the basement next to his workbench of meticulously arranged tools. Mum didn't think girls (or their fathers!) should play with trains and she gave my train set to my grade eight teacher as my punishment for failing math one term.

As a Dutchman, Dad took delight in teaching me to skate. I can still see the Export 'A' cigarette dangling from the corner of his mouth as he offered muffled words of encouragement while I clung to an old kitchen chair and pushed it along the ice, legs sprawled like a newborn calf. I was certainly no Hans Brinker, hero of the children's novel *The Silver Skates*. In any case, my skates were stainless steel, not silver.

Dad reeked of tobacco and tenderness as he picked me up, until I could glide effortlessly on my own. I loved the fragrance of fresh tobacco when we'd roll cigarettes, but detested the smell of smoke. I quit smoking at fourteen. It was no concession to good behaviour. Quite the opposite. It was a form of rebellion against my father because his nicotine-stained teeth, which he whistled through, acutely embarrassed me as a teenager.

I recall my father relaxing by reading Shakespeare or listening to classical records and radio broadcasts of the New York Metropolitan Opera on Saturday afternoons. I respected his right to do so but saw no reason why this cultural experience should be shoved down my non-musical throat, when I'd have much rather been outside playing sport. He'd happily sit at the kitchen table, tweezers and fountain pen in hand, to patiently classify his stamp collection. What a dumb hobby, I thought. (For an honour-roll student, I had many brainless thoughts.) It was only years later that I learnt he'd sold the majority of his collection to pay cash for a house when, aged fifty, he married Mum. He hadn't wanted to marry until he could afford a roof over her head.

He never had much money but even less debt. He never owned a credit card nor bought anything he couldn't afford. Like Dad, I don't advocate debt but I owe a huge one to him and Mum. We never wanted for anything we actually needed.

That said, I didn't always get what I wanted. We were the only family I knew not to own a car and I was about eight before we even got a second-hand black-and-white television. Then, we'd gather around, still in our church clothes, after roast dinner every Sunday night, to watch *Disneyland*, *Bonanza* and the *Ed Sullivan Show*. On Wednesdays, *Perry Mason* would appear in our living room. The good guys always won any show we watched but good guys like Dad didn't always win in real life.

Embarrassed by Dad's heavy Dutch accent, I desperately wanted a father like other kids in the neighbourhood. My middle name was Frederika, after my Dutch grandmother, and I was inevitably called Fred. The heritage that I once denied, I now cherish. As a youngster, sameness was so important. *Not* to be different. *Not* to be an individual. Yet, as we grow, our individuality becomes our greatest asset. A child learns this lesson the hard way.

No-one else had a father who took the number 8 bus and who wore a three-piece suit, tie, braces and expandable steel armbands. He insisted that I address the bus driver as Mister. Why didn't we have a car like everyone else? Was it because he had lost his job through no fault of his own? My father found himself unemployed with the demise of the once-great railways dining car. Retrenchment was not yet a word in anyone's vocabulary – and even if it had been, I would have been too young to understand. But I was old enough to sense despair in the household.

Dad was eligible for the equivalent of welfare, but chose instead to open a coffee shop, first in the modest Calgary suburb of Hillhurst and then 80 miles (129 km) north in the more remote town of Wetaskawin, Alberta, at a Greyhound bus terminal. We had free travel anywhere in North America but couldn't go down the road to visit my grandparents without my throwing up. This situation distressed my mother but I was happy to stay home and play with the dogs and horses, which belonged to the Mounties across the road. These red-coated Canadian icons frequented the coffee shop for Dad's tasty hot apple pies. I'm never sure if they paid or not.

His pride was as strong as his legs were weak. After years on rail carriages, shunting back and forth across the country, braking suddenly for moose or mountain goat on the tracks, his often-jolted joints became arthritic. I never heard him complain but vividly remember him holding his head high as we passed the queue of men outside the unemployment office. Even though out of work, he refused welfare payments and his dogged determination to dignify work must have subconsciously rubbed off onto me. His idealistic notion of Christian charity did not. He had struggled to build up the Greyhound coffee shop, only to sell it to some shyster who defaulted on payment. Although it meant a reduced standard of living for us, he simply told my mother that he wouldn't take legal action because, "God must have thought the other fellow needed the money more than we did."

Having lost everything, Dad then worked away from home for long stretches of time, cooking for security forces in the Northwest Territories. Like Australia's Northern Territory, it is a vast, sparsely populated landmass at the top end of the continent. After World War II, it was considered vulnerable to invasion by Russia or Japan so the DEW line (Distant Early Warning) was established in 1952 as an integrated chain of sixty-three radar and communication systems, stretching three thousand miles from the northwest coast of Alaska to the eastern shore of Baffin Island, opposite Greenland.

I never heard Dad argue about anything although I do remember overhearing my parents expressing concern that "the Communists could be coming." And it seemed to me that Dad was doing his bit to prevent that, although in all likelihood he probably only worked up there for months at a time doing whatever he had to in order to recover from the financial fiasco of the coffee shop. Later he secured a more salubrious position back home in Calgary as chef for a petroleum and golf club. After nepotism provided me with my part-time job there washing dishes, I promptly decided that my father's choice of career wouldn't be on my menu of options.

Dad was the one who discovered that a Dutch couple, total strangers, were arriving at the train station at three o'clock one morning. Who was there to pick them up? Dad. No wonder the Arends became lifelong friends, the only Dutch ones I remember. My folks' social life revolved around St. Andrew's Presbyterian Church, where Dad joined my grandfather as an elder.

That was the essence of my father. And I now visited his family knowing so little and impossibly wanting to know so much more. It was too late: I'd never find out more about his obviously close relationships with "Mum" Cool in Winnipeg and the Thackers in Edmonton, who featured in old photo albums, although I suspect they were families who took this lone Dutchman under their wing in Canada as others had me in Australia.

While in Europe I skied near the base of the Matterhorn, thrilled to traverse through powdery snow from Switzerland to Italy for lunch – another childhood dream realized. For some inexplicable reason, Switzerland was the only European country that seemed to strike a chord with me and it wasn't just the chocolate. Years later, that affinity would be explained.

In Paris, I lit a candle in Notre Dame for Mum, Dad and Granddad – the three people who'd meant life itself to me.

I didn't think that God, if he existed, would mind a Presbyterian doing that in a Catholic cathedral. Not far from Montmartre, but a long way from home, and feeling fragile, I wrote in my diary:

Where am I going? Where have I been?
What am I doing? What does it mean?
How will I get there? How will I know?
Who'll always love me? Who never will go?
When the journey is finished – When we reach the end –
I'll have answered my questions – Where, What, Who and When.
But, first to know How? And, I want to know – now.

LUCKY COUNTRY

 Surely I'd been at the back of the queue when patience was apportioned out. Frankly, I couldn't wait to get back to Australia, and feeling ill on the flight didn't make time move any faster. There was an eight-hour stopover in Bangkok. Eight long, hot, hours with no air-conditioning in the airport. Why do horrible things always happen when you're tired and not feeling exceptionally well? My suitcase split open and spilled its shameful contents right across the floor in the middle of Bangkok airport. I didn't even have the energy to cry, amid snickers from passers-by. They wouldn't be amused if it had happened to them. As I struggled to gather up dirty clothing, guards armed with machine guns supervised my every movement.

Worse was to come as the airline had overbooked and refused to let me continue on to Australia. I was turned away. Stranded. By this time, my condition had taken a decided turn for the worse. Doubled over, coughing blood in a washroom basin, I heard a little girl's voice:

"Are you all right? You look sick. What's the matter?"

I didn't feel like talking to some child but told her anyway.

"My daddy will fix it."

She ran out. You never know who you might meet in the washroom of a foreign airport. Her father was an Australian diplomat, who arranged for the airline to put me up in a hotel and find a doctor. The kindness of a young stranger saved me. When the doctor arrived and took my temperature, he declared: "Ah, you only thing in Bangkok that hotter than sun!" as my normal bronchitis had developed into pneumonia and a strep throat. I was forced to stay three more days until I was well enough to travel.

Australia is called the Lucky Country for a reason. Glad to be home, it wasn't the last time I'd be inclined to kiss the tarmac with the palpable sense of relief that travellers feel when they set foot on familiar turf. I'd gone to Canada wondering what might have changed. I'd discovered that everything had – especially me. It wasn't home anymore. Europe was exciting but it was upon landing at Tullamarine Airport that I realized that home might – just might – be in Australia.

Back at work in November 1975, we drafted more legislation with tedious technical detail. Just as well I hadn't followed through on the notion I once toyed with of becoming a lawyer, because although I've always had a strong sense of justice, I dislike conflict almost as much as my father. (But, unlike him, I've sometimes, wrongly, wanted to always be right.) Although I loved interaction with sporting groups, what I really wanted to do was find a cure for cancer but had no talent for medical research. Even if I did, my time would be spent mostly in a laboratory and not mixing with people. Maybe I was in the right profession after all – convincing others to take better care of their bodies. Living and teaching by example . . . Still, I wasn't sure. An individual's cardiovascular system might be in tremendous shape but that wouldn't save them from cancer.

Some people find their answers while taking a shower. Others find them while driving, walking, washing or gardening. I may never find mine but I usually get a little closer to moments of insight while exercising or taking a soothing bath afterwards. As I ran my way back to fitness, I finally accepted that I'd never find a medical cure for cancer, but I had other skills. I could help curb an aggressive form of sociological cancer: an inertness of body and mind that places people into prisons of their own making, stark cubicles of nothingness. Let the medical professionals concern themselves with finding a cure – I could focus on prevention. Soon I was speaking to school kids about the dangers of smoking.

At work, few took the notion seriously when two colleagues and I launched a fitness campaign. *You can't market sport like soup!*

Who says we can't?

After an enthusiastic but only moderately successful alliance with a Melbourne newspaper, Fitness Fun in *The Sun*, we discovered departmental funds that needed to be allocated before the end of the financial year. It was a bit like muscle tone – use it or lose it. We invited pitches from a number of advertising agencies who diligently paraded their sporting competencies and convictions in alignment with our own; apart from one, where the principal partner and media personality, Phillip Adams, declared unequivocally: "Fitness campaign . . . waste of taxpayers' money if you ask me." He left the room, his associates struggling for words. We'd virtually ruled them out of the running but needed to reach unanimous agreement on a recommendation for Cabinet the next morning. After much debate late

at night, we couldn't decide between the top two contenders. In jest, one of us (we don't remember who) said:
"Why don't we just go with Adams? We'll lose the money
anyway if we don't have this on the minister's desk in the
morning." Why not? Maybe his agency could use him as an
example of our target market . . . sort of a Trojan horse
approach.

Why not indeed? It was a gamble that paid off and gave
credit to the creative genius of the agency, and the courage
of the minister to back such an unorthodox dark horse.
Thus, cartoon character "Norm" was born and the *Life. Be
In It* campaign, spearheaded by one of my colleagues, won
numerous national and international awards. We were all
proud to have been involved in its embryonic stage.

It was now time to grasp some personal independence and
move forward yet again. For the immediate future I believed
my place on the planet was more likely beneath the Southern
Cross than the Northern Lights. Although I had become
comfortable living with the Jansens, I launched out and
bought my first flat on Brunswick Road. A year earlier, I'd
approached the manager of the bank on the ground floor of
our office building to determine the criteria for obtaining a
home loan. Twelve months later, I'd met all criteria so made
another appointment to see how much I could borrow.

"Sorry, but I can't help," he mumbled over his big beer
gut, obviously oblivious to our lifestyle campaign.

"But I fulfilled the requirements that you, yourself, out-
lined."

"Yes, well uh . . . times have changed and with money
being a bit tight at the moment, and all things being equal,
we save our loans for married men."

"Well, that's surprising in this day and age and I'm sure

the premier will be interested to learn that policy, as I'm on his equal opportunity committee, which meets this afternoon."

I smiled sweetly, stood and shook his hand as hard as I could. By the time I reached my office on the twenty-third floor, the loan had been approved.

After exchanging contracts, I wondered whether I'd made a major mistake. The place was filthy, with rotting food on the carpet and cockroaches the size of a thumb. I scrubbed and disinfected for longer than I care to remember, thinking that one advantage of Canada's cold climate was the relative absence of creepy-crawlies. One of the few annoying aspects of Australia was the blowfly and I found the notion of "the Great Australian salute" far from amusing as I swatted at the pests. Their spring flight on a westerly wind was an unwelcome harbinger of summer. I couldn't afford to install screens and certainly wouldn't be rescuing any of the little buggers from storm windows!

Later, after a shower, I was standing in my almost empty, yet clean, bedroom when I saw it. The hairy spider above the door was bigger than my hand. I'd never been this close to such an immense arachnid in my entire life and froze with fear, heart pounding. The phone wasn't yet connected. Who could I call at this hour anyway? What if it fell on me? Bit me? I was stark naked. Apart from the mattress on the floor, the only items in the room were a mop, bucket, broom and pair of cowboy boots.

I tried to wait it out. Twenty minutes passed. It didn't move and I wouldn't sleep with it there. I pulled on the boots slowly in case it saw me and lunged. Ever so carefully, I picked up the broom, aimed, and thumped. It didn't die, but scurried across the floor. Ready with the cowboy boots, I jumped on it until the threat was nothing more than stain on the carpet. Next day I discovered it was a harmless huntsman and the only risk of death was from a fright-induced coronary. But, dear diary, how was I to know?

> In this country, a spider the size of a dime can kill you but one the size of a saucer is harmless. Go figure! Likewise, there's no danger from six-foot goannas but almost invisible, venomous snakes would kill me in minutes if I trod on them in the bush. Who says they'd scurry away, more frightened than me? As for lethal jellyfish and sharks, what about that first time I snorkelled and nearly swallowed my mouthpiece as a dolphin approached? I'm a bit short-sighted but a triangular fin is a triangular fin! At least you can't miss a grizzly bear coming. Fear of the unknown is always greatest.

I hadn't factored in the hidden expenses of maintaining my own home. By the time I'd bought cleaning supplies, sheets, other bare necessities and paid the legal fees, land tax and bonds for electricity, I was so broke I couldn't even afford to go to the movies for six months. But having a place of my own was worth every cent and Dad's old trunk that had travelled with him from Holland to Canada became the coffee table centrepiece – in fact, the only piece of furniture in the living room.

Christmas cards from Canada heralded the marriages of many friends. I was happy for them and admittedly a little envious. Why couldn't I find someone to spend the rest of my life with? What was wrong with me? Those were my thoughts as I continued to record daily rituals in my diary. Then, a New Year's resolution: *Find myself and forget about finding a husband, until after the first objective has been met.*

Overall, life was good and I still couldn't believe I was being paid to be involved in sport. The president of the Victorian Golf Union invited me to play in what I mistakenly thought was a relaxed social game. I fronted up to the exclusive Yarra Yarra Golf Club in Melbourne with sneakers and clubs that I'd purchased from K-Mart. Before I'd even left the car park, two sophisticated women approached and asked: "What are you doing here?"

Stating the obvious, I simply said I was there to golf.

"With those?" they exclaimed, and reluctantly pointed me in the direction of the first tee. On arrival, I couldn't help but notice the tiered bleachers, television cameras and a host of people milling around. Only then did I realize the significance of a Pro–Am game whereby a professional is matched with three amateurs in the preliminary to a championship tournament. Introduced to my playing partners, I politely asked each if they played much golf and was somewhat intimidated to discover that two had low handicaps.

The third seemed somewhat bemused by my question. He was none other than Peter Thomson, five times British Open champion! I would have happily headed home, tail between legs, but he was extremely gracious and assured me it was simply a fun event.

Thomson teed off first and as expected, belted the ball straight down the fairway, although he didn't seem particularly pleased with the shot. The second guy drove a blistering shot well past Thomson, and by this time I wanted to melt into the lush green grass as I feared I would only embarrass myself. Luckily, the third member of our group beat me to it and missed the ball completely, much to his horror and my relief. More fortunately, the women's tee was about 80 metres ahead of the men's (thank goodness the fairness of equal opportunity hadn't yet extended to the fairways!). So

I headed for it. Head down with concentration, I quickly swung one of those hit-and-hope shots that saw the ball soar beyond Thomson's drive and the gallery burst into applause. I somehow managed to par the hole and by this stage, a spectator asked if he could caddy. The poor man then lugged my clubs for the next seventeen holes as I hacked my way around the manicured fairways, hardly hitting another decent shot. Still, we all had fun and by the time we reached the eighteenth green, TV cameras were rolling. Miraculously, I sank a long putt and received a kiss from my playing partners. As we left the green, a journalist approached. "It looks like we have a new golfer on the Australian scene."

"She sure is new," laughed Thomson. "Her first time on an eighteen-hole course!"

As I retired to the women's locker room to change for the tournament dinner, I again met the two women from the car park, who had only seen the first and last shot of an otherwise dismal round. "My goodness, dear, those clubs certainly are effective. What brand are they?"

"K-Mart special! Didn't your mothers tell you not to judge a book by its cover?" I smiled. I have never been one for snobbery and love the great levelling factor in sport: everyone is equal.

I played tennis at Kooyong with Davis Cup coach Neale Fraser. I was splattered with blood while seated ringside with boxing president, Arthur Tunstall. Then, a sophisticated cocktail party with Lord Killanin, president of the International Olympic Committee. All in a week's work! Water-skiing at Yarrawonga amid duck shooters' shotgun blasts. Nearly drowning in a kayak. Broken thumbs from hang-gliding. Twisted knee from a parachute jump. I literally threw myself into every activity imaginable. And, no, I wasn't at all afraid of those risks. If I died, it would be quick and painless. Long-lingering cancer was my only fear.

Most sporting administrators in those days were volunteers – not celebrities but unsung heroes working hard and tirelessly behind the scenes. I felt privileged to be associated with them, and to be nominated as a finalist in the Miss Sportsgirl of Victoria Awards. From cricket to croquet, tennis to trugo, I loved it all and was constantly busy most evenings and weekends. My job was my life, but who was complaining?

I kept up this frenetic pace as I embarked on a residential management course – one that would alter the course of my life.

10

BIG BROTHERS

 The Australian Administrative Staff College at Mount Eliza, then considered the Australian equivalent of the Harvard Business School, ran an elite business education course catering to a cross-section of industry. The chairman of the Public Service Selection Board went to great lengths to tell me that I was the only "foreigner," the youngest attendee and the first female they had ever selected; the implication was that if I screwed up, I'd ruin future prospects for others from those demographic groups!

Undeterred, I arrived on 30 January 1977 to find that for the next four and a half weeks I would be the only woman among sixty participants of a live-in course. You can imagine the inevitable innuendos. When I walked into the dining room for a black-tie dinner on the first evening, wolf whistles only added to my apprehension. How would they have felt if it had been one of them in the company of fifty-nine women? The attention was overwhelming, but I sensed that wearing a skirt meant I needed to work twice as hard to gain their respect.

As I got ready for bed after that first dinner, an inebriated participant knocked on my door and proclaimed that women had no place in management. Nevertheless, he sleazily suggested we might "get to know each other a little better." I politely assured him we would have ample time to do so over ensuing weeks. For two nights, he persisted and when he woke me a third time, I was furious but didn't want to be a tattletale to staff. So I confided with one of the other attendees in my group syndicate who suggested a plan whereby he and I swapped nametags on bedroom doors. Sure enough, Mr. Pain-in-the-Butt was too ignorant to know which room was which and his next knock was answered by a strapping six-foot male. As I finally slept soundly, he rushed down to the bar to gleefully gossip that a man was in my room, which validated his theories about women in business. Luckily, others knew of our plan and ridiculed him for the fool he was. I never saw him again as he quit the following day. Now the odds were only 58:1 and I was rapidly becoming one of the boys.

I'm convinced that a sense of humour, aptitude on the volleyball court and comfort with subsequent locker-room banter gained me more respect than any feminist philosophy or economic literacy.

The college grounds were part of an old estate named Moondah, an Aboriginal word that translates as "over the horizon." My personal vistas widened to include people from diverse backgrounds and foreign management concepts. Still, I felt compelled to study copious business literature until all hours of the morning in an attempt to prove myself.

We were told that no-one came out of the course the same way they went in, but I did not appreciate this comment until the last week. Although I enjoyed my job, I grew restless. Where would this thing they called a career path lead when I already reported to the head of the department?

Since age thirteen, I had clearly seen my profession in physical education and recreation but I wasn't the only one who now challenged their vocational path. Walking along the beach, a few of us explored these feelings. I was astounded that many of my male counterparts opened up enough to admit they felt the same as me. I thought I'd been the only one feeling out of my league but guess we all just hid our insecurities behind coping corporate masks. Our parallel footprints along the shore were quickly swept away by the sea. I wondered if the impressions I hoped to make on the world would disappear as readily. So many questions. So few answers. I felt my future was embedded in Australia and I had finally turned the corner on the past. But hadn't I thought that before?

I became the first elected female representative of the quaintly named *Old Boys Association* of Mount Eliza. Should I have objected to the nomenclature and insisted it be changed to Alumni Association? Maybe I should have taken a stronger stand about sexism; then again, maybe I was oblivious to most of it. I seldom thought about sexism in those days except in a possibly naïve way that the best way to overcome it was to quietly demonstrate ability. Despite the taunts I experienced at the beginning of the course, by the end I felt I was leaving fifty-eight big brothers behind but taking with me friendships to last a lifetime, long after I forgot fiscal forecasting. I was now comfortably one of the boys but still had doors opened for me – and many more doors would open.

At the end of over four weeks' isolation at Mount Eliza, the men couldn't wait to get home to wives and families. I would miss their companionship more than they would mine. I would also miss the warmth of college staff and dreaded returning to my empty unit. I'd often joked that men were like parking spots: all the good ones were already taken. But it no longer seemed funny and as I drove back to my Melbourne flat, I couldn't help but think that the special time spent eating, playing and learning together had been as close to a family existence as I had experienced in the four years since my parents died.

I parked the car and my emotions. There was little time for reflection because I was invited to South Africa on an all-expenses-paid trip to speak about the animated cartoon *Life. Be In It* campaign. Ironically, cartoons as a form of television advertising had originated in South Africa in order to depict characters as neither black nor white, rich nor poor. Yet, it was those same contrasts in the country that struck me almost as powerfully as the stunning landscape.

At the opening of Loftus Rugby Stadium in Pretoria, South Africa, seventy thousand fans burst into an apparently spontaneous rendition of "For He's a Jolly Good Fellow" when the prime minister arrived. No politician in Canada or Australia would receive that welcome. Still, I preferred our system of government and was less impressed when he announced that South Africa was barred from international sport because the Springboks had soundly beaten a conglomerate team of top rugby players from other countries. "We are the best so they are frightened of us," he gloated.

He made no mention of apartheid or the fact that these individual stars had not played as a team and many did not speak the same language. The longer I remained, I recognized the apartheid issue was more complex than I originally realized and an outsider like me was in no position to referee! I met wonderful people from all racial backgrounds, whether pursuing ideologies in conference or impalas in a jeep.

Even on safari, I searched for something the most powerful binoculars couldn't detect – the threads of connection. The presence of Dutch Boer accents reminded me of my father. In this land founded on gold, I had his wedding ring melted down and moulded into a small pendant.

So too, my views of politics began to reshape. I had only worked for a Liberal government and given little thought to public policy beyond sport. My brief sojourn in South Africa opened my eyes to broader, more pressing issues of social concern. I once naïvely applied for a job as press secretary to Labor prime minister, Gough Whitlam! Re-reading my diary entry, I can hardly believe my arrogance:

> I doubt I'll get the job. I respect him but don't share all his ideals and feel it would be unlikely to change him.

Change the prime minister indeed! When Don Chipp spoke at the foundation meeting of the Australian Democrats Party on 9 May 1977, I was in the audience of twenty-five hundred at Melbourne Town Hall. Although inspired by his philosophy, I felt that his vision seemed unlikely to be realized. I was proved wrong.

Having at least explored political alternatives, I decided against joining any party. It wasn't something one should rush into as quickly as I'd tried to do. Besides, there were more pressing matters to attend to. My last trip to Canada had convinced me that Australia was now my most likely home and it was time to return to Calgary and completely clean out the house for sale.

My parents had worked a lifetime to acquire modest material possessions that were sold at auction, in less than two hours, for peanuts. After the sale of the house, lawyers informed me that most proceeds would be consumed in capital gains tax and other financial matters that Mum had inadvertently overlooked after my father's death. I surprised myself to be upset over nothing more than material possessions. It wasn't so much the money but knowing much of the tax would be directed towards unemployment payments to people not willing to work half as hard as my migrant parents. I fully supported people who couldn't work but not those who wouldn't.

It was also the finality of leaving the only home I had ever known. Now, nearly five years after Mum had died, I finally went to the cemetery and arranged a headstone for her, Dad and Granddad: *Thanks for loving . . . and letting me love.*

It was too late to tell them how much I loved them. Too late to say thank you in person. But I meant it more than anything I've ever thought.

Even though I'd been gone for five years, that final goodbye to my dog Blitz tore at my heart even though I knew she was well cared for by a friend. It was hard to completely close a chapter in my life. But, to open others, it had to be done.

After this far from pleasant annual leave, I returned to my office overlooking Melbourne's Port Phillip Bay. No place would ever again be my safe harbour of home but perhaps I now had a safe enough harbour for my heart. I wrote a book on sports marketing, promotion and sponsorship to help sporting organizations generate more revenue. Responsible for government funding, I regretted that there was never enough to distribute to all worthy causes and hoped a self-help book might marginally expand the pie of limited resources by tapping into the private sector.

Launching the book, which had arrived only five minutes earlier from the printer, English fast bowling cricket legend Frank (Typhoon) Tyson quipped that I was affectionately known as "the girl who always said no . . . to government funding."

Sports marketing has since become more sophisticated and the book is somewhat dated now. But, long before one-day matches, super leagues and salary caps, it was regarded as rather revolutionary. It remains a source of surprise and satisfaction when someone from a sporting club tells me that they still refer to it.

Apart from one ski weekend, my last annual leave had been wiped out with the teary and dreary sale of my childhood home so by the time Easter rolled around, I was ready for adventure in the midst of a modified childhood cowgirl fantasy. Riding in a five-day cattle muster over the Victorian High Plains, out of Merrijig, was as wildly exciting as the African veldt. We galloped over logs and through rivers with the legendary Lovick family, and later these rugged cattle-men and women regaled us around campfires at Sheepyard Flat with tales of *The Man From Snowy River*. Years later, filmed with the same horses, it became an award-winning movie, but the one on my mind at the time was John Wayne's *True Grit*. With a wish on the wind and the wind through my hair, I incessantly sang the theme song:

> "Some day little girl, the sadness will leave your eyes ... Few battles are won alone ... The pain of it will ease a bit when you find a man with true grit."

Clutching the reins, I wanted to chase my parents' killer like John Wayne did the villains in the movie. But cancer was too elusive for even a larger-than-life cowboy hero to catch.

My thoughts were rudely interrupted when I flew over a log and my horse did not. Later, I awoke in Royal Melbourne Hospital on pristine white sheets with a hairline hip fracture, and without a shower for days. Stinking like a stable, I couldn't help but think of when I last saw my mum alive – in a hospital much like this but on the other side of the world. I tried to remember our happier times but the ubiquitous hospital smells overpowered the horsey ones.

Did I need a man with true grit to help ease the pain? Life was great. I loved my job, had established good friends, bought a flat and nice car, joined sporting clubs and was travelling the world. I was rubbing shoulders with celebrities, most of whom were just genuine down-to-earth folks. Still, there was something missing. It had to be a man. What else could it be?

11

SEASONS OF THE HEART

I had been fiercely independent; too proud to ask for help or be beholden to anyone. Meeting my new seventy-four-year-old neighbour reinforced that view when one afternoon she invited me to tea. She'd moved from the big family home following her husband's death two years earlier. As I offered sympathy over a cuppa, her reply shocked me: "Don't feel sorry for me now. I wished he'd died years ago! I've only begun to enjoy life in the last eighteen months."

She told a tale of physical and psychological abuse so awful it was barely comprehensible. "Why did you stay married all those years?" I asked. "You don't understand, dear. I was one of nine children. My mother died when I was six. My father married me off when I was fifteen. I had no education and was totally economically dependent on a man I didn't love. I had no choice."

My heart went out to this sprightly senior citizen who, in spite of her closeted existence and losing a breast to cancer, gave the outward impression of a carefree life. I admired her spirit but shuddered at her earlier involuntary dependency. I was determined to be independent, economically and emotionally. Thankfully, my generation of women has more choice, although I remained optimistic about the option of marriage.

During my recent all-too-short ski weekend at Jasper, I'd met up with my old boyfriend, Tim Park, for the first time since my mother's death. We'd stayed in touch, initially with lengthy, handwritten letters every week, which had long since dwindled to just a card at Christmas. Seeing him again after nearly five years stirred up sentiments pointless to pursue because only a few days earlier, I'd tied up the loose ends in Canada and now called Australia home. I'd just got settled, but this reconnection remained unsettling. Our latent letter exchange resumed and four months later, Tim came to Melbourne for a three-week visit. It was a long way, in many ways, from Grande Prairie, where we first met just after the deaths of his brother and my mother. Could a ski weekend and that original three-week flame of passion be rekindled? Were we the same people as then?

Within days, he proposed under a gum tree in the Royal Botanical Gardens. Happy and safe in his embrace on the sprawling lawn carpeted with April autumn leaves, I said yes without hesitation and without fully thinking through the consequences of such a reply. At that moment, I thought I was in love. But, after the initial romantic flurry, joyfully throwing leaves at each other like Canadian kids do in September, I wondered about seasons of the heart. We'd decided on a non-denominational service with the celebrant paraphrasing Ecclesiastes:

> "To everything there is a season and a time to every purpose under heaven . . . a time to laugh, a time to cry, a time to live, a time to die."

After a sleepless night, I told Tim that I thought the timing wasn't quite right and it might be best to first live together. He replied that his mother wouldn't approve and he felt compelled to return to Canada for family reasons. But I had a job here. He didn't have one in Canada. Why should I compromise my career? I knew no-one when I arrived in Melbourne, before I'd established now-strong ties among friends and colleagues. Would I want to start again in Vancouver where he was now living? Could I? Did I love Tim enough to give up what I had in Australia?

These were tough questions. Although there was no question that Tim was a lovely guy, I wasn't entirely sure I wanted to spend the rest of my life with him. Admittedly, in five years, I hadn't met anyone more suitable. And at twenty-seven, I wasn't getting any younger. Maybe friends were right. Maybe I was too fussy.

On the other hand, I'd already said yes even though I felt a little pressured to make such a big decision. Maybe it was just a case of cold feet. Keeping our plans secret, I never spoke to anyone else directly about this dilemma. Instead, I asked a married friend the hypothetical question about the consequences of such a major decision. She offered excellent advice: "If you're not sure, don't do it."

Ignoring her wise counsel, we married eight days later! I still sometimes wonder why I wed so impulsively. Maybe it was little more than a remnant from my brief flirtation with the Labor Party and Prime Minister Whitlam's campaign motto: "It's time."

Only three people knew why they were invited to a cocktail party at Kooyong Tennis Club. For the other sixty guests, it was ostensibly a farewell party for Tim. I gave my solemn vow it was not an engagement party. Little did they realize, it was a surprise wedding! In less than a week, we organized the celebrant, cake, catering, flowers, invitations, rings, music and other matrimonial paraphernalia. Yes, it was frenetic but probably no more so than if we'd had months to plan. As I purchased my dress at a classy Toorak boutique, the saleswoman asked: "And what month is the wedding, dear?"

"The day after tomorrow."

Her eyes shifted shamelessly to my abdomen. But, no, history was not repeating itself. There was little likelihood of my being an unwed or nearly wed mother.

The Jansens were the first of my friends to know. Having lived with them for two years, Frank was rather like a father so I asked if he would give me away. When we broke the news, this tough, former union representative broke into tears. I had been insensitive, expecting him to share our happiness. At his age, Frank felt he would never see me again if I followed my husband to Canada. This only increased my qualms about the impulsive decision to get married in the first place. To no avail, we both tried to persuade Tim to stay. In typical form, Frank came up with one of his classics, which I fondly referred to as a Jansen-ism: "Australia is a great place to live. The only problem is you don't live bloody long enough!"

At the office, my boss speculated on an engagement party and teased, "Tomorrow's the big day, Cath."

"Sure is . . . the Saints play the Swans! And the Swans have a chance of a win!"

Neatly dodging the interrogation as swiftly as a halfback does a tackle, it wasn't difficult to divert Friday afternoon conversation to football! Every self-respecting Melbournian needed an Aussie Rules side to support and although I was no diehard spectator, the South Melbourne Swans had always been my team since my first faux pas about "rooting." And with good reason. Their red-and-white uniforms were the same colours I wore while representing my high school and university; the same colours proudly flown on

Canada's new flag; and more importantly, the Swans were the team that Frank Jansen supported!

I was to curse all teams the next day, as I fought Saturday football traffic to rush home and iron my wedding dress. I spent most of the early afternoon in the empty office, writing letters of resignation and documenting details of projects that would need attention while I was away on my honeymoon. As I sat poised at the typewriter with a mudpack plastered on my face, a colleague surprised me. After he recovered from the shock, I could hardly join his laughter, as it was near impossible to crack a smile!

I also had trouble keeping a straight face earlier in the week when a prominent man about town asked me to dinner. "I'm sorry but I already have another engagement on Saturday." In view of the secrecy, I could hardly say it was my own!

On 20 May 1978, a couple of hours into the cocktail party, we announced our engagement. It came as no surprise.

"We thought that's what you were up to. When are you getting married?"

"Soon," we replied coyly.

An hour later, I was in the ladies locker room at Kooyong, changing into whites with the help of my bridesmaids, Chris and Jan...just like tennis players over the years, except this was in preparation for a match of a different nature.

We arrived back in the reception area to the traditional rendition of "Here Comes the Bride." Between vows, I overheard stunned guests comment: "Am I drunk or is DeVrye getting married?"

Inscribed on the wedding cake were the words, "In tennis love is nothing. In life, it's everything." I wondered if it was enough. Unlike my elderly neighbour, I had a choice but already doubted it was the right one as we flew to Fiji for our honeymoon. Far from post-wedding bliss, we were already arguing. As agreed, Tim continued eastward and I returned to Australia to tie up loose ends before joining him, just as I'd done in Canada only a few months earlier. What was I thinking? Was I even thinking? It was a stressful time because I didn't want to leave Australia but felt obliged to Tim and our marital vows.

With the honesty of hindsight, I was more bound by the oath of allegiance to Australia. A month after my wedding, on 22 June 1978, I became an Australian citizen. Again with the honesty of hindsight, I guess I wanted the safety net of being able to return to Australia if the marriage didn't work out. One hundred new Australians gathered in Scots Church on Collins Street. I was the last to receive my citizenship certificate, following Juan from Chile, who pleaded: "Let us go and make party."

I regretted rushing back to the office and leaving him alone, as friends or relatives accompanied most other migrants. Many didn't understand the literal meaning of the words they recited but their tears of pride needed no translation. Surprisingly few tears were shed during the ensuing round of farewell parties as everyone predicted I'd soon be back in Oz. "You've gone from Quasi-Aussie to Dinky-di," they teased.

Unlike five years ago, I no longer felt alone in the Antipodes. But was I making a mistake to leave my adopted country that had fostered wonderful friendships over five years? In the process of gaining a spouse, I had relinquished my job, friends, sport and lifestyle. What a bizarre contradiction. I also felt I was losing my independent identity and missed Australia desperately even before the Qantas plane had lifted off the Melbourne runway.

Touching down in Vancouver, my perspective improved when I met my in-laws who generously housed us in the ground floor of their lovely home. Used to independence, I sensed we were imposing but also felt fortunate to be part of their family. Devoid of any family environment for so long, I failed to fully appreciate the attached obligations and resented the need to justify my actions as a "young matron" – so dubbed by my mother-in-law. She meant well, but we "had our moments." On one occasion, she accepted an invitation for us to attend a christening. Through miscommunication with my husband, no-one asked me and I already had plans to play gridiron football in an all-male league on that day. My childhood dream became an adult nightmare, as did our first year of marriage, when I felt responsibility for my life slipping into someone else's hands. (Although I hasten to add that I caught a touchdown pass, we won the game and the men accepted me on the team that season.)

Never before had I felt so depressed over an event of *my own making*. . . the impulsive decision to marry. After one monumental argument with my husband, I thought I was losing my mind. I knew I was losing part of my self and didn't know what to do about it. The loss was likely my independence and I felt stifled.

> Isn't one supposed to be blissful in this *Leave It to Beaver* happy household scene? Or are happy families an endangered species like the rodents of the river had been in the days of Canadian fur traders?

Cycling around the picturesque Vancouver suburb of Point Roberts didn't help. Nor did the good company of Tim's friends. Even the stunning Pacific sunsets framed by tall pine trees from the living room of my in-laws'

Tsawwassen home didn't ease my unease. Their beauty was eclipsed by the reminder that the life I loved was on the other side of that ocean.

Our marriage had no chance of survival as long as we slept under Tim's parents' roof. Unable to find work in Vancouver, we were eventually hired by an oil rig that drilled downward over one mile into the frozen tundra of northern Alberta – one of North America's largest.

At the interview, the foreman queried our qualifications.

"Dad was a chef and Mum specialized in domestic science."

"That'll do. Can you start today?"

I was the chief cook – and Tim the bottle-washer. Five hours later, we arrived by four-wheel drive in the middle of a blizzard, the middle of the night and the middle of nowhere. Like thousands of acupuncture needles, horizontal snow stung my cheeks and from the door of the portable Atco trailer I heard the howl of wolves. Tempted to join their cries, I was overwhelmed by a long, rectangular stainless steel industrial kitchen. A la carte breakfast was expected in a few hours. We first put the oatmeal on the back burner and panic bubbled as we searched for utensils to fry bacon and eggs and make toast. Where did they hide the jam? At 7 a.m. sharp, thirty burly roughnecks tumbled into the mess but the wooden spoon steadfastly refused to budge from the pan of porridge, now solidified.

Overheard at a nearby table: "Do ya think the new cooks would give us the recipe for that oatmeal? I could use it to fix my muffler." The chief engineer ordered an omelette, which at least didn't stick to the pan but resembled a well-scrambled egg. Tim tentatively delivered the plate and apologized.

"We can make another. It looks like it's been hit by a truck."

"That's okay. It's your first day and we know you just got in." He took his plate and after one bite, asked, "Hey, was that a Mack truck?"

Dinner was no more delicious. I'd often cooked frozen vegetables but had underestimated the extra time it takes for 10-kilogram packs to thaw, so aided the process with a hammer and chisel. Priding myself on learning from my mistakes, the next night I immersed broccoli much earlier. Come time to strain, the green mush rushed through the colander almost as fast as we raced to plug the sink and return it to its rightful serving bowl.

I'd cracked the secret culinary code for my great-grand-mother's Scottish shortbread recipe. But it seemed there was a bit more to cooking than Mum's handwritten recipes, which consisted largely of a pinch of this and dash of that. My kitchen career was a series of these unforgettable "character-building" moments. I gained first-hand experience of the physical labour my father endured as a cook, but there were aspects of my personal behaviour I would have gladly forgotten.

The tension in our marriage did not ease. One bleak day, Tim fuelled a well of burning rage that even famed oil-well firefighter Red Adair could not have quelled. Like a gush from an erupting geyser, my control came uncapped with a frightening force. Within seconds, pots, pans, plates, glasses and utensils were airborne across the huge stainless steel kitchen in the general direction of my husband.

After cursing subsided, I swore that hell would freeze over before I'd ever lose my cool like that again. Shaking and sobbing, I realized I could have accidentally killed him with a knife. We often laughed about that comic episode of the temperamental chef but it was far from funny at the time. I was clearly a recipe for disaster in the kitchen and looked forward to returning to a white-collar job. Wearing a white hat, as my father had done, was too hard!

Far from that remote tundra of turmoil, our next equally disastrous venture was to crew a 41-foot yacht down the west coast of the United States with a Vietnam War veteran who fished the Bering Sea. With no radar, we were nearly killed in fog and after thirteen straight days of seasickness, I refused to budge from the dock at Astoria, Washington. There I met an old fisherman who told me he had been seasick every day for nearly forty years.

"Why don't you get another job?" I asked.

"Because I inherited my father's boat and don't know any other way to earn a living."

Like my elderly neighbour miles away in Melbourne, many of that generation felt their choices were limited. Was it just his generation?

> After hours of solitary night-watch in shipping channels on the open sea, I must choose in which direction to steer my life. Not unlike navigating in fog, I sometimes have no idea where life is going. But it certainly can't stay in this current tide of endless confusion. I'd been an only child with many choices . . . and maybe I'll choose to be alone again – but when we next stop in Portland, Oregon, I'm jumping ship to visit my friend, Ellie from Montana days.

I didn't want to lose my husband. More importantly, I didn't want to lose myself. I looked like losing both and I felt like a loser. Eight months earlier I had a career, house and friends. Now, I had none. I'd lost my temper, and previously my parents, but I'd never lost hope. I decided to return to Australia with or without my husband.

Clutching my emu-and-kangaroo-embossed passport, I sank into the aircraft seat with relief. Beside me, Tim slumped. We fought in London, Athens, Cairo and Singapore. Geography was no barrier to our sense of dislocation from our familiar territorial pasts. Still, we also shared many memorable and close moments and rationalized that things would improve once we settled in our own home in Australia.

12

A CHANGE OF CAREER PATH

Passing through customs control on 28 February 1979, I had nothing to declare . . . except my love for Australia. Perhaps the customs officer had heard it a thousand times before, perhaps not. He didn't bat an eyelid. Even with no family in this vast island continent, I felt like the proverbial prodigal daughter returning home. Unfortunately, our home was not a happy one and Tim, bereft of friends and family, was undoubtedly unhappier than I was. My old boss offered me a job, although we both knew I could never return on a permanent basis. It wouldn't be the same. In the interim, it paid the bills.

An opportunity arose three months later with the re-election of the Hamer Government in Victoria. A subsequent Cabinet shuffle created openings for ministerial staff and the newly appointed minister for the arts and education appointed me as his speechwriter/press secretary. I felt rather inept as my arts knowledge was about as colourful as a blank canvas but I imagined it would not be dissimilar to dealing with volunteers in sporting organizations. How wrong I was in that assumption. During my first meeting, representatives flaunting gold cigarette-holders and ostrich feathers called everyone *dah-ling*. I wondered what I'd gotten myself into. Again.

At least the minister seemed down to earth even if he openly stated that his idea of arts was a bush band. Though said in jest, this comment did not paint him in a favourable light with his new constituency.

Although I gained a greater appreciation of the Australian cultural landscape, and met many interesting people, refreshingly free from the pretentiousness pervading some of the arts scene, it was not a rewarding time in my career. The politics of arts administration seemed more of a minefield than the party politics of the legislative process. I found the latter fascinating and started to become almost as addicted to politics as I had been to sport. After all, it was really just another game.

Due to lack of finances, Tim and I agreed that he would visit his parents for Christmas, while I stayed in Australia. It was a good compromise and I enjoyed catching up with friends I had seldom seen since marriage.

A few of us were playing tennis the day after he departed. Sudden pain shot down my spine as I collapsed on the court. How could anything invisible hurt so much? Unable to move my toes or legs for three days, I might never play sport again proclaimed the doctors. Lying vulnerable in Casualty, terror transformed to an unusual aura of peace after a tiny jab from a big needle. Unlike the elderly Greek woman in the adjacent cubicle, how lucky I was to be able to communicate. Unlike the homeless man on the other side, how fortunate I was to sleep between clean sheets every night. Still, I wondered what good could ever come of this mishap: a fractured vertebra and ruptured disc?

"Please God, no more opportunities!" I prayed.

He must have heard me. Within weeks, I walked with only a back brace. Within months, the pain eased somewhat with the help of painkillers and chiropractic treatment. Within myself, I smiled. Anyone with such fabulous friends, like my former boss and neighbours who cared for me during this time, must be all right, I rationalized, and the guilt of my relationship with Tim temporarily disappeared. The best gift I ever gave him was one of silence, as I didn't wish to ruin his Christmas in Canada by his feeling obliged to be with me. Our marriage was often more about duty than love but neither of us wanted to run away from our commitment.

Having never run more than two miles in my life, some temporary aberration (and another bet by colleagues) prompted me to enter the twenty-six-mile Melbourne Marathon later in 1979. Of fifty-five hundred who started in the 29°Celsius heat, only half finished. I still can't believe I was one. Sunburned and dehydrated. Exhausted and exhilarated. It was impossible to remove my shoes because blood glued my socks and soles as one. Having read about the pain of the long-distance runner, I thought this was just par for the course until I was diagnosed with a stress fracture and forced to wear fluffy sheepskin slippers to Parliament House for a week! It was not a good look but the elated mental state of realizing a goal more than compensated for the physical discomfort.

I knew the stress fracture would heal in time. Not so my marriage. As important as I believe determination and commitment are to reaching a goal – any goal – I'd also have to admit that sometimes it helps to know when to quit.

Marathon fights were the norm. In the war of words, it was a truce only when we both slept. We seldom declared amnesty and Tim retreated to silence, which only infuriated me more. Did we really love each other as much as we thought or were we afraid to admit failure? Would children make a difference or only add to the problem?

Potential offspring – a real family of our own – was the subject of conversation as we drove to Queensland in our second-hand yellow Toyota Corolla, dodging dead kangaroos, wombats and the carrion-eating crows on the road. At 39°Celsius, without air-conditioning or agreement, debate heated with no solution to our dilemma. Heading north past Grong Grong and Turn Back Jimmy Creek, the outback names seemed romantic, almost quaint, provided you didn't have to live there. A flock of white cockatoos with pink underbellies coloured the sky.

Realization suddenly hit me during this trip through the middle of nowhere. My "problem" was that I had been a latent feminist for years, in denial that there was any need to be involved with so-called women's issues. After all, I'd always been one of the boys.

Tim is a super person but we're too different. I'm tired of hurting him in moments of rage; tired of being frustrated by his actions or inaction; tired of fighting and feeling guilty; and just tired. I want him to be happy and share that happiness but that's too idealistic, given he wants to have kids and live in a small Canadian town and I want a career near an Australian city. Let's not destroy each other's dreams just for each other. Let's not destroy each other. Sometimes I think that no-one understands me; that no-one ever did, except Granddad and he's been dead half my life. Are Tim and I right for each other? I love him more as a brother. Is that enough? In some ways, I now feel closer to his parents than him, especially his father who I admire. Even his mother and I get on quite well, considering she'll never forgive me for taking her little boy half a world away. I'd divorce tomorrow except I wouldn't just be losing a husband. I'd be losing a family. Still, I think I'd be doing Tim a big favour if we separated and he returned to Canada . . .

It was only a diary entry, which I wrote and kept to myself while Tim had a cool shower. Soon after, we bought our first home in 1979 – a little blue, brick, single-fronted terrace in Station Street, North Carlton. Renovation gave us a new focus. We now had something else to argue about! As well as a marriage certificate, we had another legal document binding us. A mortgage. It contained no terms and conditions of love. I encouraged Tim to return to Canada for good when his father became ill. It wasn't right that he felt obliged to stay with me.

> I'll miss him and doubt I'll ever meet anyone who loves me as much but unless I can reciprocate, I've got to let him go. If there is any question about our love for each other, and there are many, it's unfair for him to be apart from two people who love him unconditionally.

I confided my dissatisfaction with my marriage and career to one of my married male friends. His words of wisdom fell on deaf ears: *If you chase happiness like you would a butterfly, it will always be just out of reach. But if you sit quiet and still, it might surprise you by alighting.*

We were both afraid to let go. Both afraid of rushing out of our marriage as quickly as we had rushed in. Like many other married couples in crisis, we thought an addition to the family would help. It wasn't a baby but a puppy.

From the moment I first set eyes on her, Tammy brought me more joy than I ever thought possible, even though in her first night, alone in the kitchen, she wet the floor and whimpered plaintively. My own sobs joined hers, feeling the cruelty of wrenching her away from her mother and siblings. And I was determined to give my unconditional love to this bundle of golden retriever fluff now in my care, the same love my adopted parents so willingly offered me.

Tim and I made a commitment that, as an inner-city dog, Tammy deserved morning and evening walks. He did mornings. I did evenings. Arguments subsided as every nonworking, waking moment was spent renovating – or training Tammy. With guidance from fantastic neighbours who'd raised two daughters and two golden retrievers, Tammy became my surrogate child and the Whittle family joined my former professor and former boss as surrogate parents. Once Tammy was house-trained, we took her into a showroom in search of golden-retriever-coloured carpet to complete our renovations.

Tam taught me a lot about love. I remember telling the security guards at Parliament House that she was training to be a guide dog. Even a blind man could see that she, like me, lacked the required discipline. But she helped me see so many things that would have otherwise gone unnoticed in the busy world of work. We went for daily long-distance runs to better prepare for my next marathon and unwind from the stress of work and home. Her boundless happiness boosted mine. When I was out running, I wasn't in arguing.

My second marathon was completed an hour faster than the first one and with minimum pain, even though back pain had become a constant companion at work and play. Some days, it seemed to pass through every pore in lightning-sharp bursts or more usually like the duller thud of distant roaring thunder. Then, I was more likely to cause others pain, especially those closest to me. Pervasive pain was no excuse for a short fuse but on pain-free days, I felt a different person, a gentler and lighter being. Halfway through my third marathon, I decided it was too nice a day to run on boring bitumen so stopped, sipped a milkshake by the side of the road and headed off to enjoy tennis on the grass at Kooyong. I no longer had anything to prove by pounding the pavement.

Tam gave birth to ten healthy pups and we sat through the night and fed her warm milk, honey and brandy while we ate those iconic Australian chocolate biscuits, Tim Tams. Tim and Tam. The miracle of birth made us wonder, again, about children of our own. Cutting two hundred puppy toenails, I realized that the more I thought about it – and one should indeed think about it a lot – I wasn't sure if I was parent material. Strange as it may sound, I'd always wanted to be a grandmother but never had any strong maternal instincts. Maybe I should have married someone who had children from a previous marriage, as I doubted I would have the patience for kids.

I seemed to have the patience for puppies and politics, though. Gradually learning more about the process of government, I became totally engrossed; again I attended evening and weekend meetings just as I had in sports administration. This was a new form of adrenaline for me but must have been tough for Tim.

Subsequently, I worked for the deputy leader of the Upper House who had the dual portfolios of attorney-general and minister for consumer affairs. Personally acquainted with many of the Members of Parliament, I respected only a handful of representatives from both sides of the House. My boss was outstanding, but there seemed little doubt it would be easy to do a better job and make a more significant contribution than many sitting members (who did little else than sit).

Rather than work for a politician, I decided to become one. My background led me to embrace mostly Labor working-class philosophies but I joined the Liberal Party (the equivalent of the Canadian Conservatives or the US Republicans) because of Sir Robert Menzies' ideology on the rights of the individual, rather than the far Left of the Labor Party which, at that time, appeared to reduce everyone to the lowest common denominator of social welfare. I was also still appalled by the frequent strikes, as I had been when I first arrived. I dutifully served my time in the branch hierarchy before throwing my hat in the ring for pre-selection.

Within weeks, I doubted my decision to become a politician. During a doorknock, one woman screeched: "Get off my property before I kill you. We don't want any of you foreigners running this country. We don't even want you in this country!"

I was as Australian as she was; never had I considered myself a foreigner. Never before had I given a thought to racial discrimination. Never had I wondered what people of non–English-speaking background or appearance may encounter in the world out there. Although welling with unshed tears, my eyes had been opened to an undercurrent of prejudice, thanks to this woman's angry remarks. Unless stemmed, such hatred ruins a nation. Australia was my nation, too, essentially comprised of migrants from other countries with one ambition in mind: to call themselves a part of the Lucky Country.

After initial hurt, the woman's verbal attack only refuelled my desire to address injustice through the political system. I stood for pre-selection for the safest State Liberal seat in Victoria. With fifty-three contestants for the Upper House seat of East Yarra, it narrowed down to two of us at the end of a full day of exhaustive ballots.

I lost the final vote and was bitterly disappointed. Shortly after, I lost my job in 1981 when the Labor Party was swept to power in the state for the first time in twenty-six years. Even I conceded the change was for the better and, prior to the election, had already decided to seek employment in private enterprise.

I was horrified to see how quickly my former boss's so-called friends and allies dumped him when he was no longer useful in his ministerial role. I rationalized that my pre-selection loss was for the better. And I could almost hear Mum's voice in my head: *Things always work out for the better, dear,* as we cleared out the office and shredded all documents.

I no longer wanted to live my life in the goldfish bowl of politics, subject to the fickleness of others. Looking at growth industries in the private sector, I considered careers in travel and energy until one of my mentors from the Mount Eliza Administrative Staff College urged me to join IBM.

That was the second time in my life someone suggested I join the company so it seemed sensible to submit an application. I proposed they hire me as a fitness consultant, based on the dual premise that I could return stressed and overweight executives to wellbeing and, since computers would create excess leisure time, I could also devise recreational programs so employees could use that leisure time more effectively. Oh yeah – what extra leisure time, I ask myself now? What naïvety about technology on my part!

Someone in the personnel department must have been curious enough to recommend me for an initial interview. After four more interviews and extensive testing they offered me a job as a trainee sales representative.

During the first few months I almost quit several times. After the days of government limos, gala concerts and the power of politics, I didn't park happily at the bottom of the pecking order in a huge organization. What's more, much of the technical training seemed as incomprehensible as a Beijing telephone book, as I struggled with the most elementary software programming and lacked any interest or patience with machines.

However, once I left the classroom to deal with customers, my attitude changed. No longer constrained by theories of selling techniques, now I was free to help customers with technological solutions to grow their business. I was far more interested in opening a relationship than closing a sale. And, although never fully grasping technical or financial intricacies, I always knew exactly who to ask for help. Above all else, I'd finally learned never to be too proud to do so. It didn't signify I was weak or incompetent but maybe strong enough to show some humility.

Before I knew it, I had exceeded all quota targets in my first year as a sales representative. This came as a complete surprise because my only previous experience with sales at the ripe old age of eight or nine had been a disaster. I had unsuccessfully peddled Brownie cookies door to door. As soon as one neighbour politely said no thank you, I rushed home to Mum. And, bless her heart, she'd bought the whole carton, which we ate for months after.

That wouldn't be happening at IBM. My first big computer sale was to a tennis buddy, whose father owned a publishing company. I was distraught to learn, too late, that the equipment lacked the technical capacity he needed. My manager had assured me this particular model would suit. I was livid when he then admitted that it wouldn't do the job but that he had wanted the initial sale because then, the customer could be persuaded to purchase the additional upgrade. After storming out of the office, I wrote to the chairman of IBM, outlining how we had basically (and unintentionally, in my case) been dishonest with the customer. That wasn't the appropriate escalation protocol but I didn't care in the least that I was risking my job. It was far more important to preserve my integrity, not to mention friendship.

The next day, Bernie O'Neill arrived in Australia for a visit – Bernie, that stranger on the plane whom I'd met many years earlier when I was rushing home to my mother's deathbed. Bernie – a retired American insurance executive who was no longer a stranger because we'd corresponded for years although I hadn't seen him since that fateful flight. Bernie – who had fought in the Coral Sea during World War II in the same troop as the then chairman of IBM Australia. Unbeknown to me, when these two veterans of war and industry lunched together, Bernie told my boss's boss's boss about my ethical concerns. Within a week, I had a happy customer, a new manager, a somewhat bewildered chairman and had won a trip to New Zealand for my sales results.

Still, "something" was missing. Maybe I felt that I never really contributed to anything but the bottom line at IBM – not that there's anything wrong with a healthy bottom line! Perhaps I needed to feel more directly connected to helping others less fortunate than those of us in the corporate world. Unsure and still searching, I became a volunteer with Allambie Children's Centre in Melbourne.

It was a happy and sad experience. I felt fortunate to have been adopted at six months of age and not remember a single moment of life in an institution. I felt sad for those children who did and full of admiration for the full-time staff at Allambie. I felt fortunate, too, not to have come from a family torn apart by child abuse, alcohol or drugs. Although the time spent with adolescent kids was draining, I always arrived home in a happier frame of mind.

Concerns of the corporate world paled into insignificance and I felt I was making some small difference, whereas Tim felt he'd only be happy with children of his own.

Around this same time, I wrote to the Alberta Government to determine if there was an adoption registry where parents and adopted children could be matched. I hadn't thought much about my origins but my biological clock was ticking, which must have aroused my curiosity. A few weeks later, IBM sent me to New York on business. With Tim working back in Australia, I took the opportunity to visit my aunt, uncle and friends in Calgary for two days. I hadn't yet received a reply to my letter of inquiry about adoption and the records office was only a two-hour drive north, in the provincial capital of Edmonton.

Leaning on the inquiry counter, I was amazed at the apparent disarray of hundreds of filing cabinets and brown cardboard boxes. As a marketing representative for IBM, I saw an obvious opportunity to sell a computer system that would enable alphabetical matching of names, thus greatly increasing the likelihood of pairing parents with children. I'm not sure if I was more disappointed that they had no records of my parents or that they refused to discuss the possibility of buying a computer, such was my thinking as a partially commissioned salesperson.

They did, however, give me the name of a voluntary organization called Parent Finders and I subscribed to their publications for a number of years. As a support group, Parent Finders offered practical suggestions on finding families and stories about the joys and heartbreaks of successful and unsuccessful searches. It struck me that many of the so-called successful searches were only thus in terms of establishing identification. Many a Pandora's Box was opened, with subsequent heartache to emerge.

Did I want to continue? Had I actually started a search? No. I'd simply made inquiries to a government department and was none the wiser for my efforts. There was little point engaging on a quest for a past which wasn't really that important to me at that point in time. I was far more interested in the present and the future.

IBM offered me a promotion and two-year transfer to head office in Sydney. Tim and I decided this chance was an excuse for a trial separation and he returned to Canada in 1984. Although it's hard to let go, it's often more damaging not to. With many heart-wrenching trips between Canada and Australia during those two years, it became evident there was no hope of reconciliation. I knew though, that it was like facing the prospect of removing a cancerous limb to save the whole body. As painful as it was, it was best to cut loose from Tim – for him and for me.

When we finally parted at Toronto airport after yet another of my business trips, tears streamed down my face as he drove off into a blinding blizzard. I hoped he'd turn back but knew he wouldn't. I hoped it wasn't over but was relieved that it was. After eight long years, there had been more pain than bliss. I knew we were doing the right thing so why did I doubt?

Just as I'd been at the right place and time when sports administration took off in Australia, I managed to hit the employment boom in 1984, when IBM grew from hiring 60 graduates to more than 350 in one year. As national recruitment manager, I even had the luxury of recruiting my own terrific team and tried to emulate the warm family feeling in the workplace that I'd enjoyed in my days at Youth, Sport and Recreation.

Apart from meeting great neighbours, I had no time to worry about making new friends in Sydney because I travelled seven out of twelve months that year. Whenever home, I kept asking why this was supposedly such a great career move when I'd doubled the size of my mortgage and halved the size of my house. A British backpacker who had briefly been a neighbour in Melbourne came to housesit and look after the dog during my travels and eventually moved in on a full-time basis. Having a flatmate was a new experience. My husband had told me that I was impossible to live with; however, Liz Burrows and I never exchanged a harsh word. She provided tremendous support on the home front – and soon became my best friend.

As surely as jacaranda blooms in spring, personal perspective rejuvenates. Shortly, the tree outside my front gate would be covered in purple bloom and rainbow lorikeets. In the back garden, under still barren frangipani and wisteria, Liz and I chatted while Tam chased sticks. Sydney's warm winter sun soothed my soul and shoulders – the warm fuzzy feeling was like that of silky, silvery pussywillows, those first harbingers of spring in Canada to awake after a winter of discontent. I lost over twenty pounds in two months, a sure sign of being happier because I tend to gain weight when dejected.

At work, I had support from local management and we were successful by all standards set by corporate head office. My first trip to New York was one of great anticipation. When the vice president called me in, I expected praise. Instead, I was admonished for a campus poster that read: *Even if you think a megabyte is a hamburger with the lot . . . you could still work for IBM!*

In head office, this was seen as degrading to the mighty Big Blue. In Australia, such light-hearted irreverence helped attract bright graduates who might otherwise not have considered the computer industry in those embryonic days. At IBM headquarters in Armonk, there was not an executive without a blue suit and white shirt. Everyone seemed committed to flying in formation and some middle management had the leadership attributes of the dead goose that floated in the pond outside head office that day.

In spite of such lacklustre individuals, there were many more who made me proud to work for IBM. A week in New York enhanced that pride. Our office lobby, at the corner of Madison Avenue and 57th Street, was adorned with pumpkins and wheat sheaves to celebrate Thanksgiving. The lobby was a haven for tired shoppers trying to escape cold streets. Downstairs, they could view an ever-changing display in the corporate art gallery. Our IBM identification card provided free entry to many of New York's galleries and museums. I didn't work for a computer company. I worked for part of the American dream.

What about my own dreams? I saw places that were allotted the proceeds from my mother's church bake sales – including a mission in Formosa (now Taiwan) where a friend of hers had been posted as a missionary. There I was, travelling the world on a new passport without making the sacrifices of missionaries, explorers or pioneers.

In this part of Asia, my husband's surname, Park, was as common as Smith. When we married, I hyphenated mine to DeVrye-Park, which only added to the confusion of an already difficult to pronounce name. Now that we were separated but still legally married, I was simply DeVrye again. I probably should have cut my losses – and name – earlier.

Life before marriage had been a colourful jigsaw puzzle. Career, home, health, friends, sport, income and travel were all pieces fitting firmly in their correct places. Then marriage jarred the table and a few bits fell to the floor. A couple of pieces were still missing and it would take some time to get the rest of the picture back together again. As I was slowly doing so, another important piece of my past disappeared.

Frank Jansen died that August. He was a great Australian. He wasn't famous but he was honest, unselfish and a gifted conversationalist. He so enjoyed life and the company of others. He was one of a kind and kind to one and all. Forgotten by some near the end of his life, but remembered always for the rest of mine. I still see his smile and hear the laughter in his voice: *Every day above the ground is a good one.*

When I first arrived in Australia, lost and lonely, I failed to fully appreciate his words. I now had to remind myself of his wisdom. It looked like I'd be bogged down in the details of a divorce settlement and, although I'd been the principal provider, I couldn't see how I could afford to pay my husband for his share of the house.

How could I get through this?

Just when I thought the situation impossible, opportunity again came my way. I was appointed Asia Pacific headquarters personnel manager in Tokyo. I accepted the position with no sense of adventure or yen to experience the Japanese culture – the only yen of interest was that to be deposited in my bank account.

13

TOKYO TREMORS

 In four short, exciting years with IBM, my climb through the ranks was almost meteoric. Another, more senior female colleague once asked me, "Who have you slept with to move up so quickly?"

"No-one! Which is why I've been promoted and you haven't," I replied, just as cattily. "If they know you in the bedroom, they don't want to know you in the boardroom." Although I admittedly made the mistake of having an office romance, I had never slept my way upward. Without doubt, my gender had accelerated promotion at a time when Australian companies were striving to cooperate with new guidelines for equal opportunity. Again, I was at the right place at the right time and my boss and mentor, Roy Lea, gambled that I had the right background to move ahead. There was a caveat, though. Before I left for Japan, Roy cautioned, "The predominantly male, middle-aged Japanese staff won't likely cooperate because you're female. But do your best, as you'll be a role model for younger Japanese women."

With that underwhelming vote of confidence, I set off on 17 April 1986 for Tokyo and inherited responsibility for six hundred expatriate families but had to temporarily say goodbye to my dog, Tammy, who was now, again, the only family I had in Australia.

The first three months were as challenging as eating jelly with chopsticks. Frequent earthquakes reminded me that life can shift, sometimes in an instant, usually over longer periods of time. I felt on shaky ground with tremors of my own inadequacy and began to think I might be an example of the "Peter Principle," where promotion exceeds competence level. Could I only be a token female in a mainly male environment?

Twenty million people lived in Tokyo – more than the entire population of Australia – and they all seemed to cram into my morning subway station! I would board the crowded commuter train at 7:30 a.m., with someone comfortably nestled in my armpit and my bottom pinched more often in Tokyo than Rome. I'd arrive, crushed and sweaty, for another day in the office and there I remained, cheerful and upbeat, until 9 or 10 p.m. Then I'd return home and burst into tears. I expected to miss Tammy and my friends but hadn't realized how much I would mourn the absence of the wide-open Australian horizon – whether sea or desert.

Tokyo's skyline seemed the same every day, six days a week. Finally, the most senior person on my team came to me and cautioned: "You work too hard, DeVrye-san. Please go home earlier." I assured him that I didn't want to be seen as a lazy Westerner amid the hardworking Japanese. However, I had failed to understand that the key reason my staff worked such long hours was the unwritten protocol that employees shouldn't leave until the boss did. It was rather like a Mexican stand-off with everyone exhausted, trying to live up to the expectations of the other. Maybe my work habits were early signs of becoming a workaholic, stretched like an elastic band, ready to snap at the first sign of tension.

The main stress came not from Japanese males, but from

the whingeing of American and Australian spouses who longed for their acre in Connecticut or harbour view in Sydney. One night near 10 o'clock, a woman phoned my home in near hysteria.

"Send one of the Japs around immediately to change the light bulb in the kitchen!" I patiently informed her that such a task was not company responsibility and that her terminology was inappropriate. She persisted, stating that her husband was out of town and Tokyo was a hardship posting. Hardly! She eventually calmed down as I explained the difference between bayonet and screw-top fittings and instructed her to wait until morning to remove it and take it to a hardware store where, by simply smiling and showing the bulb, she'd be able to purchase a replacement. After hanging up, I congratulated myself on my remarkable restraint for not suggesting she stand in a bucket of water and stick her finger in the socket! Such were the complaints I handled as human resource manager, but I had no-one with whom I could share my own concerns about the isolation I felt.

My predominantly male Japanese staff may not have liked working for a Western woman. Perhaps they never admitted it to anyone else, either, but they never indicated any problem to me. In reality, I needed them more than they needed me and we soon reached mutual trust.

One secretary had a degree in nuclear physics while another junior administrator had a master's in English Literature from Columbia University. Although I was an oddity among executive ranks, they were extremely bright young women. Before I left, I convinced senior Japanese management to promote the first female, first-line manager in a non-secretarial role but was told that she wouldn't be accepted by male subordinates. I was convinced that her people skills would overcome traditional obstacles and told her that I believed she could succeed. To do so, she would need to be aware of barriers and have a pioneering spirit, just as American women had done in the 1960s. We didn't need the reminder that this was Japan and the year was 1987.

As time passed, I learnt to cope with daily Japanese life outside the office, thanks to my friend and language teacher, Miyoko. She introduced me to local markets and customs, and I bought a motor scooter to explore more of the culture instead of simply working from my internationally linked terminal – a common mode of work today but not in 1988.

But Tammy could not send emails and the prices of golf and fruit were as steep as Mount Fuji. The Japanese experience eventually proved to be priceless, but it took me a while to see it. Even an all-night climb for a sunrise view from the top of Mount Fuji provided no actual vista. Through fog cover, the only sight was the climber 2 metres in front of my nose. My eyes were opened in other ways.

I remained an obvious outsider and frequently embarrassed myself with language blunders. On the descent from Fuji, I met a man who appeared to have a fun run advertised on his T-shirt. As we strolled together, I asked in my halting Japanese whether he jogged every morning. He responded in broken English that he did so three times a week. The conversation continued slowly in this vein, each of us struggling to use the other's language to reply.

"Do you also run marathons?"

He looked puzzled so I explained the term marathon to the best of my ability.

". . . very difficult, very long time."

"Oh yes," he twigged. "Me marathon . . . and four children . . . very long time, very difficult!"

Likewise, Japanese toilets proved problematic at times. On the train to see a giant Buddha at Kamakura, I was squatted over the stainless steel hole in the floor when the train suddenly stopped and I instinctively grabbed the door handle for support. As I did so, the sliding door opened and I tumbled out into the corridor with purple jeans around my knees – not just embarrassed but bare-assed! The Japanese all turned a blind eye so I didn't "lose face" but my English colleague held no such reserve, regaling this tale to everyone back in the office.

What's more, the stationmaster couldn't seem to understand my simple question: "What time does the train return to Tokyo?" *Densha* is the word for train and *denwa* is the word for phone, so we both became increasingly frustrated when I repeatedly asked him what time the telephone left for Tokyo!

It was quite different to memories of myself as a little girl travelling through the Rockies securely in my father's care on the Canadian Pacific Railway. Thirty years later in Japan, I queried the bilingual announcements each time a station was approached. The Japanese message seemed very detailed and lasted a number of minutes. The English translation simply consisted of: We will now arrive at such and such destination. I always wondered what they *weren't* telling me.

I never fulfilled my fleeting childhood notion to be a missionary but my experience in Japan converted me to the wider global community. I'd travelled before but never interacted on a regular basis with businesspeople from many different countries. It was both a joy and a frustration to experience other cultures first-hand. Friends speculated that my time in Japan was divine justice meted out to teach me patience, but tea ceremonies, origami and flower arrangement remained beyond my grasp. However, in the midst of the built-up Tokyo skyline, I did manage to expand my own personal horizon of tolerance and was so kindly tolerated as an obvious outsider. Many times I experienced the practical application of that old Japanese proverb: *One kind word can warm three winter months.*

Can you imagine the reaction from a group of Australians or North Americans if a Japanese national attended an Anzac march or Legion service? We're all minorities somewhere in this world. As one of a few white faces present amid one hundred thousand at the Hiroshima memorial service, I was engulfed in a cloud of kindness from strangers as I tried unsuccessfully, then and now, to comprehend the loss of innocent civilian life in the horror of war, just as I had on my first visit to Hawaii and Pearl Harbor. "World peace through world trade" was an IBM motto but I struggled with inner peace when an old woman offered me a seaweed rice cracker and the words: "My son died here." I could offer nothing but a tear in return.

After three months in Tokyo, I thought I understood quite a bit about life in Japan. After two years, I realized just how much I still had to learn. I wrote *An A–Z Guide to Living and Working in Japan* to help others avoid my considerable faux pas. At times, my Japanese friends, colleagues and total strangers must have all thought I was a few fish short of a sushi!

14

HIMALAYAN HORIZONS

 Metaphorically expanding my personal horizons was one thing, but after eighteen months in the compact world of Tokyo, I needed real space. So in 1987 I headed off on vacation to trek in the Himalayas of Nepal. *The Japan Times* reported that K2 may have replaced Everest as the highest mountain – as I questioned my climb up the corporate ladder, I sensed it was only a matter of time until the media would report IBM was no longer the biggest computer giant on the globe.

It was rebelliously rewarding to walk out of the office in high heels and a pinstriped suit, with hiking boots dangling from the outside of my backpack. It nicely subverted my staid corporate image.

I met my Sydney flatmate and best friend, Liz, at Kathmandu airport while police brandished batons at touts. We grabbed our own backpacks from a rickety wagon and, after dodging rickshaws, bikes, people, dogs and Brahmans amid the bedlam of the narrow streets, we safely collapsed in our $5 a night hotel room.

We awoke pre-dawn to only the sound of birds. The sun and noise levels rose together to a cacophony of flushing toilets, barking dogs, tinkling bicycle bells, revving engines and the ubiquitous car horns. This was interspersed with babies crying, children laughing, women chattering, plus the revolting noise of throat-clearing as men expressively expectorated. Tokyo was positively serene by comparison.

Propped on temple stairs at Dubar Square, we organized porters and watched life pass by, relieved to be removed from our own worries that paled into insignificance beside others' day-to-day struggle for survival. It seemed incongruous that I earned more in two hours than a porter here would in two weeks of strenuous work. Was I worth that much more? Of course not. It was just a different economic system – without income tax, but without welfare for the needy either.

We set off full of enthusiasm for a three-week trek to Annapurna Base Camp, and at the end of the day concluded that physical fatigue was preferable to the mental exhaustion of staggering home from a bad day at the office. We questioned if that would be so if we were not here by choice. The answer was as clear as the azure sky above the Tibetan refugee camp we'd passed. Of all freedoms, choice is the choicest.

Already we had climbed higher than the top of Mount Fuji. Every lodge seemed to be named Namaste – the greeting of peace. We had only a cup of water per day for washing. A little pot of lemon tea, cornbread and dhal seemed luxury indeed. After some initial acclimatization, we eased into the rhythm of early waking and walking through villages so small that I don't recall mention of their names. Ever moving upward and closer to our ultimate destination of base camp, we crossed the main avalanche area at Hinku before the midday sun hit and were greatly relieved to reach the next stop, where we were assured the trail was safe.

Only 20 minutes away from our night's camp I stopped to squat, as one frequently must. My Sherpa discreetly waited around the next bend, less than 200 metres away. I'd almost caught up with him when we heard a rumble from the right that sounded like thunder. As I looked in that direction, he urged me to hurry. "Come, come – no look, no look."

I had looked to the right – but that was the wrong and opposite direction to any danger as sound deceptively echoed off the mountain wall in quadraphonic clarity. Within seconds, a massive avalanche of snow and ice swept just behind us, covering the exact spot where my bare behind had been exposed only moments earlier. We spent no time evaluating the debris. Legs that previously felt like lead in the high altitude found renewed adrenaline-induced energy as I nearly sprinted to that night's camp.

I couldn't believe Liz asked if I'd taken a photo! In spite of jokes about "quite a flush," my body was suffused with a wave of fear. The mountain was already wrapped in fog by 2 p.m., as was I – in my ultra-down sleeping bag, shivering with shock.

Coaxed to continue in the morning, we tramped on to base camp, breaking through ice crust to our thighs. I failed to fully absorb Annapurna's grandeur, as I was conscious that the only way back was across the avalanche. Heading down the next day, we met two American hikers on the way up.

"Be careful. An Australian was almost caught in an avalanche."

The next trekker warned that two Australians were caught and one died. By the time we reached that evening's camp site, another trekker insisted we lay buried beneath the snow, in spite of our assurance that the mountain version of Chinese whispers had been at work.

The novelty of repeating the story soon wore as thin as the soles of our hiking boots as we soaked blistered feet in icy streams to anaesthetize the pain. Rather than being buried alive, I felt more alive in a perverse way – but only many days later after we reached safety on the other side of the avalanche.

Rushing rivers, although contaminated with Giardia, seemed nothing less than pristine, rhododendrons bloomed redder and below us ferns carpeted canyons in vivid green. An occasional wildflower clung to our boots, as we did to the ropes on suspension bridges, aptly named because of the suspense of wondering if you'd make it to the other side! Once across, we could relax and enjoy the songs of more than a hundred species of birds – their individual notes were indistinguishable to the untrained ear but their symphony filled the crisp, thin air.

> What a pity the beautiful butterflies only have one day to live. If beset with such a fate, what a great place to live that one day; above the tree line, free of foliage and responsibility to anything but this moment.

My diary also noted that I had hoped to attain the inner peace that we in the West associate with high mountain lamas. Instead, my meagre mind was fully focused on placing one foot in front of the other on treacherous mountain terrain.

At times, the simplicity and dignity of a subsistence existence seemed somewhat noble. A smile is communication enough – no need for three-page memos and multiple copies. While trekking, you rejoice to meet others along the way and learn of what lies ahead. In corporations, those who have gone before seldom share the journey. Or, maybe we're too embarrassed to ask.

Witnessing first-hand the harshness of life in the mountains of Nepal, any fantasies of living simply off the land evaporated like morning dew on the tent. Maybe it had something to do with incidents like ducking power lines while bouncing along on the roof of a bus that was itself only inches away from plummeting to the gorge below. Or chasing bandits from a hut the night before. Or food poisoning and the absence of a decent toilet and the ensuing argument as Liz and I failed to agree on scatological standards. It's one thing to be privileged to choose to absorb another culture for a period of time but I felt more fortunate to choose to return to my own concept of civilization by simply producing a slip of paper, known as an airline ticket.

I shall never forget the parting words of my Sherpa: "I hope to see you again – in this life or another!"

As the plane left Kathmandu, I was acutely aware that although we may all sleep under the same moon, we each dream of different horizons. My next bed would be the Raffles Hotel in Singapore, an oasis in the Orient, for an IBM sales conference. There, I bubbled about my trek like a newly opened bottle of champagne to any willing listener. Then, hit with the reality of final paperwork for my and Tim's divorce when I returned to my Tokyo high-rise, I felt as flat as the dregs of that same bottle.

I'd been nearly killed in an avalanche but usually successfully buried my own fears of being alone. Admittedly afraid of dying alone, at least I've never been frightened to live. A birthday card on the fridge from Liz reminded me of the wise words of writer Helen Keller: "Life is either a daring adventure – or nothing."

15

HOPE AS MY COMPASS

 I'd travelled extensively in Asia and was appalled by the poverty I witnessed. Apart from writing cheques to charities, surely there was something tangible that I could personally do to help. I thought of adopting a child and started what became a thick file of correspondence to relevant government authorities. My last letter in 1987 read:

> Although I appreciate your logic of giving preference to two parent applicants, I would nevertheless like to apply to adopt a child from Australia or overseas. Age is not relevant. As an adoptee myself, I would like to offer another child the same opportunities and love which I would otherwise not have had. I fully realize the specific difficulties of adopting an overseas child, as well as the challenges of being a single parent, but believe I have the financial means, emotional stability and commitment to help a child.

At one stage, some well-meaning bureaucrat informed me – off the record, of course – that single people weren't allowed to adopt because there was a likelihood they would be homosexual and likely to abuse a child. I'd never heard such drivel in my entire life so appealed to the minister, who replied with a reasonably sympathetic but nonetheless

standard letter. I conceded defeat and agreed that two loving parents would be ideal. Still, I believed I could have
offered some poor orphan in a refugee camp a far better life
than what he or she had. That's all I wanted to do – give
some kid a chance, just like my parents had given me.

As my mother would always say, much to my disgust as
a teenager – *it probably wasn't meant to be.* In Japan, without
any family I could call my own, I reflected that Mum was
probably right.

It never occurred to me that somewhere I might have
family. Family that I'd not yet met. If I hadn't become seriously ill, I may never have been tempted to discover their
existence.

When I ended up in the Japanese hospital coughing up
blood, I decided to try to find my biological parents, if only
to rule out hereditary reasons for my illness. And once I'd
started asking those questions I began to want some
answers. I had never been told much at all about my beginnings. I don't remember time in an orphanage and am
grateful that I don't remember my infancy at all. Confused
by the label "illegitimate," I felt a completely legitimate
human being, whether born in or out of wedlock. I loved
my parents and they loved me and that was all that ever
mattered. I'd never wanted to know any more. Until now.
What was my medical history? Was there any hereditary
disease I should be aware of?

That's when I decided to try to find these biological parents of mine. There was nothing left to lose and since Liz
was now visiting me in Japan, we waded through telephone
books at the Canadian Consulate in Tokyo, just as we had
done through thigh-deep snow in the Himalayas. After
writing to every Bachman in Canada I only received replies
from well-meaning strangers, with no real clues as to my

origins. There was no point becoming obsessed with the search. If we were meant to meet up, it would happen.

I've already mentioned the lovely, and not so lovely, letters I received. I'd been too busy to reply to a later letter from a Bachman who had compiled a family tree. At a quick glance, most of the names on her mailing list corresponded with my master list, so I let it go, until the day before leaving Japan for my next IBM posting, in Hong Kong.

As I packed up the mess on my desk, I remembered I hadn't taken time to cross-reference Cathy Bachman's mailing list with mine. About thirty more Bachmans were scattered across Canada in small towns that weren't listed in the Tokyo-based Canadian Consulate's directories, my original information source. I posted a few more letters – just in case.

Just in case. I heard the distant echo of my mother's mantra. To be honest, I expected nothing. It was less disappointing to think that way. Continuing to clear my desk, I came across another letter and paused to re-read it.

> Dear Catherine,
> I wish we were related for you sound like a daughter anyone would be so pleased to find and believe your birth parents would and should be honoured you are trying so hard to find them. Times have changed since you were born and people are not keeping such "family secrets" anymore as we have become more enlightened (slowly).
>
> If you could find the right Bachmans, I'm sure they would be overjoyed to hear from you. The woman who bore you has never forgotten you no matter how wonderful her present life is because it is not in our nature to ever forget such an event. You are in her thoughts daily I am sure and it will be such a relief and joy to know you are well and had a happy life when

she had to give you up for adoption. We all need to know our roots and I give you a lot of credit for going about it as you are.

Did you know that the names, which were chosen for you, were very popular in that era and romantic? Marilyn Monroe was the movie star of the day. I am sorry I cannot be of more help.

I wish you well in your search and would love to hear from you one day that you have succeeded. I will be thinking of you now, dear girl, and if you are ever in Toronto, do give me a call.

Marie Nadya Bachman

Although I'd never cried at my folks' funerals, tears were nothing new to me now. Even though I hadn't found my biological parents, it was deeply touching that people half a world away took time out of their lives to help a total stranger.

Maybe everything, everyone and everywhere is strange – until they become familiar? I'd begun my time in Japan as a total stranger to the people and their culture. Although the early days had been as frustrating as pushing a sumo wrestler the opposite direction in a revolving door, I realized there were aspects of life in Japan that I would miss. Even the soba (noodle) shop on the corner with the once unrecognizable kanji characters had become an orientation point in my neighbourhood, and a landmark in my Tokyo life. People had actually stopped me there to ask for directions. Ironically, I'm "directionally challenged" at the best of times. On holiday, I seldom read maps and prefer to explore with just a vague notion of my destination. Conversely, for business appointments, I plan where I'm going and why. Car satellite navigation systems are a bonus in strange cities. Rather than a dismissive, "You missed the turn, you idiot" – a frequent refrain of Tim's on car trips – a voice calmly informs, "Please be patient while we re-calculate your destination."

As I packed the manila folder file with the final divorce documentation that couldn't be ratified until returning to Australia, I realized that there would be no more automobile arguments with Tim, since for many years we hadn't been heading in the same direction. For the rest of my life's journey, I might get lost but I would carry on with hope as my compass and optimism as my map.

Strange what you think when you're moving on. I tidied the remaining papers and continued packing. My desk was now clear, even if my mind was not. Just before the movers arrived, I finally posted those remaining letters to small towns in the wheat belt of southern Alberta. The chances of finding anyone at this stage were like looking for the proverbial needle in a haystack but there was nothing to lose.

I was returning to Hong Kong in quite different circumstances to my first visit, but it was equally enthralling – from the pace and energy of Victoria Peak to the fragrant harbour and not-so-fragrant back alleys. Colour, people, diversity, food and excitement blended to typify the magic of the Orient I'd first set eyes on fifteen years earlier. But, compared to Tokyo, it seemed strangely Westernized. Signs were in English. Caucasians were conspicuous at the American Club, Hong Kong Cricket Club, Aberdeen Yacht Club, Royal Hong Kong Club and the Jardine Matheson box at the Royal Hong Kong Jockey Club. There were more clubs than those in my bag at the Sheko Golf Club! Oh, the privileged life of the expat community! But on 26 January 1988, I wanted to be nowhere other than Sydney to celebrate Australia's bicentennial year. Work commitments prevented that. So, rather than see tall ships sail into Sydney Harbour, I improvised and hired tall transport of another sort – a double-decker roofless tram, decorated with stuffed kangaroos, koalas, streamers and balloons. We celebrated Australia Day with meat pies and beer, riding through the crowded night markets singing "Waltzing Matilda," while locals dined on their delicacies of snake and dog (no doubt an acquired taste, like Vegemite) in the Year of the Dragon.

It was a strange economy where you could buy a polo shirt in Kowloon for only HK$20 (about US$3) – cheaper than having the old one laundered! I'm not a seasoned shopper but for many expats the bargains were as addictive as the opium of old. I preferred to take a favourite designer suit to a tailor and ask them to "photocopy" it in different fabrics. What a contrast to my first Hong Kong visit, when I had virtually nothing to spend, except time. Time to satisfy my curiosity. Time to peer out hotel windows into sweatshops at 4 a.m. Time to dream. Time to sit and watch. Time to be at one with another culture rather than rush off to another cocktail party. In many ways, that's the best sort of trip to take.

I wanted to stay longer, but like most IBM employees I knew the company initials could easily stand for I've Been Moved. All too soon my assignment ended and I was heading back to Sydney via a short vacation in India.

Admittedly one of the world's most fascinating destinations, my first impressions of India were bleak, as the Delhi taxi dodged donkeys barely visible in the darkness. What juxtaposition to the bright lights of Hong Kong. Morning introduced me to a more colourful country with some 800 million citizens. How could the streets possibly accommodate even one more rickshaw, taxi, donkey, cart, truck, camel, bus, elephant or pedestrian? At first glance at the chaos, one could be forgiven for thinking there were no road rules in India. In fact, there was a very simple maxim adhered to by all. The bigger object always had right of way even if it was on the wrong side of the road!

Later I boarded a train for Agra. More than 10 million people a day travelled on India Rail as 11,000 trains criss-crossed the country on 60,777 kilometres of track. I felt much safer here than on the road, where hands begging for money had reached into my taxi. I was even more upset when the taxi driver matter-of-factly informed me that these were professional beggars controlled by pimps and that many had been intentionally maimed at birth. The driver was sleazy enough to be a pimp himself. I didn't appreciate his persistent sexual harassment, so invented an imaginary husband for the remainder of my solo trip.

The view of the Taj Mahal, across the drought-stricken river, was splendid – this monument of love had been built as a tribute to a king's dead queen, who died aged thirty-nine following the birth of her fourteenth child. It was less romantic to see pregnant women hoist picks and shovels, while young children clung to their skirts. Meanwhile, groups of nearby men shared cups of chai with each other.

Further south, the ancient desert city of Jaiselmeer was reminiscent of a scene from the sixteenth century. I've never seen anything like it before or since. It reminded me of images in my Sunday school picture books of colourfully clad women in long flowing robes statuesquely balancing jugs of well-water on their heads. Once on a prosperous caravan route to the Orient along which wealthy merchants traded their precious cargoes of silks, spices and jewels, Jaiselmeer was a resting place because of its huge lake on the edge of the desert.

That watering hole had completely dried up only six years earlier but the economy had done so in 1947, when India achieved independence. Caravans could no longer freely cross the Pakistan border so merchants left for the cities, leaving behind only poor peasants and a rich legacy of magnificent sandstone structures.

In this town where time stood still, it occurred to me that we shouldn't judge a civilization, past or present, purely by materialistic standards. Indians were appalled that we placed our children in daycare and our elderly in retirement homes. For them, the extended family was part of life's cycle.

I still had no clues about my family. A camel ride through the magnificent rippled sand dunes of the Thar Desert allowed more time for thought. Alighting from these ships of the desert, I sank past my calves in the fine sand and envisaged tales of entire caravans being buried alive, as these gangly, flea-bitten camels tucked their knees under them as gracefully as a geisha.

I also envisaged less elegant scenarios from one of the most moving books I'd ever read, Dominique Lapierre's *City of Joy*, set in the slums of Calcutta. There, Mother Teresa created an oasis of optimism in a desert of despair, while most Westerners like me were still trying to quench a thirst for self-truth. Like bananas and oranges, the safest and most sanitary fruit choice of travellers, I'd remained relatively protected in my outer skin.

Yes, I'd come a long way in a few short years. I was a grown woman now, with the world seemingly at my feet. But I had not forgotten the little girl who never quite fitted in anywhere, the little girl whose dad called her "cowboy" even though she never got the horse she desperately wanted. If she wasn't hanging around the Calgary Stampede grounds, she was dreaming about travelling the world. Where did my love of horses and adventure come from?

Maybe I would soon find out, although it seemed doubtful. Back on the plane to Sydney, I felt I was heading towards a crossroads. With no signposts in the sky, at 30,000 feet, somewhere over the Timor Sea, I wrote my letter of resignation to IBM.

16

BRIDGING NEWS

It was 29 February 1988 . . . Leap year and I was back in Sydney, jet-lagged and ill again, and wondering where on earth I'd be sent next and for how long.

I'd just picked up my dog Tam who had been cared for by wonderful neighbours. I physically felt the truth of the words inscribed at Gandhi's cremation site – *Oh God* – in every cell of my body when I opened the door to my empty house in Neutral Bay, which had been rented in my absence. It looked like the back blocks of Bombay. Tenants had trashed the place. I couldn't even wash my hands because water and electricity were cut off. Tam sniffed around, happily oblivious to the mess.

Still, compared to what I'd seen in India, this was only temporary and nothing to worry about. After all, no-one was chasing me with a cobra, as had happened the week before! And, even though there was often dreadful drought in Australia, it wasn't as bad as the Indian camel caravan I'd experienced, where school-aged children had never seen rain and where I had promised to never again leave the water running while brushing my teeth.

Wrapped in the embrace of the backyard sun, I regained perspective after the initial inspection of my house. As I was about to leave, I noticed a telegram sitting on the dusty mantelpiece. At least the mantelpiece was still there – nothing else seemed to be. No heaters, no light fittings, just the telegram.

I scratched my ear tiredly and gave Tam another pat. No doubt this ever-patient golden retriever was wondering if I'd be taking off again. Unconditional love and devotion flooded from her eyes, the only sound was her tail thumping against the floor. No wonder I'd missed her so much. I loved her more than she loved me – but at least she still loved me.

At that moment, the search for my biological parents was the last thing on my mind. For too long I'd received occasional messages that shed no light whatsoever upon my origins, and had almost given up hope. So with mind numb, I opened the telegram, half-thinking it must be for the previous tenants, even though it had my name on it.

I blamed jet lag for that. But couldn't blame jet lag for what the telegram said, unless I was suffering a mental aberration.

"You were a very pleasant surprise. Grandmother's letter en route. Would like you to phone me collect. Would be nice to phone your mother first. Love Harold and Pearl Mandeville, and mother Trudy."

I stood there, stunned for a little while. No thought at all crossed my mind. If it did, then I was unawares. This supposedly intelligent, active so-called corporate high-flyer was anaesthetized. I looked at the name and address. Yep. Definitely for me. But who were Harold and Pearl Mandeville? I read the telegram again and this time my brain fixed on the words "mother Trudy."

Mother Trudy.

"I've got a mother. I've got a mother . . ."

Tam's tail thumped on the carpet until my instant of joy

turned to tears. For so long now, far too long, I'd been in silent mourning for the only people who loved me unconditionally – my mum, dad and granddad. Now this telegram heralded the words: Mother Trudy.

Why was I crying? Shouldn't I be *happy* to have found my biological parents after all these years? Part of me was pleased, but a bigger part of me let loose with years of bottled-up emotion and feelings dammed a decade and a half. For the first time in fifteen years, I allowed myself to fully grieve for Mum, Dad and Granddad. I sank to the carpet, my entire body heaving, as sobs echoed through the empty house. It had taken all these years of warmth in Australia to thaw that sadness frozen in time. Overflowing with emotion, the dam had finally burst, but rather than drowning in floodwaters of despair, I felt my sorrow lift like a feather in a light summer's breeze.

I held Tam tight, as she licked the salty tears from my face. I wanted to curl up in a little ball and sleep forever – there on the barren carpet but there was somebody else who had to know this news.

Liz had helped get all those addresses from the consulate's directories when she visited Tokyo after our Himalayan adventure. She was still my best friend and had been my flatmate for six years after my husband left – so to Liz's workplace Tammy and I duly scurried.

Tammy wandered up and down the pharmacy's aisles, wagging her tail in greeting to all.

"Hi there, mate!" Liz squealed, like she had a hundred times before. "You're back a day early."

I thrust the telegram under her nose. "I've got a mother."

She hugged me tight, laughing and crying. Both of us were oblivious to the curious looks from customers.

My search was over, but the story had barely begun.

Other neighbours had collected my mail in my long absence and it was there I went next. Yes, as per telegram, there was a letter waiting for me, which I took to the bathroom to read in privacy.

The telegram had said "grandmother's letter en route," but this letter was from my *mother*. I sat in the bathroom for a long time and cried again. Heaven knows what they thought. Delhi Belly? Trudy, the woman who had given birth to me, wrote that she found this letter difficult to write. I can imagine it would have been more than difficult. She was sorry about my parents' deaths, would have liked to personally thank them for taking care of her baby, giving her those things which she could not . . . It was true. They *did* give me everything I needed – most of all, truckloads of love. All Trudy said about my father was his name, so now the Harold Mandeville of the telegram made a little more sense. I'd never expected to find a father. Was it a bonus? And who was this mysterious Pearl?

Trudy went on to say how her mother and sisters were supportive now but hadn't always been . . .

I read the letter half a dozen times in case I missed something important. What sort of woman was she? I wondered. What circumstances had led her to give up her baby? She didn't have to contact me. Maybe, just maybe, she occasionally wondered what had happened to that baby daughter she'd given away?

She mustn't have been able to clothe, feed or educate me. A surge of love welled up inside and it was born of gratitude to my mum and my dad for giving me what this woman could not. I can't even imagine what it would have been like to be an unwed mother in 1950. But it wouldn't have been easy.

I folded the letter and went back to the room IBM had

booked me into at the Hilton. I couldn't go back to my empty house until furniture arrived. Nor did I wish to disturb any friends, as I knew I was in for a restless night. I turned the television on and there it was – the closing ceremony of the 1988 Calgary Winter Olympics. Media coverage brought my hometown to the entire world, but only one person could see it through my eyes. McMahon Stadium where I'd once played gridiron football and cheered the Stampeders on. Shots of the crowd. Were any of those people related to me? Amid the spirit of the Olympic family, I at last had hopes of meeting my own. Did I have brothers and sisters? What did they look like? Did they know about me?

More shots of the Saddledome Stadium from Scotchman's Hill again brought me undone. So many unanswered and unavoidable questions whirlpooled. My childhood came flooding back. Scotchman's Hill, where Granddad first settled so long ago. The fireworks during Stampede Week. Hiding in the cliffs and smoking under the bridge. Scotchman's Hill and a multitude of cowboys trying to be nice to a little would-be cowgirl whose only question was, "Can I walk your horse, mister?"

I thought about my Canadian childhood – even though it felt a lifetime ago, and someone else's lifetime at that because it just didn't feel like mine at that crucial point in time. It had been fifteen years since I saw the sun set over the Rocky Mountains.

Had I known then, really known, what I knew now, would I have been a better daughter to the wonderful couple who had loved me as their own flesh and blood? What would I have done differently if I had my time over again? What if this Trudy from Canada had kept me? What then?

The memories of my childhood were mine to own – no-one else's. Why think of what could have been? I had to concentrate on what definitely was: my family, my friends. I remembered the St. Andrew's Church bake sales, all proceeds to missions scattered about the planet I so desperately wanted to see and know, while people around me were quite content with their own lives . . . My dad, all his life wanting to be an architect but working instead as a chef on the Canadian Pacific. How tirelessly he worked to provide for us. He sacrificed his dreams for us. And I took him for granted. He'd give away his last dime if he thought someone else needed it more. Tears filled my eyes when I thought about him. It was too late now to say sorry. Dad, I am so sorry. Why wasn't I a better daughter?

And my poor mother, like most adoptive parents, over-protective but patiently patching up her tomboy daughter's injuries while hoping a miracle would occur and the tomboy would no longer object to florals and frills. Still, her sports-mad daughter, not particularly athletically gifted, always tried her hardest. A broken ankle tobogganing, an exposed kneecap from a hockey puck and a sleigh slicing her face. At one stage, I had so many stitches Mum must have thought she was raising a patchwork quilt instead of a daughter! And the stitches were very different to her own fine handiwork on the trusty old treadle Singer sewing machine. She counted with horror the twenty-six stitches in my skull from a wayward ski, but she never knew the ski patrol used a fine razor saw to separate my head from the snow. Fortunately, the frozen blood prevented me from losing any more of it. That knock on the head might explain a few things! The outspoken one, always questioning and never content. Wanting a horse and getting a budgie instead. Two college degrees when no-one thought it necessary for girls to go to university at all . . . We were different, my mother and I. Her life revolved around family and home, while my horizons weren't neatly confined within four walls – never had been, never would be.

Mum had always been a carer who crocheted kindness into the very fabric of everyday living. First, she was the eldest child, helping to raise younger siblings and then the role of caring for ageing parents fell to her. Finally, she was the matriarch – family gatherings with cousins always centred on our home.

My Auntie Kay, whom I loved very much, played a central part in these. With three sons of her own she tolerated my tomboy tendencies. Her laugh lit up a room and much to my parents' horror, she bought my first rock and roll record by Bobby Curtola, the Canadian equivalent of Australian Johnny Farnham, about the time the Beatles rose to global fame.

I was never spoiled with material goods but if there was only one piece of cake left, it was mine. And although I never let on, I adored the blue velvet dress Mum sewed for me the year Bobby Vinton released a song of the same name.

When my parents died, each slowly and suffering far too much, I realized too late just how much they meant to me. So I did what both my Scottish grandfather seventy-odd years before and my father had done. I made a new life in a new country. Yet, all the while, something was missing.

Love was absent.

I'd worked and played hard to achieve those little-girl dreams of travel. Of making a difference, or at least trying to.

My life had turned full circle and I realized it as I sat, alone in the Sydney Hilton hotel, watching the closing ceremony of the Olympic Games in Calgary. I now had in my possession a letter from the woman who had given birth to me thirty-seven years earlier.

I had the chance now to know my birth mother, and it

wasn't just medical information I was curious about. Not now. And there was a father, too – someone called Harold. This mother of mine, Trudy, had a mother and sisters. There was a whole tribe of family out there that I'd never known existed. I was now an undeniable part of that family – unless of course, one of them wanted to deny it.

I chewed my fingernails and felt an overpowering urge for a big block of chocolate.

For years now I'd felt I was alone. Totally alone. There was a hidden bottomless void deep inside me. The sum total of the family I used to be a part of had been reduced to one.

The house my grandfather had built on Scotchman's Hill now provided shelter for other people. The line ended with me. And I'd taken the line's end to Australia, half a world away, to build something new.

Now I had the chance to pick up the threads of another family line. One which, biologically at least, I was a part of.

How many other people have that opportunity?

I was lucky. I'd instigated a search that I felt at the time would leave no emotional residue whatsoever upon me. So wrong about the impact of the contact, now I had to decide if it was right to pursue this path. What were my expectations here? What did I really want? Would my appearance after thirty-seven long years cause pain and turmoil in the lives of these strangers to whom I was related? How many secrets would come tumbling out of previously locked closets because of this?

And worse, was my search and its outcome a betrayal of Mum's and Dad's love?

I had only wanted to know if there were any hereditary illnesses. I kept reminding myself of that.

The closing ceremony was over and my innate practicality resurfaced. I had to go through with this. I seldom backed down. As Frank Jansen would have said: *Get off your behind and 'ave a bloody go.*

What, really, did I have to lose?

No-one was there to say, *Catherine, you shouldn't.* Be careful. This was a decision I had to make on my own. No dares. No cans and no can'ts. Mum used to look at me and sigh, as if she knew what would be waiting at the end of my next adventure.

Oh, Mum, I thought. I need you now. How I need you now. What should I do with this open Pandora's Box?

I sent a telegram to say I'd call as soon as my home phone was reconnected and I'd moved back in. And I tore up my letter of resignation from IBM. For the time being, I didn't need any more challenges to my equilibrium.

17

FAMILY TREE

 Frida Bachman was my biological grandmother, eighty-four years old and living in a nursing home in Taber, Alberta. Sometimes she would ask her family – or anyone else who might listen – *I wonder whatever happened to that little baby Trudy gave away?*

"Don't worry, Mum, you've got all of us," her youngest daughter would assure her.

"Ya, but I still vonder." Frida could never understand why Trudy was so different than her sisters. She wondered if she had gone wrong as a mother.

Frida never got much mail. Only one brother and a few cousins were still alive in Switzerland but she also occasionally received cards or letters from her daughter in Ottawa and from her many grandchildren scattered throughout the country. Mostly they were too busy with their own lives to write an old lady, she thought, so she wondered who this could be from as she fumbled with the airmail envelope postmarked Japan. She didn't recall anyone mentioning that one of the kids was going there. She paused and studied the unfamiliar return address.

This letter was different and she knew it before she'd read a word. It was typed, not like the rushed, handwritten scrawl she recognized when family felt obliged to drop her a line. It certainly didn't look like one of those dreadful, newfangled, word-processed letters that always seemed to know her name and called her a valued customer. The last one offered her a special introductory offer on a weight reduction program – and she already weighed less than ninety pounds!

Frida's fading blue eyes squinted through the magnifying glass, and slowly, she began to read. Surprise crossed her face and tears filled her eyes. Now she knew what had become of that baby her daughter had given away.

She hung her head and closed her eyes. Almost every day for thirty-seven years she'd wondered about that child. It was almost too much to bear. So tired, now. So tired.

The nurse gently shook her shoulder.

"You have visitors, Mrs. Bachman. Time to wake up. Mrs. Bachman?"

Two of her granddaughters walked into the room. What lovely young women they had become. One was as dark as the other was fair. They lived nearby and visited almost every day. Today, they had one of their youngsters in tow, who with his boundless energy was about to accidentally disconnect the cord leading to great-grandma's oxygen. The airmail letter was still folded in her lap.

"What's that, Gran? Another letter from Switzerland?"

"I swear that boy grows bigger every day. What a beautiful child."

He was one of her forty-three grandchildren and thirty-nine great-grandchildren at the time, with more always on the way. She loved them all equally. Even with her failing eyesight and memory, Frida Bachman, the matriarch, was the only person who could recall all the names and birthdays of her ever-expanding family.

She would tell them about the letter later. Maybe. First she would have to tell Trudy.

They chatted about the weather, about the food in the nursing home but mainly about the family. She was so pleased they had all "done well," without having to make the sacrifices she and Johan, her long-dead husband, had made. She was glad her family didn't have to emigrate to a faraway country as they had. During days of struggle through the Depression, she clothed her children in hand-sewn flour sacks and love. Those pioneering days near Warner, in the region known as the Badlands where dinosaur fossils are the main draw card, were long gone. Now Frida was relieved to be surrounded by the younger generation. Surrounded by love.

Once her visitors left, she re-read the letter from Tokyo.

"I can now die happy," she sighed as her arthritic fingers picked up a pen and started to write. It was the first of many letters I received from her.

I was so glad to hear from you as I think you must be my granddaughter ... I'm 84 years old and have to live in a lodge in Taber as my health isn't the best ... At the time you were born, your mother, Trudy, lived in Calgary and had two men friends. When the father deserted her after you were born, the other insisted on marrying her a month after.

My heart fell. Was my biological father a man who couldn't accept parental responsibility for his actions? Somehow, I didn't think so but I was indeed "illegitimate" – although everything in my life seemed totally legitimate.

Trudy already had a 3-year-old girl and didn't want another man's child so with a heavy heart decided to give you out for adoption. We didn't hear about it till after they got married in Banff and had 3 more children ... I phoned your mother. She promised to come and read your letter. Said she couldn't believe it until she saw it ... She promised to write.

Yes, she had written.

Trudy still has the ordeal to tell her family about you. They will be surprised ... You must have had a nicer life than the rest of the family. The father was good to them in a way but their mother had to work hard ...

How lucky I'd been to be given to Marg and Henk DeVrye. Truly fortunate. I read on with muddled emotions.

Telling her family about you will be quite a chore for Trudy ...
    I am so glad that I have finally heard from you as have been wondering often what had become of you. Never had a chance to see you but so glad you had a good home and loving parents. I'm sure all the girls and families will be glad to know you are found, although some never knew about you before. I would be happy to hear from you again. Will hope that. Trust will write soon ...

Grandma Bachman wrote often, sometimes two or three times a week:

I can't see small print anymore but many my age can't see anything so I feel lucky in the lodge as I'm not left alone like so many and can enjoy my remaining days with my family who always come to visit. And having found you means a lot to me. I have much pain but the pills help and the doctor told me years ago that I wouldn't have all these troubles if I wouldn't get so old ...
    People have to live somehow and people can't sell wheat

anymore. It is a crazy world. Too much to pay for machinery and now that silly war is on, I am glad I have not much time left but worry for the younger generations – they don't seem to though.

Guess the Good Lord will set it right some day. And I wish all my loved ones a happy life . . .

I will write again if I can . . . Grandma Bachman

All her letters to me were signed that way. Please, Frida, hold on until I can see you face to face . . .

Many letters came from this wonderful old lady whose life revolved around the family she loved. It seemed I was now a part of her family, in her eyes anyway – even though she could barely see.

Frida had emigrated to Canada from Switzerland at the same age I'd moved to Australia. Was that why the Matterhorn was the only landmark in Europe that interested me? I had more in common with her than I realized at first. There was an immediate bond between us – strong, unyielding. She wanted to know everything about me and requested a photograph. I eventually sent snapshots of me as a youngster but as all of my possessions were still in transit, the only recent photo I had was taken at the Singapore zoo – embraced by an orangutan. On the back I wrote: I'm the one in the black and white shirt in case you're worried . . .

Writing letters to a grandmother I'd never known existed was one thing, but getting the courage to pick up the phone and call my biological parents was another. My household goods arrived and I began unpacking endless cardboard boxes. Looking at it all, I realized some emotional baggage remained unopened. It took ten days to muster the courage to call. March 6, the anniversary of the day I was taken

home by Mum and Dad thirty-eight years earlier, seemed as
appropriate a day as any to make the call. My biological
parents were probably wondering why it was taking so long
for my phone to be reconnected.

I took a deep breath and picked up the receiver. I'd try
my birth "mother" first, since that was what my "father's"
telegram had suggested I do. I dialed, not quite sure what I
would say.

It rang. It rang. It rang. She wasn't home. I hung up,
almost relieved. Two hours later I dialed again before my
resolve failed. Then it was picked up and I heard my own
voice nervously say: "Hello, this is Catherine DeVrye calling
from Australia."

"Oh, uh, hello," Trudy replied. There was a thick silence
for a moment, before the questions began, one after the
other:

"What time is it there?"

"What do you look like?"

"Are you married?"

"Any children?"

"Are you healthy?"

"What do you do for a living?"

On and on and on, we asked innocent questions, as one
would a stranger. There were so many other questions on
my mind that I didn't dare ask.

Why did you give me up?

Are you glad I called?

Did you love my father?

Our conversation was very strained and by the time it
was over, I had almost lost the nerve to call this man,
Harold Mandeville. The one who had supposedly deserted
my mother. What had I expected? It was a question that
had no answer. I went outside, hoping that fresh air would

clear my mind. Tam looked at me expectantly and perhaps it was the look in her eyes that prompted me to return, pick up that telephone and make another overseas call.

I rehearsed this time. I knew exactly what I'd say and how I'd say it.

So much for plans. The moment I uttered my name, a deep, warm, friendly voice cut me off. "We've been worried about you. We've been watching every Australian on TV to see if we could recognize you."

Like me, my biological father had been scanning the crowd at the televised Olympic Games, wondering . . . At that moment, I felt an energy, a connection more powerful than any telecommunications satellite could ever produce. I was talking to the man who was at least 50 percent responsible for my existence. Talking to him was easier than talking to Trudy.

"What do you do for a living?" he asked.

"I work for IBM."

"Oh yeah, what's that?"

I duly explained, thinking this could be a bizarre conversation, not aware he was a little hard of hearing. Then I asked: "What do you do?"

"Oh, I do a little farming now but most of my life, I was a cowboy."

What do you say when your father tells you he's a cowboy?

My mind flashed back to the Stampede. Me in my cowgirl's costume. *Can I walk your horse, mister?*

Had I asked that question to the man I was now talking to? Unlikely. I breathed deeply. The only cowboy I knew was Malcolm Jones, who had since married my girlfriend, Carole. Carole, the college friend I'd met up with at Nambour, Australia, on Boxing Day, 1973.

"A cowboy? That's . . . interesting," I said, struggling for small talk. "You don't by any chance know Malcolm Jones?" I thought there was a chance he would have at least heard of Malcolm who was a previous Canadian Bronc Riding Champion.

Not a word came in reply. I thought the line had gone dead. Again, I asked: "Hello, hello . . . Do you know Malcolm Jones?"

"Yep, as a matter of fact, I sure do," he drawled.

Another long pause: "I helped raise him from the time he was fourteen."

Tingles ran up and down my spine and goose bumps appeared like moguls on a ski field. Was this really happening?

"I saw him and Carole last week . . . Cath? Cath, you still there?"

It was an unreal, haunting experience. Was this why I'd been mesmerized by rodeos? Was it in my genes, right from the beginning? What are the odds that a girlfriend from university, who I'd travelled with in Australia years earlier, would marry a cowboy who was almost part of my biological father's family?

It's difficult even now to fully express the flood of feelings. I couldn't comprehend this powerful and somewhat spooky coincidence. Perhaps I never will. Was it anything more than mere coincidence?

I assured Harold Mandeville that I wouldn't tell Malcolm and Carole. After all, he was a leading citizen in a small town and likely wouldn't want anyone to know he had an illegitimate daughter on the other side of the world. After all, my birth father wasn't just any old cowboy. He'd won eight Canadian championships. Surely he wouldn't want this news to leak . . .

"I'll call 'em right away," he enthused.

He told me that he and his wife, Pearl, had apparently been searching for me since I was six months old. Of course, I asked about hereditary illnesses on his side. There were none that he knew of.

I wasn't quite the same for quite some time after that phone call to Harold but I told no-one at work, not even my boss. Anything personal was still confined to the privacy of my diary.

Also diarized were an inordinate amount of trivial annoyances after moving back into my home. A flat tire. I burned my never-fail chocolate cake made from a recipe in *Women's Weekly* magazine and ruined a shirt with dirty water from a steam iron, while waiting in vain for a tradesman to show up. Decided to paint those shelves myself. Little things, which normally I'd take in my stride, were driving me crazy and worse were the twelve-hour days, especially when two of those hours were unproductive in commuting time. Was it worth it? Why didn't I resign from IBM when I'd planned?

Rather than any rush of excitement about being appointed to a plum job at IBM as manager of special events and communications, the highlights of my week were more letters from my newfound grandmother, mother and father. I wasn't sure how to react to a letter from my father that addressed me as: *My dear little girl.*

I was anything but dear or little and hoped he'd accept me as I was.

I was upset to learn Pearl was in hospital. I didn't want anything to happen to them before we met. I'd made arrangements to meet sooner rather than later. That thought was reinforced when I received a letter from Carole and Malcolm Jones. Carole wrote:

He's thrilled. You couldn't have picked a better Dad. You're going to like him. We're so happy for you both and would have put you in touch years ago if we had known.

Malcolm added:

He guided me as a teenager and taught me how to ride broncs. I lived with Harold and Pearl and they treated me like a son. If I had a wish for a father, I would ask for Harold.

I'd booked a flight to Canada but first had some business travelling to do. Most people would have been excited to spend two weeks on Hamilton Island, North Queensland, but for me, it was hard work staging IBM's sales incentive events.

One of our conference speakers was a diver who'd discovered booty of sunken treasure. He too was adopted, had recently found his father and been an emotional wreck long after. My heart sank. Should I do this? I wondered. What if my experience would be like his? Could I take it?

I was already in too deep and couldn't back out now. What about Frida, my grandmother? For months now we'd corresponded. I was sure she was hanging on to life so that she could finally meet me, face to face. Carole and Malcolm had only kind things to say about Harold. And Trudy? What about her? Had she told her own family about me yet?

Two days after swimming with the dolphins on the Great Barrier Reef, I was at Expo 88 in Brisbane. As it happened, my biological father had two brothers, each with a son living in Australia. Outside the IBM pavilion, a good-looking man told my boss he was my long-lost Canadian cousin. "A likely story," my boss laughed cynically. But there, at Expo,

I met the first of my newfound family. Wayne Mandeville looked like a lovable teddy bear with smiling eyes. He told me that my father was a non-smoker, played poker, made his own bread and was known for his conservative ways. "Heck, he was so straight, we nicknamed him Uncle Prude . . . until now!" Wayne laughed.

I only hoped that the rest of the family were half as nice as Wayne.

On 7 May 1988, the fifteenth anniversary of Mum's death, I didn't feel as sad as usual. Pearl called to say that my homecoming was the best Mother's Day present she could receive. After all, she said, she'd been waiting thirty-seven years to meet me, too.

18

MEET AND GREET

When are you coming home?

My Auntie Kay from Canada asked me that question a lot of late. It was hard to make her understand that Australia was now my home. It was equally difficult for her to explain why my Uncle Frank wasn't at the airport to greet me, as he normally did.

Tentatively, Auntie Kay indicated that she thought it best to speak with me alone. In my excitement about discovering my roots, I had totally forgotten that my uncle had an adopted son from his first marriage. Naturally, he was not too thrilled about my forthcoming reunion. I had read about the need for sensitivity towards feelings of adoptive parents, but since my folks were dead, I had inadvertently and selfishly overlooked the feelings of my aunt and uncle whom I also loved dearly.

I was surprised and upset that my mother's best friend, Grace Robertson, shared their apprehension.

"To be honest, Cath, I was disappointed you felt the need to find this new family when Marg and Henk loved you so much."

With a lump in my throat, again I wondered if I had done the right thing. I was in Canada and wouldn't turn back now.

What Grace said next surprised me. "Then I gave it a great deal of thought and realized I couldn't possibly understand what it felt like to be adopted and wonder about your biology. I came to comprehend that you had to do what you felt you had to do. You belonged to Marg and Henk but I felt you also belonged to me. But I know your mum and dad raised you to have sense enough to do the right thing. You've got my support."

Like my adoptive parents, "Auntie" Grace wasn't related to me. She and Mum had met aged eight. She'd given me insights into my mother, the very person that I hadn't thought to ask about myself. Although I had yet to meet them, finding my biological parents had helped me be more open about my own parents, rather than bottling everything up, as I had when they died. Grace and I talked for hours, about all sorts of things.

She and my mother used to do the same and as a little girl I amused myself during their conversations by playing with Grace's dogs, Freckles and Landy. Freckles was an obvious name for the tan-and-white spaniel, but she'd had to explain to me as a child why the black dog was named Landy: "One day we were driving in Kananaskis and this black spaniel followed us for miles along the road. He was obviously lost, so we picked him up and named him Landy. It was just before the 1954 Commonwealth Games in Vancouver and in Canada we all desperately hoped that John Landy would be the first to break the four-minute mile – anyone but an Englishman."

I likely didn't even know where Australia was in those days. Years later, I met John Landy and he was most amused when I recounted this story. Grace was even more amused when I told her of my meeting. I related how I'd bumped into Landy again some years later, when he'd proven not only did he have remarkable athletic talent, but he also had a great memory.

"Would you believe when we next met, he asked if you'd picked up any more stray dogs?"

"You know Cath, Marg never let you keep any of the strays you brought home as a kid, but when you were older and finally convinced her to let you keep Blitz, she loved that dog to bits. Maybe by then she realized you were a bit of a stray yourself." Grace laughed.

It all seemed light years away from my old neighbourhood – to where I next made a pilgrimage. It seemed imperative to first tell old family friends how important they had been and always would be in my life, regardless of the outcome of the forthcoming reunion with my newfound family.

I sat on Scotchman's Hill for ages, looking down on the Stampede grounds, the Rockies on the distant horizon. The last time I saw that sight was via satellite, when I had watched the closing ceremonies of the Olympics three and a half months earlier. The television cameras had vanished but the picture of me sitting in the Sydney Hilton was permanently recorded in my memory. That night, I'd wondered if anyone in that crowd was related to me.

Well, come tomorrow I would meet the father I'd first learned about that very night. He'd been looking for me, too. Wondering, just as I had wondered . . .

It was 16 June 1988. What on earth would I wear? I was going to meet my champion cowboy father and I did not have a pair of jeans in the suitcase. The tailored suit, high heels and Gucci briefcase were totally inappropriate but so was the notion of buying a new wardrobe and pretending to be anyone but myself.

"I can't believe I'm worrying about what to wear to meet my father. It's more nerve-racking than a blind date." I joked but deep inside I was anything but the cool, controlled executive I pretended to be.

I can't recall what I eventually wore. Clothes were the least of my worries. I hardly slept the night before.

What will I say to him?

What do I call him?

Will he like me?

Will I like him?

What about his wife?

Will we have anything in common?

Will we regret this reunion?

Will I need Kleenex? Should I wear mascara or will it run if I cry? I won't cry. Will I cry?

Will he be as nervous as I am?

We were to meet at 5 p.m. at the Blackfoot Motor Inn, a few kilometres from my childhood home. At four, he called up and said, "Get your little self over here."

I'd travelled hundreds of thousands of miles around the world but that ten-minute drive to the Blackfoot Inn seemed farther than the nineteen-hour trip from Sydney to Calgary.

I parked. Still inside the car, I combed my hair and re-applied lipstick, oblivious that Harold Mandeville was watching from the window of his room on the third floor and pacing like an expectant father awaiting the arrival of his newborn baby.

The elevator was out of order, so I walked those three flights of stairs. My heart was pounding, but not through any lack of fitness.

The door was ajar. What to do? Knock? Right. Knock. Then I'll see him, and . . . what next? Do I shake his hand? I took a deep breath and tentatively knocked.

A tall man wearing a cowboy hat appeared in the doorway. There must have been a three-second pause before his arms reached out and silently drew me in. It was a hug I hoped would last forever. If I'd expected Clint Eastwood, Roy Rogers and John Wayne rolled into one, I would not have been disappointed.

My father was a handsome man who still looked good in a pair of jeans. His huge hands were calloused. His heart was not. I'd never hugged my own father quite like the first time Harold and I embraced. Much to my surprise, I didn't cry but we were both near tears.

Behind him stood a petite brunette with big hair.

"This is my wife, Pearl," he said. She also gave me a hug. I liked her instantly and we all proceeded to chat about anything and everything for about three hours. Whenever I spoke to Pearl, I saw Harold watching me from the corner of his eye. I did likewise when he talked to her. Was there any resemblance between father and daughter? I couldn't see any. Maybe I looked like Trudy?

I learned that when my mother was pregnant, she had written to him. At the time, he was on the rodeo circuit in the United States and never received the letter. He had no idea she was pregnant until he was back in town and bumped into her mother, Frida Bachman, on the street.

"How's Trudy?" he'd casually asked.

He got an earful from my feisty Swiss grandmother.

It appeared likely that his own mother had intercepted the letter. Years later, it was good to know that there were no hard feelings between the families still living in the same town. In fact, Harold and Pearl had visited my grandmother, Frida, the week before to talk about my unexpected appearance.

The ease of our first meeting was surprising. Conversation became more strained when Harold and

Pearl's son and his girlfriend arrived. I sensed my half-brother, Bryan, wasn't overly pleased about my arrival, speaking only when prompted by Pearl. It didn't worry me much. I fully appreciated his apprehension.

He had spent some time on the rodeo circuit in Australia and knew one of my former boyfriends in Calgary who was also a rodeo cowboy. Bryan and I had a fair bit in common so I was certain that with time, we'd get on fine.

I was surprised when his ex-wife also joined us at this first meeting. She had remarried and adopted a little boy. I hadn't realized how many people had adopted or been adopted. As I finally opened up, so did a whole new world of relationships.

After a few hours in the hotel room, I took Harold and Pearl to meet Auntie Kay and Uncle Frank. It was worse than bringing a prospective teenage boyfriend home to meet your parents and hoping for their approval. I needn't have worried. Harold broke the ice instantly by shaking Frank's hand. "Thanks for sharing her with us."

The next day, Kay, Frank and my favourite little cousin, Dale, who was now over six feet tall, golfed in the nearby town of High River. In the relaxed swing of things, I broke 90 for the first time and we shared lots of laughter and flapper pie, a rich Canadian custard cream and wafer desert – a rather distant cousin of the Australian signature dishes of pavlova and lamingtons. When we returned to the car, a note on the windshield startled us. From a distance, it looked like a parking ticket, but it was from my father.

Don't you ever try to lose us.

19

EXPECT THE UNEXPECTED

How incredibly happy I felt as I borrowed my aunt's car to continue another 70 miles south to Lethbridge. Now it was time for the next step, to meet my birth mother, Trudy.

Clouds hung lazily in the vastness of the twilight sky. The flat prairie spread endlessly in one direction, framed by a fireball sun over the Rockies in the other. So open and free. So different from sharing my Sydney existence with more than 3 million people. I turned up the Country-and-Western station, turned off the air-conditioning and rolled down the windows to hear, smell and feel in order to be closer to the landscape my biological father now farmed, as uninterrupted golden wheat fields waved in the warm evening breeze . . .

I thought I'd forgotten my apprehension about meeting my birth mother and was running late when I pulled up in front of her house. It was in a nice suburban street, with a well-kept lawn. Obviously more anxious than I thought, I leapt out and in my haste promptly locked the keys in the car. When I knocked, a petite woman with curly brownish hair and tortoiseshell glasses appeared at the screen door.

"Hi, I'm Cath," I said. "Do you have a coathanger?"

It should have been a more momentous reunion. But I don't remember a hug or kiss – or even a handshake. Trudy found a coathanger to break into the car. Thankfully neither of us broke into tears. Still standing out on the street, we cautiously chatted about nothing in particular. She seemed pleasant, if not more nervous than I was. Once inside, in her living room, she told me a little about herself and each of her other children and kept apologizing for not keeping me as she chain-smoked a pack of cigarettes.

My birth mother had named me Marilyn Darlene, after Marilyn Monroe. I thought of the letter I'd received, how Marilyn was a common name at the time, and why. But I was born with a full head of nearly black hair, so I wasn't quite sure why I was named after the blonde bombshell, unless my mother had a vivid imagination.

Christened Gertrude May, Trudy said that even as a girl she never seemed to fully fit into the tidy two-storey house with its somewhat tired coat of whitish-grey paint and bright flowerbeds. As an unmarried mother, when she had her first child, some of her sisters had ostracized her. Their friends at school made snide comments. It was a disgrace in a small town in 1947 to give birth without being legally wed. When I arrived three years later, her second illegitimate child, it would have been even more difficult for her.

According to Trudy, when I was three months old, the cold Canadian winter had set in. My half-sister, mother and the man she was about to marry were living in a rented, poorly built house where the freezing north winds blew snow right through the cracks in the timber. I lay coughing and crying, while snowflakes landed on my makeshift cradle – a wooden orange box. In desperation and concerned for my life, my mother bundled me in a blanket and gave me to a welfare organization.

I wanted to believe that this was why she gave me up.

Mum and Dad (Marg and Henk) on their wedding day,
September 1946

Granddad with me, shortly
after I was adopted

Aged five with Mum, outside
the Greyhound Bus depot
at Wetaskiwin

Still horse crazy at thirteen

*Dressed as a cowgirl for the
Calgary Stampede, aged six*

With Dad and Smokey, before my 1968 high-school graduation

Powder-puff football at the University of Calgary. I'm in the back row on the far right. (Who said shoulder pads weren't fashionable?!)

Back in Canada visiting Uncle Frank and Auntie Kay

At the University of Montana, 1971, with my roommate Helen, friend Ellie (who both went on to adopt girls) and another friend Diane

*A fun run with teammates from the Department of Youth,
Sport and Recreation, 1974*

*With the Jansens, at
the Miss Sportsgirl of
Victoria Awards, 1975*

*At the Australian Administrative Staff College at Mount Eliza,
1977. I'm in the middle of the front row – the only woman!*

With Tim and Tam, 1979

*IBM colleagues in
Japan, 1987*

*The day after an avalanche
at Annapurna Base Camp
in the Himalayas, 1987*

Three generations of Bachmans at a barbecue, 1988.
Back row, right to left: Aunts Rose, Alice, Cec, Shirley, Louise.
Front row: me, Grandma, birth mother Trudy

With my rodeo-champion biological father, Harold, 1988

Celebrating Val's fiftieth birthday away from her grandchildren in Canyonlands, Utah

Celebrating fifty with fifty fab friends, including Liz and June

Torch-bearer day of the opening ceremonies at the Sydney 2000 Olympic Games

With: John Landy (far right), 1976

Sir Edmund Hillary, 1991

Prime Minister Bob Hawke, 1993

John Denver, 1994

Rugby Captain Nick Farr-Jones, 1994

Bryce Courtenay and Ian Kennedy, c. 1995

Jean-Michel Cousteau, 1998

Evonne Goolagong, 2000

Cathy Freeman, c. 2000

Others in the family had a different take on this story, as I would later learn. It also didn't quite explain why I was given up for adoption while my mother kept my older half-sister. Trudy claimed that her husband said they could only afford to feed one screaming child and it would be easier for an infant to be adopted than for a toddler. This seemed somewhat inconsistent with her first version of the snowflakes on my cradle. Whatever the reason, it doesn't really matter now. I know she made the right decision and forever thank her for it.

After I was adopted, three more children arrived. Life went on. For Trudy, I was no longer a visible part of it. She said that she still thought about me every September but never mentioned the subject again. Her husband had forbidden it and none of her other children needed to know about a sister they'd never see. They had enough worries raising a family over the years.

Then history repeated itself. Trudy couldn't believe her ears when her first-born announced she was pregnant and not married. Part of Trudy wanted to reach out and empathize, to share her own secret of the past to ease her daughter's pain. She didn't. My existence was only a vague memory, so why dig up the past unnecessarily? She could only offer a shoulder to cry on, Trudy said, as she lit yet another cigarette. Marilyn Monroe was long dead and so was her own little Marilyn for all intents and purposes. Trudy, over the years, had convinced herself of that. She wasn't living the glamorous city life she dreamed about as a young woman, but it wasn't so bad. She loved her kids and had reconciled to a large degree with her sisters.

Thankfully, community attitudes towards unwed mothers had mellowed marginally, and they now lived in a larger town. Frida Bachman was delighted with the birth of Trudy's granddaughter. She rejoiced in becoming a great-grandmother, while Trudy initially lamented her fate in the midst of generations.

Repeatedly I assured Trudy that she had made the right decision. She still wasn't sure. Her husband had died of a stroke a few years earlier and she was left to wear the guilt of giving up a child whose existence had never once been mentioned again.

And then, from nowhere, my letter had arrived.

Both biological parents seemed to feel guilty, just as I had felt guilty about how poorly I treated my own parents. My birth mother seemed a good-hearted person and I only wished that she wouldn't be so apologetic. As far as I was concerned, she had nothing to apologize for. We all chose to lead different lives. I'm pleased that she chose to have me. Equally I'm pleased that she chose to give me up. She need never apologize for giving me the gift of life. There was another choice that I'm thankful she never made.

Trudy was quick to mention that she hoped I didn't think she was a tramp. *I just wanted to be loved.*

I assured her that's what we all want and shared Mother Teresa's observation: "The greatest disease today is not leprosy or tuberculosis but the feeling of being unwanted."

In a similar circumstance to my birth mother, I wondered what I would have done. Would I have found myself in such a situation? I might well have done. I took some risks in my younger days, wanting to be loved and frequently confusing it with lust. Fortunately, I'd never had to face such a heart-wrenching decision.

I felt sorry for her. I felt for her. But that was all and the mother/daughter bond I'd anticipated was absent. We drove east to Taber for a barbecue at the home of her youngest sister, Louise. Her eldest sister, Alice, had flown from Ottawa for this family reunion. Trudy said they were all excited and felt it was like having a new baby arrive in the family.

"I hope they're not disappointed that I'm not cute and cuddly." My attempts at humour did little to disguise my nervousness and it was overwhelming to walk into a backyard packed with total strangers who were all family. My grandmother and all five of Trudy's sisters were there. So were their spouses, children, grandchildren and great-grandchildren, the latter bouncing away noisily on a nearby trampoline.

Carrie, an excited ten-year-old, was the first to greet me, but wanted to know why I didn't bring the orangutan from the photo taken at the Singapore zoo.

I liked all my mother's sisters, especially Louise, who looked after my grandmother, and Rose, who had similar sporting interests to mine. I looked more like her than the others but still couldn't see any other obvious genetic links with my birth mother or father, although everyone else seemed to. The sisters all talked and laughed a lot. It seemed a loving happy family with its normal share of triumph and tragedy over the years.

It wasn't a strained reunion at all, nor even emotional until they presented me with a hand-embroidered photo album: *Welcome to Our Family*.

The photos would help in years to come, as I knew I couldn't possibly remember all these relatives coming out of the woodwork. From being an only child, without family for years, I was now one of over eighty grandchildren and great-grandchildren. So we know what folks do during those cold winter nights in Canada!

I was introduced to Louise's eldest daughter, Marilyn,

who looked no more like Marilyn Monroe than I did, but she wasn't named after the actress. She was named after me.

Video cameras rolled and enough photos were taken to fill another album. I was part of a family now – two extended families in fact. Harold's and Trudy's. It was nice to belong even though I didn't really feel I belonged specifically to either. It didn't matter. I just sort of belonged to something larger than myself and felt grounded.

My newfound aunts' children were at the barbecue but none of Trudy's were. She explained they had already made plans to be out of town. Fair enough. I certainly didn't expect anyone to alter previous arrangements just because I breezed into their lives. Truth was, she hadn't told them. At the time, I suppose it was enough for Trudy just to face her sisters.

After the barbecue, we returned to sleep in Trudy's house, where she insisted I stay. After all these years, it seemed strange, but she went out of her way to make me welcome. She invited her other four children for dinner the next evening. "My kids are finding it a little difficult to understand why I could have given up my own flesh and blood and believe me it wasn't easy."

She cooked a lovely roast dinner for 5 p.m. I'd forgotten how early most Canadians ate. I felt sorry for her when, by 5:30 p.m., no-one had turned up; I even worried I might have alienated her from them. Fortunately, it was just a misunderstanding on time, and around 8 p.m. my four half-brothers and sisters arrived in dribs and drabs with their spouses and children. At best, conversation was stilted. It came to a complete halt when one half-brother innocently asked: "So, how do you know Mum?"

Trudy hadn't said a word to anyone about me. In those

few seconds of agonizing silence, I nearly choked on my dinner and gaped, open-mouthed towards her, willing the nearby sofa to swallow me up. Why hadn't she said anything to them? According to Grandma, when Trudy first saw my letter, she had denied my existence. Maybe she was still in some sort of denial. Or was she leaving it all up to me? All eyes stared at her in disbelief. I couldn't have been more stunned if I'd discovered a chili in a lemon meringue pie and I remember little of what was actually said, except for Trudy constantly apologizing to everyone. At some stage, the conversation resumed to small talk. Small talk was always safe. For everyone.

Pat and her daughter doted on their dog. I could relate to that. Merv worked at a shoe shop in town and lived in the country with Sheila and their two children. She had a brother in Australia, in Yallourn, Victoria, so that provided a frame of reference. Ken was a motorbike enthusiast and enjoyed other sport, as did Debbie and her husband Tim. I liked them and there was no shortage of mutual interests despite the obvious tension in the room. They seemed a happy enough family but we were all too frightened to delve into anything but superficialities until Merv's wife eventually said, "I can't believe she gave you away. She adores children."

It was obvious that Trudy's grandchildren loved her in return. I assured them that I understood her reasons and held no grudges whatsoever.

As I left the next morning, Trudy gave me a lovely card with a crisp bill enclosed: "What we've just started, I never want to finish."

It was as close as we got to expressing any emotion. I appreciated the sentiment but didn't want the money. I wanted nothing from her except acceptance. I was glad to have met Trudy and her other children, but relieved to get into the car to return to the life I knew.

I visited my grandmother in Taber the next day. She had vacated her family home of sixty years only a few months earlier. As we sat in her single room at the nursing home, she lamented, "I didn't want to come here but knew it was for the best as I couldn't manage on my own anymore. When they made me move into this little room, I had to get rid of everything we had in the big house. I had a collection of spoons. Each of my grandchildren and great-grandchildren received one as a memory of me."

Taking my hand in hers, she continued, "I was afraid I might not live long enough to see you but I always knew you would turn up one of these days, so I saved this one for you, Cath."

With that, she took the spoon from her pocket and her tiny arthritic hands pressed it into mine. Even though she had cataracts, I was the one with clouded eyes that afternoon.

Frida Bachman was as hard of hearing as she was soft of heart. She told me (and anyone within earshot) that Trudy had moved back home when she had her first daughter. She patiently explained, even though I never asked, that Trudy had always been different from the rest of the family. This was not said in any judgmental way. It wasn't right or wrong. That's just the way it was. That's the way everything was with Grandma – so loving and accepting of others. She admitted that wasn't always the case and there had been much tension when, in the early years, they felt Trudy had brought shame to the family.

Time heals many wounds but also produces different

recollections of the same events. What did it matter, now that everything was out in the open and no-one needed to feel guilty anymore?

Both my biological parents told me separately that they wished they could have met my parents to thank them for doing such a good job of raising me. They're not alone. Finding my birth parents made me love my adoptive family even more!

I can appreciate that many adoptive parents fear that their children will reject them if they discover their biological roots. This may well be the case in some circumstances but was the exact opposite in mine. It was wonderful to find my biological parents but Margaret and Henk DeVrye will always be Mum and Dad and I love them more than ever. The best definition of adoption I've found is within *Chicken Soup for the Soul* by Jack Canfield and Mark Victor Hansen. A little girl explains, "You move from the tummy of one Mummy into the heart of another." My adoptive parents held my hand for a short while – but my heart for a lifetime.

Later, I set out to visit my father in his own home for the first time, the neutral territory of the hotel having helped us through our initial meeting. I drove slowly, looking for the house number. A neighbour flagged me down and said he recognized me from a photo Harold had proudly shown around the neighbourhood. And I'd been worried he wouldn't want anyone to know.

Pearl had cooked a lovely meal and invited Trudy, who I think felt more nervous than ever. I doubt I would have been as open and accepting of my husband's child and former lover and it seemed rather peculiar seeing my biological parents together.

It was unsettling sleeping under my father's roof. I was

afraid that the feeling would vanish like a dream upon awakening. He periodically peeked through the door to check on me. I couldn't remember when anyone last did that.

Sleep is a stranger when love awakes your heart. I expected no such emotion. I simply expected to close a chapter in my life but felt a magnetic pull to know these people better. I awoke to the aroma of freshly baked scones, which Harold had made with his own wheat, topped with homemade crabapple jelly.

The next day, 19 June 1988, was a Father's Day I don't think either of us will forget. Rummaging through a pile of sickly sentimental cards in the shop, I had quickly discarded ones containing clearly inappropriate messages such as: "Thanks for everything you've always done" or "Thanks for always being there over the years."

I finally found one which read: *Happy Father's Day . . . from the kid who taught you to expect the unexpected!*

In one of his letters, he had written, "I don't know what you called your deserving Dad but I would be very proud if you called me Dad, Pop or whatever."

Trudy suggested I call her Mum. "Half of Debbie's ball team call me Mum and they aren't even my children. It's really up to you."

I managed to avoid calling either of them anything! It seemed strange to address these two people as Mum or Dad. My father signed me in as Kathy Mandeville at the Raymond Golf Club and then asked if that upset me. How could I be upset with anyone who had his arm around me, introducing me to friends as his daughter from Australia? But, in my heart, I'll always be Catherine DeVrye.

The couple we golfed with asked me about Harold's other children and must have thought it strange that I couldn't answer the most basic questions. I'd always wondered what it would be like to have a sister or brother and now that I had several, I wasn't sure how to react. What would they expect? Pearl confided that Vicky, her daughter, admitted to being a little jealous and they would have been disappointed if she wasn't. I sensed my arrival made my siblings appreciate their parents more than ever before.

After golf, Harold showed me his workshop. He was quite a tinkerer. He'd even invented an automatic car ignition so Pearl didn't have to go outside to start the car in winter. We then walked through his wheat crop near Skiff, his birthplace and the source of his rodeo nickname. He didn't ranch cattle because he could never kill anything. Until then, I'd never thought of cowboys as sentimental types, just tough guys on TV. How wrong can we be with assumptions? He didn't have a mean bone in his body and remarkably had most of them intact, after all those years of falling off broncs.

At a barbecue, I met my father's sister, Dixie, who'd come from Minneapolis. Dixie took me aside and whispered, "I haven't seen Harold this happy in years. Not many men stand as tall as your dad." Their brother, Bill, had driven from British Columbia for the occasion and another, Fred, was a Member of the Legislative Council. At my father's first rodeo, the brothers had shared a pair of boots and spurs because the family had lost everything, except their indomitable spirit, in the crash of 1929 and again in the blizzard of 1938.

I met so many half-cousins I lost track of who was who but thought they were good people and lots of fun. Carole and Malcolm were also at the barbecue and it was great to see them after so many years. We had exchanged Christmas cards but had not met since Nambour, Queensland, some fifteen years earlier. Our chat was interrupted by the arrival of a Welcome Home Cath cake. It was at that barbecue where I finally met my half-sister, Vicky. I wanted her to like me but was uneasy because it was her birthday and there they all were, making a fuss over me. But she was easygoing and I instantly felt closer to her than to any of the others.

Vicky and I leafed through old scrapbooks like a couple of kids. I knew half-brother Bryan was both handsome and handy on a horse but didn't know that Vicky was once crowned the Miss Alberta Rodeo Queen. I was fascinated by old black-and-white newspaper clippings of our father in action on his horse, or off – in the dust of the rodeo ring. His home was adorned with stunning bronze sculptures of cowboys and livestock – all the trophies he'd won over the years. In the basement were many engraved saddles. I was honoured when he gave me one of his gold and silver championship belt buckles. He'd won it steer-wrestling in 1957. I was seven years old at the time and I thought of that letter Mum had kept, and had shown me after my Dad had died. *Hello Cowboy . . . Dearest Sweetheart . . .*

"You can't be part of our family without one," said Pearl, interrupting my daydream.

I looked at her, confusion in my eyes.

"The belt buckle," she said. "You can't be part of our family without one."

"Sorry," I said. "I was miles away."

"You seem to have made our life more complete. We were worried you might not take to us or our way of life but we think you'll fit in just fine."

There was an uncomfortable silence when my father added: "I was a bit of a jerk when I knew your mother. It was kind of . . . a bad year for me."

To which I replied, "Well, it was a good one for me!"

Any tension soon shattered.

There was a lot less laughter when, all too soon, it was time to say goodbye. I was in bad enough shape but at least I wasn't alone. Cowboys and corporate executives aren't supposed to cry but I knew love was in the Alberta air the moment I wiped a tear from his cheek. Nothing could stop my tears, though. Heading back to Calgary after this emotional journey, I almost had a head-on collision but never told anyone. I ran out of gas and slept in the car at a closed pump until the service station opened in the morning.

"Why didn't you call me?" asked my father the next day.

It never occurred to me to ask for help. I had been self-sufficient for so long.

"You oughta learn to be a little less independent."

He was probably right. I should learn to let others help me. Learn to accept assistance. Learn to admit it's all right to need someone. Learn to love again . . .

20

OPENING UP

 From that very first phone call, I'd never expected to feel that emotion called love. It was frighteningly powerful. I wouldn't contemplate living permanently in Canada again because my home was Australia, but part of me didn't want to leave these people, my newfound "family." I'd visited, simply intending to meet my biological parents and close a chapter in my life. But now, torn between two shores, there was an inexplicable urge to be a little closer to them all – even if not in the geographic sense.

I hate airport farewells and we had an unwritten agreement there would be no tears. As the plane took off, I hoped the novelty of loving each other would never wear off. Stopping in Vancouver, I had a good visit with my former in-laws who suggested I no longer call them Mum and Dad. Now I was totally confused about the use of the names.

I arrived in Bangkok on 1 July and was amazed the newspapers ran feature articles for Canada's National Day. It was a relief to check into the Shangri-La Hotel and be rid of the taxi driver, who couldn't understand I had no interest in fooling around with either boys or girls!

I knew we would have a challenge to prepare for the arrival and safe stay of eight hundred IBM staff for our sales incentive conference in recognition of top-performing employees, with astronaut Neil Armstrong as the guest speaker. We booked a temple for a gala dinner, rented portable toilets and hired elephants and tigers for a show. We also contracted five hundred plainclothes security guards to patrol Pat Pong and keep unregistered guests such as my enthusiastic taxi driver and his associates at bay. AIDS awareness was in its infancy and, responsible for the wellbeing of mainly young male delegates, I left nothing to chance and asked the manager to make condoms available in the rooms.

"You must meet so many men in your travels," one of my girlfriends said enviously, upon my return to Australia after the conference.

"Yes. Bellboys, taxi drivers, waiters, married men . . ."

Now that I had found my parents, I was less preoccupied with finding a man. Having married for all the wrong reasons, I was determined not to repeat that mistake. Next time, marriage would not hastily replace a missing piece of an emotional jigsaw. I had now found that missing piece. It wasn't just one man. It was an entire family. Two families. I felt more complete as an individual and now understood why one adoptive organization is aptly named Jigsaw. Yes, I still wanted to fall in love and live happily ever after but at the moment, there were enough emotions to cope with. Just as friends had proudly inundated me with photos of their new babies, I bored them with happy snaps of my new parents!

Life returned to normality – be there such a thing. I often worked late on strategic plan figures but reached the point where I became more certain that the corporate fast track was not my calling. I detested financial detail and desired more creative freedom. Long walks with Tammy and the aroma of lemon blossoms in the garden provided welcome stress-relief on weekends.

At work, stress was part of daily corporate life and my secretary had unwelcome trauma at home. Her mother was diagnosed with cancer. For the first time in fifteen years, I finally felt strong enough to offer support to someone else. She was nineteen and I knew exactly what she was enduring. Sharing the experience is one thing; lessening the burden of watching a parent slowly die is another.

In September, I received a Happy First Birthday card from my father and a lovely one from my mother. (I have called her every year since on my birthday to thank her for giving birth to me.) Other postal, phone and electronic mail greetings arrived from around the world and Liz baked the now traditional chocolate birthday cake. I felt lucky to be alive. Lucky to have been raised by such wonderful parents. Lucky to have found my biological ones. It felt as if I'd truly been born again – but certainly not into any particular denomination.

Now, I had more inner faith in who I was. Through finding my family, I'd discovered much more about myself. I was a more complete person but wondered which parts of my make-up were environmental and which were hereditary. Obviously, my physical composition was genetic and I took some comfort in the longevity of my biological grandparents. But what about personality and mannerisms? After much soul-searching, I was convinced that at least 90 percent of my character came from the value systems of my adoptive parents. From my biological father, I may have gained my love of action, sport and of course, horses – and possibly a little horse sense. From him, I may also have inherited a bad memory and an inability to sit still.

A steady stream of letters arrived from far-flung relatives in Canada. Many had slightly different recollections of events and emotions surrounding my adoption.

Grandma Bachman often wrote twice a week. Her information was repetitive, but always consistent, so I chose to accept her account of the adoption circumstances as the most reliable.

By then Frida weighed less than thirty kilograms, but she was an extraordinary little woman with a huge heart. I comfortably called her Grandma because I had not felt the warmth of a close relationship with a grandmother before. My own had died when I was eight and she hadn't wanted Mum to adopt me in the first place, so although we lived in the same house, it's understandable we were never close. Yet I had a loving bond with Grandma Bachman who lived ten thousand miles away.

She saved all my letters and postcards in an album and wrote that she especially enjoyed postcards of places she would never get to see. Of course, I kept all her letters. They were a combination of daily nursing home routine, comments on the past and occasional observations on current affairs. There was also a chronicle of updates on various family members as she helped one of her daughters compile a family tree. Grandma's mind was sharp. Although her hearing and eyesight failed and she needed oxygen and medication for constant pain, she never once complained.

After a stroke, her writing became more illegible. I cherished those letters even more. Each word was written with effort and love, and I felt guilty about my hastily scrawled postcards and word-processed letters. Grandma's youngest daughter, Louise, comforted me: "Don't worry if Mum says she can't read your writing. She makes me read it to so many people, I almost have it memorized. When she received your first letter, it was like a light bulb turned on inside her."

Later letters from Louise were more sombre. It was largely through them that I became aware of Grandma's deterioration.

"She has flashbacks to her childhood when her stepfather abused her. She screams for help . . ."

No-one could change the unspoken past but Louise and her sisters helped out as best they could and kindness has at least as much power to heal as cruelty has to hurt. Letters and phone calls told of frequent reunions with much laughter. There was little I could do from afar. Still, I was glad to be part of this close-knit family. It hadn't always been so. My mother's sister, the one I thought I looked like, Rose, wrote a very touching letter:

> When Trudy had the first baby and brought it home – my gosh – we were a condemned family. It seems so hard to believe the way people thought in those days but believe me; they didn't want their kids associating with us! I can understand how overwhelming this has been for you. I'm sorry for any hurt we may have caused and hopefully, we'll now all be a more understanding family thanks to you.

I was constantly assuring everyone that they hadn't caused me any hurt. I was pleased that circumstances had worked out as they had. Society has changed, giving Western women more choice. I do not think ill of those who choose to abort. Whatever the decision, I believe it is the individual woman's choice to make it and to live with the consequences of her actions. Likewise, adoption laws have changed. Some people want to know where they come from and have a right to know, but – conversely – they also have an obligation to respect the privacy of others who wish to keep their secret.

I thought back to 1982 when I was one of fifty-two candidates in pre-selection for a safe parliamentary seat. At the end of more than ten hours of exhaustive balloting, the remaining four contenders were called back for further questioning. The Right to Life issue split voting delegates down the middle and I knew there was no easy answer to the question when it was asked of me. I drew a deep breath and simply responded: "I'm adopted . . . You can draw your own conclusions on the personal choice I might make."

I had summoned all my courage to say it. It was the first time I'd laid it on the line publicly, even though I didn't directly answer the question. As we awaited the results, a leading politician congratulated me and exclaimed, "That's the best answer I've ever heard. Whatever made you think up something like that?"

"Because it's true."

"Is it really?" he asked.

When the other candidate won the final ballot by two votes, I cut affiliations with all political parties – not because I lost. I almost certainly "had the numbers" to win the next seat but if telling the truth was such a novelty, a party political path wasn't for me. I became a swinging voter.

Until then, even close friends did not know I was adopted or that my parents had died. Over a decade later, I was telling everyone. After enduring years of bottled-up emotion, I could finally talk freely about both sets of parents.

Lives, like flowers, continue to open up with warmth. It was amazing how many acquaintances had some connection with adoption and shared similar stories. My cousin's wife was adopted. So were many friends, with whom I shared common interests for years, all of us unaware of this other kinship called adoption.

From University of Montana days, my roommate Helen and great mate Ellie have since adopted children themselves. So have other friends, both locally and overseas. I was touched that one couple not only adopted two children but also fostered a number of babies who otherwise would have spent their early life institutionalized. One girlfriend wrote of the love she felt for the birth mother of her three daughters: "She was adopted herself and became pregnant in the middle of a divorce. We promised to keep her posted of her daughter's development."

The most enlightening conversations were with girlfriends who had given up a child. Some I had known for years – I thought well. Not their secret though. Now that I'd opened up, they were eager to explore my emotions and asked if I held any resentment. I was equally keen to more fully comprehend their feelings. Maybe it would help me better understand my mother. Maybe I could help them better understand as well. Some were angry and felt that at the time they had been given no choice. There were no counselling or support groups in those days. Twenty years on, some were now reconciling with parents who would say, "We never realized you were so alone because you seemed to cope."

Oftentimes, those who seem to be "coping" are the people who need help the most.

Each situation was different and dominated by varying emotions. But there was one constant – guilt. I reassured those birth mothers as best I could. After all, what had they done except give a kid a chance in life? A kid like me.

Reassurances bounced across dinner tables like a lengthy rally on a tennis court. It was easy enough to talk about the guilt of others but inside I still felt guilty about the way I treated my own parents as a rebellious teenager. One mother, who had given up her son, and since had other children, assured me: "Don't worry. Parents are very forgiving of kids. When they're asleep and looking angelic, a parent feels nothing but absolute love and overlooks all the trouble they caused during the day."

As my friends were now at the age where they had rebellious teenagers of their own, I realized that I wasn't quite as terrible as I'd beat myself up for being over the years. I gradually recognized that neither mothers, fathers nor adoptees had much to gain by being angry, sad or guilty about the past. Nor are these emotions unique to those who are adopted. I have little patience for people who make excuses for their lives by blaming their parents, teachers, friends, employers – or anyone else. Forget the blame game. None of us can change what has been by wishing for what was not. Quite simply, being responsible means we must take personal responsibility for our own actions, even if we're not always proud of what we've done. It's okay to say: "Hey, I goofed and won't do that again."

It's important to acknowledge mistakes and move forward. In sharing my story with others, the ghosts of my own past became friendlier. I allowed myself to become more conscious of my feelings and increasingly open to exploring my emotions. And I was no longer secretly envious of the adult friendships that many of my contemporaries now had with their parents. I started to notice newspaper articles about famous people who had been through similar circumstances. I wasn't such an oddity after all.

Adoption or abandonment certainly hadn't curtailed the success of prominent Antipodeans Brett Ogle, Kerry Stokes, Jack Thompson, Layne Beachley or Dame Kiri Te Kanawa. Sportsman, entrepreneur, actor, surfer and singer: each had excelled at their chosen career. I was also surprised at the hundreds of international celebrities who had been adopted, although there was no logical reason to be so: household names such as Aristotle, Eleanor Roosevelt, Nancy Reagan, Jesse Jackson, John Lennon, Bobby Darin, Greg Louganis, Steve Jobs, Halle Berry . . . not to mention my original namesake, Marilyn Monroe.

Many more had adopted children: not only Angelina Jolie, but also Walt Disney, Bob Hope, Julie Andrews, Bette Davis, Mia Farrow, Barbara Walters, Nicole Kidman, Tom Cruise, Michelle Pfeiffer, Kris Kristofferson, Steven Spielberg . . . The list goes on but only a handful of celebrities, like Joni Mitchell and Roseanne Barr, were courageous enough to admit to giving up children for adoption.

Charles Dickens, Leo Tolstoy and James Michener were also adopted and there must be untold tales of countless others. I could never write like them, so ignored requests from both friends and strangers to document my story. Apart from immediate family, who would be interested?

I'd put my grief on the back burner for a long time. In doing so, I had not come to grips with the deaths of my parents and my emotions tended to overflow at the most unlikely moments. I was too proud to seek professional help when I should have. Although I appeared to cope, it was a disguise so masterful that I even fooled myself most of the time.

Now people were telling me that they were inspired by my story and wanted me to put it all into a book. How? I was still frantically climbing the corporate ladder at IBM although I had no idea where this ladder would lead – or even if it might be up against the wrong wall.

21

NEVER ASK "WHAT IF . . .?"

Although I sometimes questioned the viability of a long-term future with IBM, the corporation offered countless prospects in return for long hours and commitment. Perhaps there was a glass ceiling, but I saw only windows of opportunity – although in retrospect, we few women near the top should have been less competitive and more cooperative.

I still travelled extensively and decided to renovate my home. "We've never seen a sheila up a ladder before," the builders exclaimed.

"Well, you better get used to it because I'll be checking every day."

Management experience at IBM had not prepared me for this supervisory role. Like most renovators, I swear I'll never do it again but was ultimately pleased with the result – especially the central heating. Was Sydney's climate ever cold enough to warrant the expense? I thought so. Even in my working-class family home in Canada, we always had central heating. Now financially comfortable, I saw no reason to deny myself that creature comfort.

A long way from once washing dishes at Canyon Meadows Golf and Country in Calgary, weekends at New South Wales Golf Club provided exercise, relaxation and snob-free camaraderie on the shores of Botany Bay. No-one cared what you did for a living and everyone shared the same joys and frustrations of the game. I experienced plenty of the latter. One day, I found myself on the same fairway as famed golfer Greg Norman. I wasn't meant to be on his fairway but had an incurable slice! We chatted briefly and for the rest of the round, I wondered if amateur cowboys once idolized my champion father, as golfers did Greg Norman. Did my father see conversations with fans as an intrusion or an ego boost? I'd ask next time I saw him but had no idea when that would be. In the meantime, I called to wish his wife Pearl a happy birthday. I'd left it too late to send a card.

"What are you up to?"

"We're off to Edmonton next week. Your dad's being inducted into the Rodeo Hall of Fame."

Having accumulated about a bazillion frequent-flyer points, I impulsively asked how she'd feel if I flew over to surprise him. There would be a price to pay at work, as we were very busy. But I had never shared any of my biological father's achievements and it seemed a once-in-a-lifetime opportunity to show him I cared. My feet hardly touched the ground over the next two days, although I must say it was a relief to be on terra firma when my flight safely landed in the middle of a blizzard only a few hours before the ceremony began.

I assumed there would be a hundred or so folks in a draughty community hall. What a surprise to find more than twelve thousand fans packed in the bleachers for the Canadian Indoor Rodeo Finals.

During a break in competition, a red carpet was unrolled onto the dirt floor of the arena and the announcer asked the crowd to welcome Harold Mandeville, "A man who has made an outstanding contribution to the sport, with the unparalleled achievement of eight Canadian titles over a twenty-year span between his first and last championship. He is joined tonight by his wife Pearl from Lethbridge, son Bryan from Calgary, daughter Vicky from Red Deer and daughter Cath who just flew in from Australia to surprise him." Yes, I had been a surprise!

We all watched proudly as he ambled, bow-legged in handstitched leather boots, down the red carpet to accept his award. One of his many gold and silver belt buckles glistened in the spotlight and of course the cowboy hat was firmly in place, these days to hide his receding hairline.

"A lot of you didn't know we had a daughter, Cath, in Australia because when she was little, she was too damn ugly to take to rodeos! But, now thanks to the support of my wonderful family, she has turned into a little princess."

He received a standing ovation and there wasn't a dry eye in the house.

Back at the hotel ballroom we square-danced till 3 a.m. Inundated by well-wishers whom Harold didn't know or couldn't remember, it was Pearl who graciously handled social niceties, introducing me as "our" daughter. That night, sharing a room with my half-sister Vicky, we nattered for hours in the darkness. She dozed off, but as exhausted as I was, sleep remained as elusive as a runaway steer.

I was pleased to be a part of both the Mandeville and Bachman families. I was particularly proud of my father and all he'd achieved, proud of the person he was. I suspect he was just as proud of me although we'd spent our careers in quite different arenas.

I had once dreamed of being a world champion athlete but the closest I ever got was winning a national university title in field hockey, once representing Canada in international volleyball and attending graduate school in the

United States on a partial basketball scholarship. By the time Canada first entered Olympic women's basketball and volleyball in 1976 and hockey in 1980, I was living in Australia and no longer competing. So the dream of becoming an Olympic athlete, like so many other childhood dreams, remained only that. Even if I'd been competing at the right time, I was never a gifted athlete, although I'd joke that in my heyday, I could have beaten basketball great Michael Jordan one on one. Admittedly he was only seven at that time!

I'd always been the kid who tried hardest and just made the team by the skin of my teeth, often contributing little more than enthusiastic support from the bench. My parents never encouraged me in sport and we had many domestic arguments when I was forced to forgo valuable athletic practice time to be sent to the more ladylike pursuits of accordion, piano and singing lessons.

Now that I had shared in the reality of my biological father's attainment of sporting excellence, I couldn't help but wonder, what if? What if he had raised me? What if, unlike my adoptive parents, he had encouraged me in Saturday afternoon sport, instead of opera? What if, as a professional athlete himself, he had fuelled my dreams? Would I have participated in the Olympics, rather than watched them on TV?

In the darkness, as snow softly fell outside the window, these questions drifted in my mind. Such thoughts were as short-lived as an icicle in spring because fortunately, I quickly came to my senses and started asking "what if" in a different context.

Yeah, Cath, but what if you'd been born a poor child in Nepal with a life expectancy of thirty-seven? What if you'd been born an unwanted girl in China? Or without legs? What if you hadn't been born at all?

At that point in my life, I knew categorically that the only place for a "what if" analysis was on a spreadsheet. There is absolutely no point being shackled by the past. Life is never about "what if's." Life is only about what is.

I'd been raised by the best parents imaginable. They'd always be Mum and Dad.

22

SAFARI WHISPERS

The puzzle of my past had been solved, except for one small area of uncertainty. Where had I been between the time that I was placed for adoption and the time my parents got that phone call? What had transpired in that six-month gap?

I thought the answer might lie in Scotland with the now retired Presbyterian minister who had baptized me. Returning from my next business trip to New York, I made a detour. For years I had longed to see Granddad's birthplace in Airdrie, just "doon the rood from Glasgow" as he'd have said. Mum's cousin, Janet Smart, the nurse who, in my childhood, had sent me postcards from afar, had an excellent knowledge of local Airdrie history. It was just as I'd once imagined: row upon row of identical brown tenement flats. I'm sure it hadn't changed much since my grandfather walked miles out of town to court my grandmother at nearby Mossywood Farm. Janet's sister and brother-in-law drove me to the original stone buildings that stood as they had for centuries, with yellow gorse in full April bloom. There was so much I should ask, but it was enough just to stand in the places where Granddad had grown up.

A shopkeeper offered me shortbread as I asked directions to Oban. It was to this idyllic fishing village of seven thousand perched on the west coast that the Reverend John

McLeod had moved after leaving his parish of St. Andrew's in Calgary. We'd corresponded for years and the address was simply Old Parish Manse. A woman in the gift shop gave me directions. "You go down to that pub and turn left. You dinna need to go into the pub, though!"

I found their home and tentatively knocked. It was nearly thirty years since we had seen each other. Within minutes, there was a cup of tea and homemade scones on the table. "God bless this hoose and oor friends. Thank you for this meeting here today."

In the brogue I remembered so well, Reverend McLeod pointed out, with genuine affection for my family, that I was but a wee bairn when we last met. In the interim, they had lost a daughter of my age to leukemia. I looked at Mrs. McLeod. Such a gentle soul, a trace of sadness still there in her eyes.

Since the reverend had signed my adoption papers, I hoped he could tell me where I had been for the first months of my life. He didn't know but pointed out Lull Island on which Calgary Beach is located, and Lismore Island, after which a town in northern New South Wales is named. The countries where I lived were somehow linked to this breathtaking, isolated region, a mere dot on a map of Scotland. I came away knowing no more about my first months on earth, but with friendships from my childhood renewed and strengthened.

Life seemed to be getting better by the day. Golf at St. Andrews, playing gridiron at the home ground of the Dallas Cowboys, walking the Great Wall of China and Colorado's Grand Canyon, elephant rides in the jungle of Thailand, scaling Aztec ruins in Mexico – all courtesy of IBM. Well, IBM actually paid me to work in an office and manage a team of diverse and talented human resource and communication professionals – but there were frequent overseas conferences and I always tried to incorporate some of my annual leave on those trips.

In September 1989, IBM invited me to attend a short leadership course at Harvard University, which was an eye-opener. One professor predicted the fall of the Berlin Wall and we thought he was delusional – until it did indeed come down two months later. I may have been the crazy one because rather than be inspired to further scale the corporate ladder, which was IBM's intention, for the umpteenth time, I questioned whether I wanted to do so. I had so enjoyed the brief time-out in the hallowed halls of academia – time to reflect what I really wanted to do with the rest of my life. Carefully sidestepping any major career-altering course of action, I simply planned another adventure for my fortieth birthday, the following year.

Less than twelve months later, I was beneath Victoria Falls on the wildest commercial whitewater rafting trip in the world, both frightening and spectacular as we catapulted down rapids while hungry-looking crocodiles guarded the banks. Sipping lime and sodas afterwards at the old colonial hotel in a courtyard of roses, azaleas and bougainvillea was equally splendid, but it was sad to see what the Mugabe regime had done to Zimbabwe, even back in those days.

More spartan, but no less memorable, was a camping safari in Kenya and Tanzania, where a young Canadian backpacker and I headed into the Serengeti with two African guides. Not a lime or soda in sight, only the eyes of a hyena peering through the darkness at our campfire. Although I was bursting to go to the loo in the middle of the night, I held on till morning because I had no idea what else might be out there.

Ngorongoro Crater was a 700-metre-high Noah's ark of animals dwelling in a time warp. At the rim looking down into mist, you couldn't see a thing. But, once at the base, it was like sitting on the bottom of a giant soup bowl with white fluffy clouds of meringue on the top. Hippos and lions at play; flamingos in flight. It was time to think, well away from corporate life, living life in the raw. Our guide asked what we did for a living.

"I work for IBM."

"What's IBM?"

Seems I'd heard that question before.

"It's the world's biggest computer company."

There was silence for a little while. "What's a computer?"

It was another humbling perspective – often in short supply in my high-tech life.

Safari. The Swahili word for a journey that entails leaving the comfort of civilization to venture into the wilderness. Now I was pleasantly lost in a wilderness of thought with the luxury of time to listen to the inner whispers that only the heart can hear.

These thoughts travelled with me eastwards to the coast. As the night train to Mombasa pulled slowly out of the station, it all seemed so romantic until the Nairobi skyline gave way to shantytowns.

It suddenly occurred to me that no-one in the world knew where I was at that particular moment. What if something happened to me?

Something did happen. I started this book. With words as wobbly as a newborn giraffe, I took the first tentative step towards understanding my ongoing journey of self-discovery. Deeply lost in thought, I tried to find meaning in the midst of Africa.

For the first time, tears felt fine as I remembered happy family times, previously eclipsed by sadness surrounding the deaths of my parents. Orphans in the wild have little chance of survival and on safari, one witnesses death daily; it's simply one part of life's circle.

Naturally, on the train, my thoughts turned to Dad and memories of when, as a little girl, we rode on the Canadian Pacific across the Rockies. I'd sit in the dome car watching for bears and moose, mesmerized by seeing the front of the train disappear into a tunnel and emerge from the other side. As it wound its way around the next mountain curve, the rear of the train would disappear into that same tunnel. Now, there were no curves on the rails, no tunnel on the flat plain and there was no need to search for wildlife – not a sole moose or bear in sight but herds of giraffes, elephants and antelope bounding alongside the clickety-clack of track. I wondered again if I was on the right one in my corporate life. Dusk turned to dark, and doubt to peace, as the rocking lulled me to sleep.

Just south of the equator, about the same latitude as Singapore, warm Mombasa breezes wafted through my consciousness. Returning to Nairobi in high spirits, I enjoyed a round of golf at Royal Nairobi Golf Club and looked forward to meeting up with Liz, who was taking time out from her two-year assignment in Malaysia. She was like the sister I'd never had and we'd have lots to catch up on. But, first there was the pressing matter of laundry.

As I headed back to the hotel from the laundromat, a neatly dressed young man approached. "I am a journalist and wish to practise English. Can I speak to you about life in your country?" Although suspecting a con, I thought, why not? Within minutes, one of his friends joined us and I was now certain it was a scam – but felt rather charitable and mellow after my train trip and was prepared to spend a few dollars on Kenyan coffee and cake. Sure enough, as I got up to leave, there came the expected plea for money along with their rather unconvincing story about being refugees from Sudan. I simply paid the bill and left, wishing them well and offering to send these budding journalists some newspapers from Australia.

Before I'd walked a block, a plainclothes police officer flashed his rather tatty badge and called me by name: "Catherine, you are under arrest for collaborating with terrorists from Sudan." Only somewhat unnerved, I assured him I had done nothing of the sort and explained the circumstance, without breaking stride. By then, two colleagues joined him and insisted I accompany them back to the station. My bravado was fading as fast as the late afternoon light but I had no intention of leaving the main street and kept heading for the hotel. By now, five big black Kenyans marched alongside, all claiming to be police officers. Intuition told me otherwise. Rather than follow them to the station like the law-abiding citizen I am, I verbally attacked them for allowing the so-called terrorists to pose as students and suggested they follow me to my hotel, where I would call the Australian government. An old gridiron strategy stood me in good stead. A strong offence beats a strong defence.

"You must pay a fine and give us your passport," they insisted. Fearing they would grab me at any stage, I lied, "My passport and money are back at the hotel. I'll meet you in the lobby." The general manager was about to become my new best friend. I headed through the revolving door and never saw them again. What I did discover was that they were all likely part of the same gang responsible for the rape, theft and even murder of other tourists. Maybe a guardian angel hid amid the clean laundry?

23

ON TOP OF AFRICA

Two days later, Liz and I set off to climb Mount Kilimanjaro. Facing my fortieth birthday, I was determined to avoid a mid-life crisis and replace it with the experience of climbing the highest mountain in Africa, 19,340 feet (5896 metres) high.

They say that life begins at forty, but I became convinced that everything else begins to wear out, spread out or fall out! I wasn't really the rugged outdoors type and my normal idea of roughing it was when room service was late. As for the joy of sleeping under the stars, give me the creature comforts of the five stars!

Imagine for a moment standing atop the highest mountain in Africa. Dawn breaks on a crystal-clear morning as you inhale fresh, rarefied mountain air. You gaze down on the vastness of Kenya to one side and Tanzania on the other, 360-degree views over Africa, as far as the eye can see. The sun bounces an opalescent, pinkish-blue light off the ice-capped glacier formations at the summit. A freak of nature for these magnificent pinnacles to be located at the equator, it was the most beautiful sight I had ever seen and it's sad to think that they have since diminished – and may disappear completely – with global warming.

At the same time, imagine shivering at minus 18°Celsius

temperatures, feeling nauseous and battling a crashing headache from the altitude. You're hyperventilating and gasping for breath in the thin air. I'd completed full marathons but never remember feeling as simultaneously elated and exhausted as after the final ascent of Kilimanjaro.

We commenced the final climb in the middle of the night. The guide alleged it was to avoid avalanche danger when the sun hit the snow. But I think the real reason he woke us up in the middle of the night was because if we'd seen the full extent of what we had to do during daylight, we might not have done it – and perhaps the same could be said of many projects!

Walking among sheer shale was like traipsing through black butter as over and over we took three steps forward and two steps back. It seemed a metaphor for life. Just when we feel we're making progress, we sometimes slip back. Yet those who achieve their own summit of success, however they define it, keep focused on their goal.

Although I couldn't see the top of the mountain, I pictured it in my mind's eye and knew that was where I wanted to be. Yes, there were times during the night when I felt like turning back but I reminded myself that I hadn't come this far to quit. Liz became ill and had to do so with her guide, but urged me to carry on.

At the highest point in Africa, between the Atlantic and Indian oceans, a plaque reads:

> We the people of Tanzania would like to light a candle and put it on top of Mt. Kilimanjaro which would shine beyond our borders giving hope where there was despair, love where there was hate and dignity where before there was only humiliation . . . Julius Nyerere, December 9, 1961.

Hope, love and dignity abounded with the first shimmer of sunlight on the summit of this extinct volcano. I felt nothing but the sheer joy of being alive to greet the dawn of a new day. My mind seemed separate from my body, as I stood alone on the top of Africa, no other person in sight except my Chuga tribesman guide, named Godbless. It was a breath of fresh air for the brain and soul.

I knew then that life doesn't begin at forty. It begins the moment we're born and every day is an important one, a new miracle to be celebrated. I remembered waiting until age sixteen so I could drive, and then waiting until I was twenty-one so I could drink. Since my folks died, I no longer waited for much of anything and had grabbed most every day as if it were my last. Crosses on the descent reminded me it might be. The last climb of the adventure was a welcome one between clean sheets.

As my tightly braided head hit the pillow, my last thoughts were of a Swahili saying: *Hakuna Matata*, which roughly translates as "no problems."

No problems, only opportunities awaited as my plane landed in Paris and I ventured back into the corporate jungle. Swapping hiking boots for high heels, I looked forward to taking my place in a series of IBM meetings in Paris, Belgium and London, and catching up with a very special friend from Sydney.

On New Year's Eve 1990 rather than greet the new decade with my usual anticipation, I wondered how the 1990s could possibly be better than the 1980s. How could anything top discovering my biological parents, attending Harvard, living in Japan, travelling the world, moving back to Sydney and climbing Kilimanjaro?

I met another long-lost cousin of my biological father's in

Noosa, Queensland. His daughter had a friend staying and when this teenager overheard the story of how I'd found my family, she shyly mentioned that she'd always wanted to contact her father but was afraid of rejection. I assured this beautiful and sensitive sixteen-year-old that no-one could possibly reject her for herself. If they did so, it was their problem. She found the courage, made contact and was welcomed.

I was about her age when I first started scribbling in my diary after Granddad died and I had no-one to talk to before bedtime. I sometimes still missed his wisdom but my diary had become somewhat of a cathartic evening ritual. Nightly entries over the years had recorded good times, bad times and mostly, the everyday times in between – friends, dinners, movies, laundry, Saturday papers, walks: life's little incidents and insights.

I've never had a particularly good memory or imagination and have long been an advocate of the old Chinese proverb that the weakest ink beats the strongest memory. I'm amazed when a friend recounts what we ate for dinner in 1986. I'm hard-pressed to recall last night's meal unless I wrote it in my diary, but it's a fair bet that it was Thai takeaway or scrambled eggs.

> Old friends find funny moments buried like a bone of bittersweet nostalgia in the backyards of our past. Underneath the surface of superficial personas, we chew the fat for hours. And although there's always one person who insists on digging up the dirt of bygone days, for most of us, what was once a bone of contention no longer matters now that we face the possibility of osteoporosis. Why do we no longer want to change the world – but just the appliances in the kitchen?

"That's weird to write in your diary every day," comments my cousin. Maybe he's right – but it's kept me honest with myself.

The damned diary was both a curse and a blessing – it jogged my memory but was a marathon task to distil. Frankly, I had made little progress on the book since I first put pen to paper in Africa but as I glanced through old dusty diaries in brown cardboard boxes and sifted through sentiment, it was reassuring to realize that much of what I had recorded as major concerns would have long been forgotten if I hadn't re-read the words on the yellowing pages. After a few weeks, I again shelved the notion of writing a book. I was too busy.

24

DARE TO BE DIFFERENT

On 8 February 1991, the phone rang. It was my next-door neighbour. "Are you frightfully busy in the next hour?" she tentatively asked. She knew I was always busy but I sensed something out of the ordinary, as she'd normally just knock.

"Why? Anything wrong?"

"No, but would you mind driving me to hospital? I think the baby might be coming a bit early and I'd rather not take a taxi."

Her water had already broken by the time I turned on the answering machine and put Tam outside. "But the baby isn't due for another two weeks," she repeated as I fumbled for change on the Sydney Harbour Bridge, hitting every pothole on the road between home and the hospital. Pulling up to Admissions, I promptly dragged the first able-bodied man I saw to help Diana from the car. Only later did I discover he was a visitor himself.

The necessary forms were completed without much ado and I followed her wheelchair to a bedroom, where she was told to don one of those impeccably fashionable hospital gowns and wait until a nurse came. The baby had no intention of waiting for anyone.

Before I knew what was happening, her contractions had

become more intense and a midwife was urgently summoned. Diana was in gut-wrenching pain and I felt totally useless, trying to comfort her.

"Everything will be fine. Tam had ten pups so don't worry. You're only having one."

What inane banter, for which Diana has since forgiven me! I didn't have a clue what to do and wasn't even sure if I should be present at such an intimate event. I had little time to ponder because less than an hour from the time of the phone call, I had the unexpected joy and privilege of witnessing the birth of a beautiful and healthy baby girl. Overcome with emotion, it was the only time I'd been to a hospital for the beginning, not the end, of life. The midwife smiled and said she loved to see people misty-eyed.

Why isn't the baby crying? I thought to myself. Surely something was wrong. I believed a newborn would scream the moment it saw daylight. Within a few minutes, I wondered if she would ever stop.

When Diana was offered a cup of tea, I was offered the baby. I must confess no particular fondness for young infants until they're old enough to walk and talk. But as I looked down at this tiny bundle in a blanket, I decided she was the most beautiful baby that had ever been born. Her name was Harriet Catherine, after her parental grandfather, Harry, and me.

I doubted I'd ever be a mother. My time for that was fast running out.

A few days after witnessing Harriet's arrival into the human race, I was snorkelling at the Great Barrier Reef, pondering my childhood and feeling incredibly close to my adoptive mother. Mum always used to say, "There's lots of fish in the sea, dear," as consolation when I was dateless for a prom. It then occurred to me that these legendary fish could also symbolize endless opportunities lying just under the surface. Swimming amid colourful schools of fish, it struck me that Mum had never actually seen a fish in the sea.

I was restless at work, unhappy about the one-hour commute to and from headquarters and disillusioned with the prevailing corporate culture. I confided my restlessness to my mentor Roy Lea, without actually saying I wished to leave. Reading between the lines, he offered me a three-month assignment as CEO of Young Achievement Australia. A non-profit organization that is funded entirely by the private sector, it aims to teach students about the creation of new wealth versus the mere redistribution of existing wealth. My assignment was part of IBM's sponsorship and my company career plan dictated that I spend some time outside the confines of Big Blue.

My predecessor had died of a heart attack in office and there were times when I wondered if that fate went with the position of running a non-profit organization, which ironically excelled itself at being non-profit! In the absence of an annual report and financial statements, it appeared close to bankruptcy. Two major sponsors withdrew their support before my appointment, so I faced the challenge to return the organization to a surplus and ensure the continued employment of twenty staff.

After a few days, I desperately missed the infrastructure and management discipline of IBM. I'd never thought about basic business issues such as payroll, pension funds or insurance. Suddenly, I was confronted with these, as well as tedious decisions such as what type of toner to buy for the photocopier! There was no "other" department to refer any matters to. I quickly learned that Post-it notes and paper clips didn't magically breed in stationery supply cupboards.

I'd easily managed a US$72 million budget but never worried about generating revenue from which to make such an allocation. Once again, like my first few months in Japan, I was out of my depth, trying to turn a small, relatively unknown non-profit organization into a progressive, well-recognized business unit.

I'm sure my boss at IBM had employed reverse psychology in placing me there. The comfort zone of IBM was now looking pretty good! However, the enthusiasm of staff, employers and young Australians eventually compensated for the absence of those corporate conveniences I'd taken for granted.

I was immersed in the entire strategic and operational direction of a worthwhile product, which had not reached its full potential. Young Achievement was Australia's best-kept secret, whereas our counterpart in North America, Junior Achievement, established in 1911, was a household name. Schools were partnered with businesses in a practically based mentorship program.

The three-month assignment was extended to six and I visited the United States with the top four students, who were guests of the New York Stock Exchange, IBM, Amway and Disney. While gazing down on Wall Street from the top of the World Trade Center Twin Towers, a sixteen-year-old from Blacktown High exclaimed as only a teenager can, "This is totally awesome!" No-one in three generations of her family had been outside New South Wales. Not only did the Young Achievement experience raise her hopes, but also the hopes of others at Blacktown High.

Blacktown High was not unlike Broadmeadows High where I first taught. Neither was it unlike my old school, Ramsay, where the principal said we'd never amount to anything. I had shared that story with Prime Minister Bob

Hawke, and now wanted to share some of my experience with kids of similar backgrounds to mine.

Still, I wavered about leaving IBM. I'd miss many colleagues but very little of the bureaucracy. Big Blue had been an excellent employer for a decade, and a small not-for-profit organization was an unknown quantity. Once again I was at the right place at the right time, and the availability of a voluntary retrenchment package in 1992 to all employees made the break from the corporate umbilical cord less painful.

My accountant and bank manager expressed their concern and I met with a financial planner to determine how best to invest my payout. He perused my spreadsheet of assets and liabilities, the only place where "what if" analysis belongs in my life.

"You've done pretty well . . . for a female. Tell me, was it an inheritance or a divorce settlement?" I informed him that I'd arrived in Australia with two hundred dollars and would have had more funds if I hadn't needed to pay my husband in the divorce settlement.

"No need to get on your feminine high horse." Needless to say, I trotted off to find another planner, one less saddled with stereotypes of women in the workforce. To save other female colleagues the same annoyance, I had his name removed from IBM's preferred supplier list before I left to join Young Achievement.

People often ask how I became a professional speaker. I'd like to say it happened overnight but there were many circumstances conspiring to point me in that direction and more hurdles than I would have imagined along the way. Certainly, it wasn't a career I'd ever consciously considered and I had been in the workplace over twenty years before even contemplating the possibility of earning a living by opening my mouth.

While at IBM, I had signed cheques for the trainers and motivational speakers we used for our management programs and sales incentive events. Some represented money well spent and others were a dubious investment, to say the least. Prior to a conference, one cancelled at the last moment because of a family emergency and it was impossible to obtain someone of similar credentials at short notice. As the topic was stress management, I volunteered to fill the void. Rather than be pleased that I had offered to do something well outside my job description, my boss chastened me. "Don't be ridiculous. We need an expert."

In spite of assurances that my physical education degree covered stress management, he insisted I find that "expert." A couple of days later, I informed him that we'd located a visiting professor from Harvard University who was on sabbatical in Australia. Much to my relief, he asked no further questions. There was no such person because I had planned to don wire-rimmed glasses and a short curly blonde wig over my brunette bob to pose as the "expert," Professor Barbara Nixon.

It initially seemed a good idea but I was more than a little nervous when I finally stepped on stage in front of two hundred colleagues and customers. After the first few minutes, I enjoyed every second and was relieved to receive laughter and applause. The executive, who had initially hired me years earlier, took notes in the front row and didn't even recognize me! I left the podium but remained on stage while the master of ceremonies took the microphone.

"Thank you, Professor Nixon, for sharing that wealth of information. We're honoured to have such global expertise here with us in Australia."

I again stepped up to the microphone and flung off the glasses and blonde wig to again become a brunette. "Following Watergate, would anyone believe an American named Nixon? It's me – and I'm just like you. Oftentimes, we know this stuff ourselves but feel we need an outside 'expert' to validate our beliefs."

Laughter subsided, and the audience was content to learn that I did, in fact, have a background in stress management. But, it became obvious just how difficult it is to be "a prophet in your own land."

Only my immediate boss remained stressed. "That was risky. What if it had failed?"

"But it didn't" I protested. His paternalistic approach reminded me of my mother. "Be careful, dear," she'd always say. Our parents seldom encourage us to take risks and I know I certainly never heard: "Go out and play and take lots of risks, dear." From an early age, we're conditioned to play it safe and certainly do so in a conservative corporation. Yet playing safe is sometimes the riskiest thing we can do.

Everyone is good at something. Too often we may be frustrated because we're not in our niche, not suited for what we're doing and missing our true potential. As John F. Kennedy once said: "There are risks and costs to a program of action. But they are far less than the long range costs and risks of comfortable inaction."

My boss seemed unimpressed when I quoted Kennedy. I knew it was indeed risky to pull a spoof like I did but I knew it was more risky to have someone else with questionable credentials or a gap in the conference program.

Soon, I was speaking to IBM managers throughout Australia and New Zealand at our annual management forums – but never again with a wig and glasses! Word spread and IBM started charging me out to their clients on a fee-for-service basis. If they'd pay IBM, maybe they'd pay me directly? After all, I believed that with risk, comes reward. I was more interested in making a difference than making money and believed I could supplement my non-profit salary at Young Achievement by simultaneously establishing my own speaking business. Had I been in the clutches or the comfort of the corporation? Only time would tell. And belief in ourselves is like a muscle – strengthened by constant and careful use. Once a phys ed teacher, always a phys ed teacher!

I named my start-up CDV Management, three little let-ters, like IBM. They symbolized not only the initials of my name, but a promise: Clients Deserve Value. The IBM acronym had its own irreverent alternatives but as far as I was concerned, It's Been Marvellous.

I'd spoken to IBM employees and customers about serv-ice quality but lacked confidence that clients would actually pay me for offering what I thought was common-sense advice. Fortunately, I was wrong. But I was also wrong about the financial fluctuations of Young Achievement and the amount of hours required of me there. It was certainly not a part-time job, as the board had anticipated.

A former assistant and friend from Victoria's Department of Youth, Sport and Recreation days, now working at the Australian Institute of Sport, invited me to be part of his support team for the Barcelona Olympics. I didn't feel I could afford to take time off.

> How can I possibly feel so snowed under – when I live near an idyllic harbour that has never even had a light flurry? Chances can melt away almost as quickly as a single snowflake touching a warm cheek.

Next morning I decided I could ill afford to forgo the opportunity of a lifetime. Lifetimes are too short and since it had always been a dream to attend the Olympics, being part of the support team seemed almost as good as being an athlete. Besides, dreams often need to be reset or modified in the course of a lifetime. With only a few days to plan the trip, this *señorita* was bound for Barcelona – maybe not fulfilling the childhood dream of actually competing in the Olympics but at least participating, although one friend unkindly suggested I was being sent as a javelin catcher!

Ten thousand athletes from 168 countries competed in twenty-eight sports. Over 6.5 million tickets were sold to spectators, while billions more around the world witnessed this spectacular event. It was magic from start to finish. The closing ceremonies were a reminder that winning wasn't everything in the Olympic spirit of participation. I felt privileged to be part of the live audience at Montjuic Stadium underneath that Olympic flame as tenor José Carreras, his throat recovering from cancer, sang "Amigos Para Siempre." Amigos – I had many friends for life, although it was a lifetime's distance from my childhood when I first saw fireworks at Scotchman's Hill.

A financial fiasco awaited my return. We discovered that the accountant at Young Achievement had paid neither creditors nor tax, in an endeavour to make our figures look better than they were, despite a "satisfactory" audit. I fired him immediately and endured the worst period of my career. If the organization went bankrupt, my dedicated staff would lose their jobs and I would lose the credibility I'd worked so hard to build over the last twenty years.

Although I only planned to stay at Young Achievement a year, I had no option but to remain and help transform it into a viable financial entity. I'm still not sure how we did it but thanks to the marvellous dedication of staff, we traded out of near bankruptcy. The new accountant and the honorary treasurer were a tower of strength at a time when I felt everything collapsing around me. As I lost sleep and gained weight, they calmly suggested strategies and implemented checks and balances, while others and myself secured additional revenues. Although finances were a constant struggle, we tripled the number of students in the mentorship program to sixteen thousand and modestly increased staffing levels to thirty-one people throughout Australia.

In the midst of this melee came a phone call out of the blue, asking if I would be interested in being considered for a government board position. Could I please send a résumé, but only if I was "squeaky clean." I assured the caller I had showered that morning. I assumed the unannounced board position had something to do with education and promptly forgot the call, as it was made clear there were a number of others being considered.

A few months later, on a business trip to Melbourne, my secretary called in a panic. "The police minister wants to see you urgently."

25

EXECUTIVE WOMAN
OF THE YEAR

My secretary assumed the police minister's request had something to do with our deposed accountant. I didn't know what to think and was not at all certain about the dubious honour of being appointed to the New South Wales Police Board – the third largest police service in the world. I was reluctant to take on a greater workload in order to acquaint myself with unfamiliar issues of policing and corporate governance. However, I was assured it would only involve one monthly meeting and that my human resource experience would prove useful when dealing with promotions procedures. I remained unconvinced and was also concerned about my personal security, as I envisioned phone taps and men in trenchcoats.

And what did they mean by "squeaky clean"? I thought I'd better 'fess up to such things as two speeding tickets, a love affair with a married man and stealing a pack of cigarettes as a twelve-year-old. Plus, when I was about five, I pocketed a spool of brightly coloured thread from the display in Calgary's landmark Hudson's Bay Company department store. Proudly giving it to my mum as a gift, I still vividly remember being marched up the escalator by the scruff of my neck to the manager's office on the top floor. In tears, I apologized to a serious-looking retailer who was probably more bemused by my mother's fire and brimstone ranting about jail and the commandment, "Thou shalt not steal."

Although it was unlikely police background checks would ever expose these "crimes," I felt the benefits of a clear conscience, thinking what a pity that confession played no part in my Presbyterian upbringing. As an ancient Persian proverb so aptly reminds us: "There is no saint without a past, no sinner without a future."

Like me, one of my mentors, a high priest of the business community, was apprehensive about the prospect of this board. Still, deep inside, I felt a strong obligation as a citizen. Thoughts swam back to another time on the other side of this ocean. I'd always been told, and believed, that police, unlike those impostors in Kenya, were my friends. After all, way back in Calgary on the wrong side of the tracks, our next-door neighbour was a cop and helped me stay on the right track by teaching me how to swim and play baseball. Police were also role models when I served as a school crossing patrol, even though the local bully insisted on hitting me over the head with my stop sign. He stopped teasing me after I won a trip to the Canadian Grey Cup football final. Only thirteen at the time, this citizenship award was my first real honour and I still remember the names of those police chaperones.

So, although I shared community concern about corruption allegations, I firmly believed – and still do – that the majority of police are honest men and women, risking their lives on a daily basis with precious little public appreciation. I reluctantly accepted and almost regretted doing so on the first day, when my photo was splashed across the front page of the paper with the headline, Clean team appointed.

Naturally, with this new responsibility, my speaking business did not take off as fast as anticipated, but some weeks earlier I had been asked to share with a group of three hundred international sportswomen the story of finding my parents. It was the first time I'd spoken publicly about it. It was a very private thing as far as I was concerned, but a friend convinced me the story would inspire others. I'd always been guarded about my personal life but told my story, surprised at the depth of emotion present in that auditorium. Noticing a few people in tears, I almost broke down myself, because I'd just received what would be the last letter from my grandmother:

> My relatives back home have all passed away. I join them soon. I am so happy to know you are alive and well. I have always loved you as much as the others . . . I can hardly see to write anymore as my eyes are dim, but I'm so happy that you found us and I wish you and all the girls all the happiness and God's blessing. It's not much of a farewell but I love you all.

On Canada Day – 1 July 1993 – Frida Bachman passed away, but not before passing on the gift of her love to me – and, of course, the rest of her family. My grandmother had been tough, yet flexible, all her life. Some might even say she was stubborn, but now she had no fight left. She simply wanted to end the interminable pain of the cancer eating away at her body. She was ready to go. Having passed her ninetieth birthday, Frida had no regrets. Surrounded by daughters, grandchildren and great-grandchildren, she was finally at peace with the world. She told her younger daughter and carer, "I can die happy – because now I know what happened to that little baby of Trudy's."

She could never have imagined that I was planning the annual Young Achievement black-tie dinner and selection of the top four from a field of sixteen thousand. On occasions like this, conversing with the cream of Australia's youth, all the hassle of running a non-profit organization paled into insignificance. There was unanimous pride that these young men and women would grow into outstanding citizens.

Still, teenagers had a way of asking difficult questions. "If you had one wish, what would it be?" inquired one.

Prompted by her refreshing frankness, I responded with the same honesty. Part of me said I should unselfishly state a desire to erase famine, discover a cure for AIDS, for cancer, formulate a peace solution for the former Yugoslavia . . . the list was endless. But truth prevailed as I confided my simple, selfish wish to be granted the impossible privilege of taking my parents to a concert and dinner. To say thanks. To tell them how much I loved them because I'd not always demonstrated that love. I later learned that this Young Achievement Student of the Year had recently lost her father to cancer and I knew then that our chat had meant something to her. No-one was prouder than I when she went on to be a Rhodes Scholar at Oxford University.

The day after the dinner, I was on the other side of an awards interview panel, as a finalist in the Telecom-sponsored Australian Executive Woman of the Year Award. Unlike the sixteen-year-olds, there was no time for nerves as I arrived in Melbourne thoroughly unprepared and exhausted. As I left the three judges, I felt I should at least put a few words together on the back of a tram ticket in the unlikely event I won. Doing so, I felt saddened at the very prospect of accepting an award without my parents present. After all, they'd always been there for school awards nights.

When my name was announced as the winner, I promptly forgot what was scribbled on the tram ticket and a succession of extempore interviews with journalists ensued.

"What are the secrets of success?"

Unprepared, I resorted to the words of someone else: "The only time success comes before work is in the dictionary."

Reading it in black and white the next morning, I thought to myself, surely I could have said something more original. But in truth, those words of British hairdresser Vidal Sassoon seemed as apt as any because hard work has always been part of my life – indeed, sometimes too big a part!

"Are you a feminist?"

"A feminist? Well, there are twenty-six letters in the English alphabet and depending on how those are arranged, we are able to label people. Unlike a jigsaw puzzle, there are many appropriate combinations and connotations. So, my reply is in that context. I'm a human being first, an Australian second, a woman third and if you insist on yet another label, yes, I'm a feminist." I'm not comfortable with labels of any sort – or high heels. Although I admittedly love to wear Prada, Gucci or Zampatti, I much prefer hanging out with "uniquely designed" people in my favourite old Nike trainers!

After the whirlwind of the awards presentation, I sat on a park bench, comfy in my thoughts and tracksuit. Strangely, I felt not the least bit elated but rather as flat as the takeaway pizza that I idly munched on. The weighty responsibility of role model now rested firmly on my shoulders. I questioned whether all my faults and frailties qualified me to live up to the expectations that others suddenly seemed to have of me. I knew only too well I was far from perfect.

Reflecting on twenty years in Australia brought back memories of how wonderful this country had been to me. I was aware of the need to put more back. Donating my prize money to Young Achievement wasn't enough. I wanted to do something more lasting; I wanted to not squander the opportunity to say the things that needed to be said.

But how? Inspiration remained elusive as my head finally hit the pillow.

Next morning, a group of friends drove to a Mount Buller ski lodge for their annual Thanksgiving dinner. It occurred to me we should really embrace this marvellous North American celebration in Australia, not because of any Pilgrim past but simply because we have so much to be thankful for.

I clambered up Mount Buller not once, but twice, to the point of exhaustion: the silence of solitude on a peak always a spiritual retreat. I looked into the heavens and my heart – as millions have done for thousands of years.

What do any of us seek when we aspire to greater heights? Or is the ascent itself half the fun? Why am I so emotional? So wanting of personal love in my life rather than public recognition? Why am I still missing my parents after twenty years? Why do I feel so empty?

What is success, anyway? I wondered, and gazed down over the blue hills, layer upon layer of landscape. I'd made it to the top. Physically and literally. But had I really made it? What's the point if you can't share such so-called success? I always missed my parents more at times of triumph than tragedy. I felt both powerful and powerless, a peculiar juxtaposition. Overlooking the Victorian High Plains, I thought back to Scotchman's Hill and imagined how proud Dad would be of this award. He'd probably show it to the waitresses and coworkers in the kitchen, just as he showed my school report cards. Tears of sadness turned to joy. Although I still regret they're not here, I knew at that moment part of them would always be with me wherever I go. Everything I do is a tribute to Mum and Dad.

Back in Sydney, I dusted off old family photo albums full of musty memories. Browsing through, I laughed and cried but mostly smiled. I removed their wedding portrait to my bedside table. It was the first time any family photo had been out of the album and I can now thank them every night before I go to bed with a smile, not sadness. They were young then, younger than me today. Life goes on – until it doesn't.

I still wasn't excited about my award because it was something I never aspired to or consciously worked towards. It just *happened*. However, I was thrilled the following Tuesday when former premier, Nick Greiner, launched my book, published by Prentice Hall. I felt unashamedly proud of *Good Service is Good Business* because I'd deliberately dedicated every spare moment over the previous three years and was convinced it could benefit businesses in delivering better value to customers.

In March 1994 I was asked to speak at an International Women's Day function at the Regent Hotel in Melbourne. From the luxury of my forty-seventh-floor hotel suite, I looked down past the *Herald Sun* building, across the Yarra River to Caroline Street, South Yarra, where I'd spent my first cold night in Australia on Val and Rod's floor.

Below lay Flinders Street railyards. With over thirty sets of concurrent tracks, it reminded me of my father and my childhood toy train set.

Embracing these distractions, I struggled with the final preparation of my presentation. Although I'd recently shared my story with an audience of three hundred, this was the first time I had been paid to talk about my life's journey. As applause gradually died down, I need not have worried about audience reaction. What did worry me was the overwhelming intensity of response.

"You changed my life today," exclaimed more than one.

"Oh, sorry," I replied. Although the comments were meant as compliments, I wanted no responsibility for changing anyone else's life. I had enough trouble managing my own, thank you very much! Only we can change our life.

I was wary about just how much credence some attendees placed on my words. The following speaker was Sara Henderson, the 1991 Australian Businesswoman of the Year, who also told her life story in an entertaining and inspirational way. She'd been doing so for a couple of years and seemed unfazed by such comments about changing lives, as we shared thoughts and the same flight back to Sydney.

"If we'd said the secret of success was to jump out one of those high-rise windows to the railway tracks below, some would have done so. Doesn't that frighten you?" I asked.

Sara calmly replied, "It used to. But I only tell my story the way it is. I can't help it if they read more into it than that." We both questioned why people were interested in hearing our life stories. After all, in the face of what may have appeared tragic to others, we felt we had no choice other than to get on with life. Calamity and courage have always been close cousins; although I never felt at all courageous and was amazed that one audience member asked how I coped. Frankly, I'd never really thought about it. What choice did I have? Cope or crumble? The latter wasn't an option, as the only crumble I had a taste for was that which Mum prepared with the rhubarb from our back garden. And, who had time to bake these days?

I was a full-time CEO, part-time speaker, board member and weekly broadcaster on a drive-time radio show. At a time of high unemployment, I basically had four jobs when over a million Australians had none. To coin a favourite Aussie colloquialism, *I was flat out – like a lizard drinking.*

After nearly three years as head of a non-profit organization, I decided there was a use-by date for most people in such positions. I had stayed a year longer than planned and it was time to move on. A new executive would be good for the staff, the organization and certainly for me.

My successor was finally appointed and for the first time in my career, I felt not just nettled, but positively stung by discrimination when the new CEO was offered a substantially larger salary package. "He's a married man who needs to put bread in the basket," the chairman of the board explained to my utter incredulity.

26

SMALL-BUSINESS DIRECTION

On 1 April 1994 I became fully self-employed. Many commented on the appropriateness of the date because I've certainly done some foolish things in life! Only time would tell if this was another. Some thought I was going through a mid-life crisis, or was plain crazy to resign in the height of the worst unemployment since the Depression. Oh well, everyone thought I was reckless to leave the security of a university job in Canada twenty-one years earlier.

As a child, I was always told little girls should be seen and not heard. Today, people would find it hard to believe that I was once somewhat shy. Likewise, my parents and teachers would be stunned to learn that I now get paid to do what I once got punished for doing – speaking.

Good Service is Good Business was on the way to becoming a best-seller, which provided a niche on the speaking circuit, with subsequent audio and video sales. Like most small businesses, mine slowly evolved. In addition to service quality, clients asked for presentations on change, success and doing business with Japan. I had no strategic plan and everything revolved around client demand.

As the previous year's winner, I was asked to judge the Business Women's Awards – and became convinced it was a fluke to have won it the year before. The finalists seemed so much smarter than I as they described their struggles of revenue-raising, hair-raising risks and child-raising – all at the same time. I had previously affiliated success with a big corporation and, ashamedly, was somewhat condescending towards small-businesspeople. A huge mistake that I'd never repeat!

I had much more to learn about small business and sometimes the learning curve was so steep, I should have been strapped in with safety ropes. For instance, the time I awaited payment for my first presentation. Three months later, still no cheque had arrived. I'd noticed in the paper that the company, one of Australia's Top 500, was having some downturn in business and asked a friend if that was the reason they hadn't paid. "Of course not," she replied. "What was the date of the invoice?"

"Invoice? What invoice? They laughed. They clapped, surely they'll send money!"

Such was my small-business naïvety. I'd managed a multimillion-dollar budget for IBM, but had never needed to worry about the responsibility of actually getting any funds in the bank! Thus, a valuable lesson in cash flow. I never missed the "security" of corporate life as was predicted. The irony was that in theory, I had less financial security than ever in my working life, and security was something I had always considered important. But in reality, even with high risk in small business, I'd never felt more secure – secure about my future, my past. Well, almost.

I still lack that "security" of a long-term relationship with someone special. Fine to share a laugh about the magnet on my fridge: "The more I know men, the more I love my golden retriever." No wonder a male golfing buddy teases: "Not exactly a man-magnet, but why do you need a man, Cath? Tam sleeps in your bedroom and snores and farts all night long!"

Diary entries aside, strictly speaking, I had many men in my life, albeit on a platonic level. I was a member of a predominantly male Rotary Club and in those early days, most of the conferences I spoke at were quite "blokey" (macho). Apart from a few occasions, I was never hassled and, apart from one occasion, was never tempted to mix business and pleasure – and even that never progressed beyond temptation.

A few days after one presentation, the CEO of a major company invited me for coffee and, I assumed, to discuss repeat business. However, one coffee turned to many. He chatted about his divorce and three daughters and emphatically stated how much he'd like to see me again. Rather thrown by this and uncertain of the ethics involved, as I'd just started working with a speakers' bureau, I called the bureau and sought advice. This was the first man I'd been interested in for some time.

"No worries. Go for it, Cath, as long as we get 30 percent of everything he's got," they laughed. That hurdle cleared, I happened to have a social function to attend so gathered my courage to ask him along. It was a fun evening and he remained a perfect gentleman with a peck on the cheek good-night. A few days later he introduced me to one of his daughters and asked me out for another dinner amid more phone conversations. By this stage the hormones were hopping over a candlelit dinner when he reached across and held my hand: "Cath, I've got something to tell you." I braced myself, thinking there must be another woman. "I'm gay."

Choking on Thai green curry, I tried to remain composed. "Oh, that's interesting . . . so why are you asking me out?"

"Well, I mistakenly thought you were a lesbian and, like me, needed a discreet cover."

"Good grief, whatever made you think that?"

"Well, a sister of one of my staff plays golf at your club and she's a lesbian, so I assumed you were as well, being a strong independent woman who obviously doesn't need a man."

Although I have gay friends, I hoped he didn't draw such irrational conclusions in his business affairs. We've remained close ever since – and he's since "come out." Ironically, my next date was with a golfer I quite fancied but he was still hurting too much after his wife had left him for a female lover.

Meanwhile, I headed off to the Royal Australian Air Force's Edinburgh Base where I addressed the officers' mess at a silver-service dinner. My life was far removed from the mess it once was. Business was booming and I was too busy to give dating a second thought. A handsome young pilot took me on a tour of the F18 fighter jets and munitions dumps. An old photo of my father popped into my mind and it occurred to me that he, too, had been a good-looking young air force recruit, serving in the Royal Canadian Air Force during World War II. The next morning, the squadron leader dared me to abseil off the air traffic control tower. No worries. He then dared me to do it frontwards. This involved trusting the team to hold the rope as I teetered at the top edge. It seemed unnatural to let my body freefall at right angles to the tower before again gaining a foothold.

Like most things, the first step is the hardest until you're committed past the point of no return. Fear lessened only somewhat on the petrifying descent and it was far from elegant, as I indelicately dangled from the harness like a wayward spider. I later learned that most officers hadn't attempted it themselves. What was I trying to prove? Why did I buy into this macho competitiveness? To build rapport with the client by putting myself in their shoes? Was it the challenge? Just ego? Or all of the above, perhaps?

27

HORIZON OF HOPE

 In 1994, Liz, another friend and I set ourselves a goal, which at times seemed to be a rather unattainable one: to ascend over 17,000 feet from Argentina to the border of Chile and then head downhill from the summit to the Pacific Ocean, over 800 kilometres away – on a bicycle, without a support vehicle.

Well-meaning friends cautioned: "Aren't you worried about the Shining Path guerrillas? What about avalanches? Political instability?"

"You're doing what!" exclaimed a disbelieving client.

"Can't afford the airfare," I joked, and added for good measure, "Hey, life is like a 21-speed bicycle – and most of us have gears we never use."

We three intrepid amigos looked at the map for a preliminary plan, one which admittedly seemed somewhat daunting until the overall project was broken down into manageable chunks – estimating how much ground could be reasonably covered each day, making allowances for inclines and questionable road conditions.

After obtaining visas and security clearances, it was now time for the physical preparation. In some ways, we'd inadvertently started when we first learned to ride a bike all those years ago. Most of us hadn't cycled much since, but the basic skills, like many we possess, lay dormant and it was no longer necessary to get out the training wheels.

Encouraged by the fact that Tolstoy, author of *War and Peace*, didn't learn to ride a bike until he was sixty-six, we remained convinced we could do it. Ageing muscles would need to be eased into a training regime rather gently so we started with short rides on cycle paths. Soon we rode 40, 50, 60 or 70 kilometres on weekends and then added telephone books to our saddlebags. Cappuccino and cake stops were welcome. Don't we deserve little rewards on any journey?

In bad weather, we'd resort to stationary bikes in the gym but it was less motivating to busily pedal and get nowhere. Sometimes it seemed the same as my newly formed business! I wondered if I should have a partner, but like a tandem bike, decided I didn't want to risk the equivalent of doing all the pedalling up front, while someone coasted pleasantly along behind.

Full of unbridled enthusiasm, and wearing some rather eccentric green-and-purple striped leggings, we arrived at Sydney airport, with only our bikes and saddlebags. No wonder I didn't get my usual frequent-flyer upgrade! The customs official quizzed, "Are you going for business or pleasure?"

"Pleasure – we're cycling over the Andes."

"Doesn't sound like pleasure to me!"

Passports sternly stamped, we headed happily off – more like the Three Stooges than the Three Amigos – and most certainly not like the Three Tenors as we hummed "Don't Cry for Me Argentina."

Jet-lagged, eighteen hours later we assembled our bikes in the airport arrivals hall at Buenos Aires and met, for the first time, three men who'd signed up for this adventure plus our tour leader.

Any previous concerns about mountain bandits quickly vanished in a vapour of fumes. We were more likely to succumb to pollution and potholes on the streets of the eighth largest city in the world. In spite of planning, nothing prepared us for death-defying pedalling through twelve lanes of Buenos Aires rush-hour traffic.

Our fearless tour leader from Melbourne had never led a tour in his life. He promptly lost his passport, wallet and hotel details, but never his boyish sense of optimism, which had seen him emigrate to Australia after his father, along with thousands of other middle-class Argentinians, had committed suicide during times of high inflation that made it impossible to meet debts.

"But don't worry. Argentina is stable now. Just don't mention the Falklands," he warned, as I gradually warmed to his sense of adventure.

How much had changed since Juan and Eva Perón founded their party on the shirtless ones – the underdogs? We visited her tomb, amazed to learn she was only thirty-three when she died of cancer. It now cost over $US50,000 just to be buried in this country. It seemed a strange juxtaposition, as the streets of La Bot neighbourhood were so alive with fire jugglers, artists, accordions and tango dancers.

Confidence waned when we set out for the mountains two days later and our bikes arrived damaged. Tires and spirits were both flat but we hadn't come this far to give in easily. For the next three weeks, we would no longer have contact with the superhighway as we slowly wound our way along remote dirt tracks.

After nine hours of an uphill battle against snow and gale-force winds, we wondered if we'd made a serious mistake but as we hadn't seen a single vehicle that entire time, there was no choice but to continue to our evening destination. Heavy panniers gave the bikes the aerodynamics of a brick. If we stopped pedalling, we'd fall over. Arriving cold, sore and dirty, we wondered if we should have trained more rigorously in the first place. It was also one of those moments when we wished we were at home in our own comfortable everyday environment, but yet knew, if we were, we'd have been wishing we were off on an exciting adventure! I consoled myself that I was fortunate enough to experience this much temporary pain through choice. But where was that espresso machine?

Vaseline was invaluable to prevent friction on our backsides while Tiger Balm eased neck aches. We rubbed in copious quantities of both, careful not to confuse the respective hands applying the ointments!

As we rolled into the rhythm of the road, I came to appreciate the joie de vivre of our eccentric tour leader, who spoke of the body being little more than a company car for the spirit.

How do we handle those headwinds of everyday life back home? Are adventure and adversity aligned as one? Where are we going? Who are we? Questions we asked for many more revolutions – of our wheels – not the political type, so frequent in the cycles of change in this country.

Following days seemed saner as we gained some relief by riding close together in each other's slipstream, the front rider providing marginal protection from the elements.

Condors glided effortlessly above while we battled 80-mile-per-hour headwinds. Our goal seemed impossible as the snow was now horizontal and I wanted to be likewise – in a warm bed. A military courier took us the remaining few miles to the hostel and after an impromptu fiesta with rocks in empty beer cans, he carried on his way. I dragged my weary body into a hostel bunk. Eaten alive by bed bugs, I vowed to never again visit a developing country – but where had I heard that before?

Through sheer persistence, stupidity (or both) we found ourselves, a few days later, at the top of the summit pass marking the border of Argentina and Chile.

"Why would anyone in their right mind cycle over the Andes?" you might ask. Customs officials must have thought likewise and body-searched us for drugs, convinced we "*locos gringos*" (crazy foreigners) had to be on them! But the rush we felt coasting downhill was nothing but a natural high. We easily covered twice the daily distances than on the ascent and took time to stop and enjoy the magnificent mountain scenery. Why "going downhill" is always referred to in a negative light seemed somewhat inexplicable as we enjoyed the easier cruise through fertile fields of flowers and vineyards.

Likewise, "over the hill" assumed more positive connotations on this trip. Now well past forty, maybe I should enjoy coasting downhill a little more; taking more time to absorb the scenery rather than racing through life. Maybe it's not always necessary to be driven to climb the next hill.

We stopped for an impromptu lunch on the ocean at Vina del Mer, where the maître d' in his tuxedo is still undoubtedly recovering from the shock of witnessing the worst case of helmet hair seen since the Spanish invasion!

So much had changed since I first rode a bright red bike with whopping big white training wheels. They're long gone but I'm still learning and maybe need them for better balance in life. It's so much harder to maintain balance when you slow down on a bike. Yet slowing down in my everyday tracks is exactly what I need to do to regain that precious balance; that fine line which allows us to change gears without loss of momentum as we head towards that distant horizon of hope.

We'd done it! Dared to dream and dared to fail! We'd stepped outside our comfort zones and tested our limits. Dwarfed by majestic mountains, we couldn't help but be reminded that we were all only part of a much bigger picture, as we were both an intimate and invisible part of the vista from afar. In our normal environment, it was easy to lose perspective about minor roadblocks along the way. In the vast mountainous splendour, there was no space for personal delusions of grandeur.

One of our group was having hassles within a large organization back home and commented: "Well, I got my rear into gear and if I can endure the discomfort of a sore backside while cycling over the Andes, I can easily cope with people at work who are a pain in the butt!"

There would be no more back-pedalling, and our companion returned to Australia with renewed vigour to embark on a fresh mid-life job change. As for me, having been told I might never play sport again after that vertebra fracture years ago, the journey had been especially satisfying.

So, how did ordinary, middle-aged people cycle over the Andes? Exactly the same way we should all approach challenges in everyday life – one pedal at a time. Good goals, like exercise, should stretch us a bit.

I can now look back on the trip with fond nostalgia, but at the time, only necessity kept me going. I'd been ill with a respiratory tract infection since day one and although my friends were annoyed with me for lack of stamina and I likewise resented being called a wimp, all was forgiven when back in Buenos Aires for my birthday, they gave me a bouquet of roses and the opportunity to be first in the hot shower.

We also visited Iguazu Falls and Perito Moreno Glacier, but by the time I got home to Sydney they were little more than distant memories, as every ounce of energy was spent in fits of coughing, in spite of the emergency antibiotics in our panniers.

My doctor prescribed more antibiotics, also with minimal impact. I staggered onto the stage a week later and had a coughing fit in the midst of a presentation on client empathy to partners of one of the world's largest accounting firms. Like the audience, I wore a dark suit, so the fact I wet myself coughing thankfully went unnoticed as I swigged cough syrup throughout. One delegate actually thought it was part of the "act."

This was drama I hadn't counted on and I headed straight to hospital – breathalyzed by police on the way. Soon I was hooked up to Ventolin and oxygen. The young intern took one look at my age, resting pulse rate of 116 and didn't believe I'd just cycled over the Andes. I guess they see all types in Emergency and I was just another nut case.

My wimp status was vindicated when the lab announced how excited they were to discover a new strain of bacteria, not to mention the parasites they had found in my blood. In spite of our hospital system being imperfect, I felt safe and relieved not to be in South America.

I also believed our police service was far better than the press perceived but far worse than the board would ever admit.

28

POLICE OPERATIONS AND STRANGE ENCOUNTERS

I often wondered why I remained on the police board in the midst of my concern over preliminary royal commission findings into corruption. In the same way, I had questioned the wisdom of plunging down an air traffic control tower with men in uniform – after the event.

Such were my thoughts one sunny Sydney spring afternoon in 1994. Heading home from a board meeting, I stopped at a red light on the Pacific Highway. An adjacent motorist suddenly leapt out of a white four-wheel drive vehicle, knocked on my window and before I had a chance to close the open roof, gave me his card and a cheeky grin.

"You're gorgeous – call me for lunch." We both drove off, me somewhat flabbergasted but admittedly flattered and wondering if I would accept this latest dare . . . or would it be diving into another painful, ego-induced disaster?

I had too many other things on my plate. I had confronted my first heckler who, among other things, berated me with: "All my sisters were pretty and feminine." I could hardly believe my reply: "All my brothers were smart." I'd never even had a brother. My mouth earns me a living but gets me into trouble as well. A few days later, I feared a repeat performance when I disconcertingly noticed the man I'd dated immediately before my marriage sitting with arms folded menacingly in the front row of an all-male audience. No worries. He had also since married and we parted that day with a peck on the cheek.

Thank goodness for that, as there was more than enough angst among New South Wales police, media, politicians and our board. My home phone was checked for listening devices but I was more bugged by the apparent deafness of some fellow board members to the rumblings of corruption allegations.

I'd long since stopped relying on information contained within the bulky binder of board papers, delivered prior to each meeting in brown paper wrapping. Wading through reams of useless briefings that killed countless forests, we drowned in information but gasped for truth, as most pertinent facts lay buried deep within the documentation. It was not unlike a vignette from the British television series *Yes, Minister*. I'm not saying that anything incorrect lay within those papers, but it was more a case of what they *didn't* say. Just as one can't learn how to ride a bike by simply reading about it, I sensed I needed hands-on experience.

The police commissioner arranged for another board member and me to visit local stations, lockups and operational units but it was soon apparent that this was little more than a PR exercise where officers exuded politeness over scones at morning tea. Eventually, I was reluctantly allowed to go on operations, and my eyes were opened not just to inadequacies in the culture but more so to the tremendous work done by most police on a daily basis. You learn stuff you never want to know when you hang out with highway patrollers, who end their shift with relief that there were no limbs protruding from car wrecks that particular night. You find out what it's like to pursue an armed robber down the alleys of Kings Cross; to attend domestic violence scenes with naked children screaming amid a flat filled with cigarette butts, broken bottles and fear; to walk in the notoriously dangerous Redfern district at night while bricks are hurled at you from darkened windows and youths shout abuse in your face.

You learn more than you want as you chat with a prostitute on the stairs of a brothel about schooling for her child; pick up used needles on the streets of Cabramatta or remain holed up with eight men in a single hotel room with surveillance cameras on the room next door in a futile attempt to bust a drug dealer. Sharing pizza and a loo in a hotel room for twelve hours, the officers, especially the younger ones, gradually took me into their confidence. This triggered me to ask more probing questions at board meetings.

I never had and never will reveal a source. Thus, my comments were mostly dismissed but where there was smoke, there had to be fire. I felt a blaze about to ignite when I was barred from attending operations "for my own good."

Weeks after the failed drug bust in the hotel room, police persistence paid off and it was immensely satisfying to have been "on the scene" when the drug squad finally apprehended the dealer in a McDonald's car park. I'd served as a volunteer behind the counter at McHappy Day but this experience added a new nuance to the phrase: "Would you like Coke with your fries?" The sort of "coke" on this crook was worth over $4000 an ounce!

Tension at police board meetings had built up more than a television cops and robber drama before a commercial break. If it hadn't been so serious it would have been a joke, but the only humour was from the constable on security parking at police headquarters. As I drove in one morning, he informed me the Pope-mobile was parked in my parking spot for the duration of the papal visit to Sydney: "Looks like you board members have enlisted the big guy to pray for us all!"

Thank goodness for the sanctuary of my own home and Tam always there with her welcoming tailwag.

I hadn't counted on obscene phone calls at night, which kept me awake and sleepy for weeks. Around the same time, a parcel I'd left for a friend was stolen from my front porch. No evidence indicated these incidents were related to my role on the board but they were still somewhat disconcerting.

Studying board papers late one humid night by an open upstairs window, I heard what sounded like a shot just above my head and the house turned pitch-black. I crouched to the floor and waited for what seemed an eternity, crawled across the carpet and gingerly peeked out another window. Tam thought it was a new game and nothing seemed untoward on our quiet Neutral Bay neighbourhood street. Then, with relief, I realized it was nothing more than an exploding light globe that shortcircuited the electricity. My nerves were more frayed than a live wire. I deferred my diary entry till morning:

> At least I got a good night's sleep and no reason not to – as I know I've acted with total integrity and the best available knowledge at hand.

Still, it was hard to juggle these events while trying to build my speaking business and the workload was far in excess of the estimated one meeting a month: now more than three a week. It wasn't easy to be all that motivational to a group of human resource managers when I felt preoccupied with my own health and safety issues.

Maybe I was a softie and not cut out for this sort of work, as I had trouble concentrating on broader police board issues after hearing gruesome details of a sergeant killed on duty.

His widow had her twin disappear as a child, her first husband was killed in a car accident and her son had been diagnosed with a brain tumour. Why had life dealt her such dreadful blows? It was hard to debate the corruption of a few when I knew so many like this sergeant risked their lives on a daily basis. We take it all for granted. I didn't intend mascara-coated droplets to stream down my cheek at a board meeting, but there was nowhere else for them to go. Male colleagues stared in dismay and I later kicked myself that I'd bothered to apologize for displaying emotion – pleading exhaustion after a less than twelve-hour turn-around flight from Auckland, New Zealand. I then headed back to the airport to try to inspire some other organization about the merits of customer service, all the while thinking about how this sergeant had died in service to his job.

The following morning brought more emotional turmoil and my own moral dilemma.

29

A GIRL'S BEST FRIEND

Tam was ageing and the vet suggested she be put to sleep. After a sleepless night, I couldn't do it. Nor could I concentrate on work.

She doesn't seem to be suffering but her incontinence is turning the house into a health hazard. Sure, she's deaf, arthritic and partially blind but enjoys her food, walks and cuddles. I feel torn with the responsibility for her life in my hands and although others are encouraging me to end her days I don't want to cut short the life of such a loyal friend of sixteen years.

It was three days before Christmas and Tam's deteriorating health gave me yet another reason to shun the so-called festive season, which often brings out the worst in families. Police statistics recorded the highest incidence of domestic violence at Christmas, a sad statistic that I'd fortuitously never experienced first-hand.

Granddad and Dad had each died in December and as kind as others have always been to invite me to join their families, I could never force jolliness because tinsel had long since stopped sparkling for me. I'd grown up too quickly from the little girl who used to help Dad put the angel atop the tree and leave cookies for Santa.

Tam's once deep brown eyes had clouded with age. Mine blurred with tears. Never in her sixteen years did she miss her two walks a day and swims on Saturday, followed by a warm shower, cream rinse and blowdry in winter. Excessive possibly, but pets are like kids – if you don't train and pamper them, why bother?

Her last years, when I worked from home, were hopefully her happiest and I often found myself talking to her. She was a good listener with nary a sound apart from the protective bark if a courier came, although she'd likely only lick an intruder to death. It's a wonder I wasn't charged for false advertising when I nailed a "Beware of the dog" sign on the gate. After all, she'd been home on three occasions when the house was burgled.

But no-one could ever steal my memories of Tam. Though "just" a dog, ever since she was eight weeks old, Tam was my surrogate child. I joked that both my husband and dog attended obedience school but only she returned house-trained! – a somewhat callous comment. Although there's nothing funny about feeling sad, humour helps heal and was one way of coping with my failed marriage. More love than ever was showered on Tam, who had been my constant companion. At IBM she'd frequently lie beside my desk if I worked late at night. It certainly wasn't the "done" corporate thing in the land of navy blue suits and white shirts but Tam and I had a deal that took precedence over any business rules.

She'd join me on jogs or sit patiently at the tennis net, knowing that after the game, she'd be allowed to chase the balls. How I ever managed to convince the prestigious New South Wales Golf Club to allow her on the course remains a mystery but the manager took a shine to her, as most people inevitably did. She'd sit motionless on the tee. Sometimes I'd be totally engrossed in the game and realize she was 200 metres behind, patiently obeying the command to sit because I'd forgotten to call, "C'mon Tam."

Now deaf as a doornail, she still chased balls and stopped to literally smile at old people and young kids – or anyone else with the time and inclination. Even people who didn't like dogs loved Tam. She had a way of radiating it. Loving so unconditionally and asking for nothing except some food, water, walks and pats. We could learn a lot from dogs. She was always there for me – through my everyday ups and downs, my divorce, the discovery of my biological family, welcoming me home from hospital and now providing a silent sounding board for police issues. With my hectic travel schedule, I always worried that I wouldn't be there for her when she needed me most.

She always slept by the side of my bed. On 21 December 1995 I woke at 4 a.m. to find her sprawled in a puddle on the kitchen floor, whimpering just as she did the first night she came home as a puppy.

Life had come full circle sixteen years later and I knew the time had come. I lifted her back to the bedroom where she still couldn't stand and stroked her through the rest of the night until the vet surgery opened next morning. Joined by Liz and my Canadian flatmate, Lorinne, I held her as the vet peacefully put her to sleep for the last time. And, aged 122 in doggie years, Tam hopefully headed for some big kennel in the sky to retrieve tennis balls forever.

She'd been with me in my twenties, thirties and forties – from the time we ran marathons to the slow arthritic walks around the block. Unlike for my parents, at least I'd been there for her at the end and knew she'd lived a full life. I felt no guilt – a strangely comforting thought, even though it was the saddest day of the last twenty-two years.

I'd dreaded this day and knew it would hurt but had no idea it would hurt so badly. Now I was totally alone again. Although I had wonderful friends, I had no family and had enjoyed a longer continuous relationship with Tam than any other living creature.

As I picked up a tuft of golden hair from the carpet – the same hair that used to annoy me when it was deposited on dark business suits – I realized that her leash, ball, bowl and teddy bear were her only material possessions. She asked for little – but gave lots.

Christmas morning came. Predictably, Santa didn't. But as I opened a card from my flatmate, Lorinne, I realized that my time with Tam had, in itself, been a precious gift. Man's best friend had given this woman a lasting love to linger in my heart through many New Year's.

As 1996 started, and in the midst of the ongoing police board drama, my secretary encouraged me towards a more romantic sort of soap opera. I finally met up with the red-light man, over coffee. According to my diary, first impressions were of:

> a rugged outdoors type – funny, direct and refreshingly free from bs – unless I'm being totally conned. He's apparently lost a testicle to cancer but I'm not sure if he's sincere or simply wanting to test his remaining one. He makes me feel like a woman but am not sure I can totally trust him as a man.

Maybe the police board had honed a sixth sense of suspicion in me? Possibly overly suspicious?

There was something unnerving about the way his cell phone was often out of range. I had no home number for him and had only met one of his friends. He spent part of his time in Sydney and part in the country. In spite of his irregular visits, I was sure he wasn't married because I often saw him on Saturday nights. I'd also visited his property and helped him and his farm hands separate and count 1446 sheep travelling along the stock route.

Still, his unreliability caused consternation. Part of me felt he was honest and needed some breathing space because he was going through a difficult time with his health and his business. Another voice sensed he wasn't quite all he claimed to be. When I confronted him, he laughed and said an ex-girlfriend once sent him a card to thank him for making any future man look good! His laughter lightened my day. When he met me at the hairdresser's, he had the entire salon in stitches, asking if he was the cause of my grey hair.

"No, likely causing me to pull it out with frustration!"

"He makes me laugh," I'd protest to Liz, who had since moved in with her boyfriend, Alan. "Yes, but he also makes you cry," she replied.

I missed Liz as a flatmate and, with admittedly more than a little self-interest, didn't think Alan was good enough for her. I was wrong, in spite of his endless taunts that my love life was more entertaining than anything on TV. Friends seemed simultaneously appalled and enthralled with the saga of the red-light man. Would he or wouldn't he turn out to be the man of my dreams or would I allow his on again/off again presence to upset my equilibrium?

Mr. Red Light teasingly asked whether a picture of a man would ever replace the one of Tam in my wallet. "Only if I ever find one half as loving and loyal!" I replied.

He begged me to be patient, not my strong suit at the best of times, but at the time I was preoccupied enough in trying to separate fact from fiction with the police board — let alone do the same in my personal life.

I was now living with another man – purely on a platonic basis! A friend's younger brother-in-law had been transferred to Sydney and asked if he could stay for a couple of weeks. What would the neighbours think?

"They'll think you got lucky!" he cheekily replied. His two weeks turned to two years. My ex-husband was wrong. I wasn't impossible to live with after all, although I readily admit to being set in my ways.

I'd had no twenty-first birthday party the year my Dad died so I celebrated a different anniversary of twenty-one years Down Under. It was hardly a rebirth but did mark a new life in a new country. On Australia Day 1995, friends suitably dressed in T-shirts, stubbies (shorts) and thongs (footwear, not underwear!) enjoyed the sunshine on a glorious summer's day. I still marvel that Canadian summers are not unlike Australian winters!

By February, all hell had broken loose with the Royal Commission into Police Corruption interim report. I was fed up with the media chasing me, while I chased my tail in circles, devoid of persuasive power to convince fellow board members that we were a toothless tiger. History, dating as far back as the founding of the colony, suggested it would be naïve to ever contemplate the complete eradication of corruption. There was no doubt in my mind that the majority of police were honest. Nevertheless, the culture needed change. Frustrated with bureaucracy, there was nothing else I could do to change it from within the system so I decided to risk venturing beyond normal channels. If I wanted to sleep soundly, there was little choice but to break board solidarity and make a private submission to the royal commission.

Clandestine meetings followed and I steadfastly refused to speak to the media, knowing it would be a matter of days before I was asked to resign. I didn't wait to be asked and my actions were later vindicated, although I ended up forgoing blue-chip boards to focus on my fledgling business. It may not have been as glamorous and certainly not as lucrative, but at least I swam or sank by my own actions and not those of anyone else.

One of these days, I may write more about my time on the New South Wales police board during the height of the royal commission into corruption. This is not one of those days – nor will it be for many years. Possibly it's a project for my old age, which I intend to reach!

Would the red-light man be around for the journey or was he more of a con man than any criminal? Was he believable or maybe, like certain policing scenarios, do we simply believe what we want to believe, in spite of all evidence to the contrary?

30

ALMOST ON TOP OF THE WORLD

 With or without a partner, life was good and I was privileged to meet one of my childhood heroes, Sir Edmund Hillary, at his home in New Zealand. I stood in awe of this tall, well-built man, then well into his seventies, who still maintained a larger-than-life presence. What most impressed me was that this international icon, the first man to stand on top of the world, remained so down to earth.

"Just call me Ed," he encouraged.

I stammered, "Did you always visualize yourself as the first man to climb Mount Everest?"

"No," he replied. "Of course we had a goal. Tenzing [Norgay] and I weren't just tramping around and found ourselves at the summit but I didn't know I would make it because there were so many uncertainties. But what's the point of having a goal if you know you're going to make it? What's the challenge in that?"

I realized the wisdom behind his question – that we often don't set our personal goals high enough, settling instead for mediocrity. And, although most people have no desire to risk their lives climbing, we still face figurative mountains in everyday life, looming large overhead, those seemingly insurmountable barriers.

Around this time, I received a fax from mountaineer Michael Groom. One of his climbing partners, Tenzing's grandson, was interested in putting the first Australian female on top of Everest. Would I be interested? Would I be interested! It was the first thing that had interested me since Tam's death. However, I recognized that as important as it is to set high goals, it's equally vital to feel in a strong position to achieve them. I'd broken my sacrum (at the base of the spine) only eight months earlier and doubted whether I could attain the required fitness and finance soon enough.

My accident was one of those metaphorical mountains that I certainly hadn't expected but one that I nevertheless had to overcome, with the help of doctors and friends, who naturally made me the "butt" of many a joke. The most hilarious was one of my own making when still heavily medicated; I informed a puzzled health insurance call centre representative that I'd broken my scrotum – not my sacrum.

"Could I confirm your gender, please?"

In a brace for months, it was the second time in my life that I was lucky not to have been paralyzed. Only months earlier, Superman hero, Christopher Reeve, was less fortunate. A fraction of a centimetre's difference and I may have faced a similar fate but doubt I could have faced it with such courage as he did.

Ironically, my injury was not sustained during any risky recreation. In fact, I'd never even broken a fingernail bungee jumping, so was there a reason for plummeting down an innocuous set of stairs on my way to speak at a conference that morning?

> Risk is relevant and life is fickle. Nearly 600 people have reached the top of Everest while 100 have died trying. How

do such statistics compare with traffic deaths we seldom notice unless it's someone we know? Or the bombing in Oklahoma City, only a few weeks after the terrible gas massacre in a Tokyo subway – innocent civilians killed, simply on their way to work or working within the safe environs of a government office block while we had cycled over the Andes. What about innocent children in Zaire dying of cholera? Or those gunned down in Columbine or Dunblane? Or sleepy Port Arthur in Tasmania? Or sleepier Taber, Alberta where teenagers were shot at a school a stone's throw from where my biological grandmother first received my letter in the nursing home: "My, oh my, what is the world coming to?" Words I'd heard her and my parents utter in the past now passed my own lips.

I reluctantly reached the decision not to attempt the expedition after exchanging more faxes and speaking with the New Zealand expedition leader, Rob Hall. Everest is risky at the best of times and I intuitively didn't believe my odds of success on this occasion were good enough so we agreed on a training program for the next climb.

I was shocked and devastated to learn that Rob Hall and eleven others perished in a freak storm on Everest on 10 May 1996. John Krakaur recounted the tragic expedition in his book *Into Thin Air*.

Rob's last words were to his pregnant wife in New Zealand, from a mobile phone at the summit. Mountaineering technology has changed since Sir Edmund's ascent in 1953 but the determination of the individual to succeed against the unpredictability of the elements had not. Technology continues to embrace new frontiers and there are always those pioneers at the forefront of discovery. Later, speaking in Colorado with the chief of the US Mars space exploration program, I learned that less than fourteen months after that fateful climbing expedition, volcanoes three times the height of Everest had been discovered on Mars.

Two weeks after Rob Hall perished, I received a postcard he'd previously sent from base camp. As world media debated the pros and cons of commercial expeditions, I just looked at his simple signature on the card and wondered about fate and about how often we make mountains out of molehills, with relatively minor problems we encounter along the way in our everyday lives. Although my broken sacrum hurt like hell – whatever the hell, hell hurts like, it was only one such molehill. It truly had been a blessing in disguise and put everything at the police board into perspective.

After the Everest tragedy, I again ventured into the mountains, although in this case it was to ski *down* slopes in the Rockies on a crystal-clear day with my half-sister Vicky and my biological father, now in his seventies and facing his own challenge of prostate cancer. It was a bittersweet visit to Canada as I visited my "Auntie" Grace, Mum's best friend from primary school, who had helped me fill in many gaps of my mother's past. A woman with impeccable good taste in décor, she, together with Mum, had drummed into me that it was better to have one solid piece than many flimsy ones; the same could be said of our thoughts. Always appreciative of an aesthetic home environment myself, my heart went out to her as she now saw only the bare walls of the hospice room she inhabited, but never complained.

"I stopped getting the paper, Cath, as it was nothing but bad news. I only read it for the obituary column, or, as your Mum would say – the hatches, matches and dispatches of the classified column. Everyone I know, apart from my son's family, has already died."

It was hard to imagine Mum being that old but harder still to think I'd never see Grace again as she waved good-bye from the frosted window.

The next night, Auntie Kay and Uncle Frank ordered Chinese takeaway but when the deliveryman arrived, Kay asked: "What's the postman doing here at night?" It was the beginning of Alzheimer's, although at that time she was still well enough to laugh at herself. Her memory was going but her infectious laughter remains unforgettable.

My biological mother seemed to have memory loss of a different kind. Her sisters had piled into a van and driven 180 clicks to meet me for brunch. It seemed somewhat strange that she was absent as we all squeezed into a restaurant booth.

We chatted about nothing in particular until, over stacks of pancakes dripping with maple syrup, I was somewhat flattened to hear that the circumstances surrounding my adoption were almost as sticky – and certainly not quite as romantic as the version of snowflakes on the cradle my mother first told me. According to her sisters, my mother and partner had crossed the nearby US border where drinking and gambling laws were more liberal than conservative Canadian ones. Apparently, my elder half-sister and I were left asleep in a motel room while they chanced their hand. Another guest complained about the screaming brats on the other side of the paper-thin walls prevalent in 1950s motels and police turned us over to a welfare agency.

Certainly, there's a chance that the collective recall of my new-found aunts could be as confused as Auntie Kay's Alzheimer's – but I doubt it. All memories, including mine, become clouded amid the mist of time but remain always true in our own minds. At least my diary serves as a compass point in what could be a storm of contention. Nothing Trudy does or doesn't do surprises me anymore and I just accept her gratefully, for who she is.

We're all products of our past but don't need to remain slaves to it. Sometimes we're not even honest with ourselves. Maybe the only time we're truly honest is when we're alone, because we don't want to hurt others. Someone asks: "How are you?" We usually reply: "Fine, thanks," even if we're not. That's technically dishonest but preferable to those people (and we all know them!) who whenever you ask the question, burden you unnecessarily with their true feelings – usually ones of misery.

So, maybe honesty isn't the best policy. I've been told that I've been too honest for my own good – or the good of others. If more diplomatic, maybe we wouldn't hurt others, intentionally or otherwise, with words.

Whoever said that sticks and stones can break your bones but names will never hurt you surely wasn't on my playground. Certainly, some words, whether true or not, stick to our soul like peanut butter to the roof of our mouth.

Only universal truth travels without a passport. It criss-crosses cultures and countries like a finely woven tapestry of certainty. The only borders are frames of reference from which we view that truth because it moves not in a linear fashion from A to B but zigzags the course of our imagination like an imperfect time line. Our own version of truth is transitory as memories sidetrack in our mind. Like boulders alter the course of water in a river – so too rocks of consciousness detour the flow of truth.

Trudy and I lived in different worlds and with relief, I headed home to mine.

31

WAVES OF CHANGE

 The house wasn't quite the same without Tam in it and an apartment for a family unit of one would be more secure and suitable to my travelling lifestyle. Liz, Lorinne and I scattered Tam's ashes in Sydney Harbour. They felt more like porous pebbles as we loosened them from our grasp and watched them settling into the sand of her favourite swimming spot. I was about to settle elsewhere. It was time to move on.

A shift nearer the airport seemed sensible but after months of relentless real estate inspections in the eastern suburbs, I reclaimed a Saturday afternoon for a swim at Manly beach. I had no intention of living there as it was another bridge away from the airport but I noticed an open house that boasted uninterrupted ocean views (if one had a periscope placed outside the bathroom window!).

"We have another unit not yet on the market if you can wait until four," the realtor urged. I had no intention of doing so but returned to a flat battery in my car. By the time it recharged, I figured I might as well look at the unit. To my disappointment, it also lacked the promised view.

"If you can extend your budget further, there's another in this same building with a great view, but it needs a bit of work."

"No thanks."

"What do you have to lose since you're already here?"

Fair enough, I agreed, until he opened the door to green carpet, orange wallpaper, yellowish chandeliers and tattered drawn drapes. A bit of work indeed! Before I turned on my heels, he drew back the drapes to reveal a sparkling blue Pacific vista. In spite of the décor and distance from the airport, it just "felt" right. Maybe this was another journey on the serendipity road.

In my mind, I bought it on the spot but it took days to arrange the extra finance and negotiations continued as the realtor agreed to make the necessary renovations before I moved in. It was all too perfect – which should have been my first clue. In spite of constant telephone reassurances that everything was progressing nicely, the removalists and I arrived on the appointed day to discover the stove and dishwasher in the middle of the living room, and no electricity, water or toilet. Tradesmen swore at each other and us, while we collectively cursed the realtor. The movers stoically stored stuff in the garage. In spite of written confirmation that the phones would be installed, there were none for nine days. I lost the plot, screaming obscenities that could have made the tradesmen blush. It was not a good look for a motivational speaker, but neither was it a good thing that the customer service expert couldn't be contacted at my non-existent home office.

Millions live their entire life with no phone or running water so why should I stress over this? Or did our forebears feel similar stress when their plough broke?

I was not a happy camper. Then again, I had not expected to be camping on the tenth floor of a luxury apartment block! Nor did other residents appreciate the noise but the move and its associated chaos proved worth the effort when I met my elderly next-door neighbour, June, who was to become my next "honorary Mum."

Relocation is seldom smooth and until now I'd been too exhausted to enjoy the waves at my doorstep. On my way back from another trip to the hardware store, I popped into one of the many surf shops in Manly. It seemed I was invisible to the young sales assistant as I looked at the wide array of wetsuits available. When I beckoned, he reluctantly ambled over and asked, "Is it for your daughter?"

So much for building customer rapport! When told it was for me, he simply shrugged his shoulders and pointed at a rack. I left, none the wiser, but certainly bemused by the sign on the door: "Our normal hours are 10–5 but that's not always the case because if surf's up, we believe surfing comes first and everything else comes second."

So much for the customer coming first!

I hesitantly entered the next store, spotting yet another salesman young enough to be my son. This surfer lad might have looked like the stereotypical dude in the first shop, complete with blond ponytail, earring and dolphin tattoo, but had a totally different attitude and suggested I try on a wetsuit. Emerging from the fitting room, he thankfully didn't burst into fits of laughter.

By now, he'd surmised that I was new to the surf and conscious of both warmth and safety. He suggested that I buy flippers for more power while learning to bodysurf and then asked, "You don't want to lose them, do you?" An obvious question; I replied in the negative and found myself purchasing ankle straps.

As I was about to pay for these three purchases, he added, "You look like a fun sort of lady and we've got a sale on boogie boards."

I laughed and replied, "Thanks, but this upselling [of which he was a master] has gone too far."

But, guess who now owns a purple-and-yellow boogie board! Having spent a small fortune when I'd simply wanted a wetsuit, I handed him my credit card and jokingly asked, "So, what else does a middle-aged surfie chick need?"

With a cheeky grin, he replied, "A middle-aged surfie bloke!"

"Okay, I'll take one of those too! Do you have a father?"

About a year after I became comfortable on the boogie board, I upgraded to a surfboard and it doesn't take a rocket scientist to know which shop I returned to. On the far side of forty, I had the dubious distinction of being the oldest enrolled in the surf school. Having spent considerably more time in IBM blue suits than wetsuits, I was about to be taught some valuable business lessons by the surf culture.

Frustrated at my inability to catch a wave without being dumped mercilessly, I'd find myself out of control, churning around beneath the waves like a limp rag in a washing machine and finally struggling to the surface for a gasp of air before the next wave tossed me under again. In fact, it seemed a bit like my business. The harder I tried, the worse it got and I'd return to work feeling defeated rather than energized after a spell in the water. Maybe I should grow old gracefully, rather than try to turn surfing into a body contact sport, with my head buried in the sand.

What could I be doing wrong? I'd taken lessons, read a book, practised, watched others and technically knew exactly what to do. So why couldn't I surf?

Surely there comes a time when too much struggle only strangles. Pounding surf below reminds me that valuable energy is used to fight tides of turmoil beyond our power to control.

Whether surfing the waves or surfing the Net, it's wiser to know when enough is enough and go with the flow.

Going with the flow is not my natural instinct and the hardest lesson to learn was to wait patiently for just the right wave to suit my skill level. Patience is a word not often used in business and IBM encouraged us to go out and find new opportunities – not wait for them to come to us. I wasn't about to sit in the office and wait for the phone to ring but I realized that sometimes frantic activity makes no difference whatsoever to the bottom line because of circumstances beyond our control. Timing is everything in surfing, too, and catching a wave was impossible, until I got the timing right.

An average ride on a wave, like a schuss down a ski slope, lasts only seconds, so it's important to be immersed in those moments. Surfing gives us no choice and my mind was magnificently clear of any distractions – just the pure joy of that wave before even thinking about the next one. Balance is vital – as it is on land.

Surely, both work and surfing should be fun. Truth be known, the only water in which I truly felt at ease was a bath brimming with aromatherapy oil – one of life's little low-cost luxuries, guaranteed to soothe muscle and mind.

How many people never enjoy riding the waves of modest success and constantly fear an imaginary tidal wave of trouble about to drown them in depths of despair? Had I been one of those people? A life without positive energy is like an ocean without waves. A life without hope is like a seagull without wings. And, a life without joy is like surf without sound.

As for that middle-aged surfie bloke, I'm afraid the red-light man was still on the scene. I hadn't seen him in months so when we met for coffee, the attraction was stronger than a triple shot of espresso, almost addictive. He suggested we spend some time together during my next trip to Perth. He arrived at the airport without his luggage but certainly not without baggage!

On the return flight, we were assigned separate seats. The woman next to me sat down for the five-hour flight across the Nullarbor Desert to Sydney and gushed: "What a small world. My friend's husband is in 1C. Isn't that a coincidence?"

I would have told her I didn't believe in coincidence – that everything happens for a reason, but I nearly reached for one of those little airsickness bags, as nausea gripped my gut. If my client hadn't been seated in the row that separated me from this lying jerk, there could have been a mid-air incident. Or maybe I was too stunned to react after learning that his wife, like my seat companion, was a flight attendant. This explained why I'd sometimes see him on weekends. The flight seemed longer than a train trip I once took from Kalgoorlie to Sydney.

The woman in the window seat continued to gush about "six degrees of separation." The plot of the Hollywood blockbuster of the same name, directed by Australian Fred Schepisi, involves the premise that we're never separated from any other individual in the world by more than six people. With Australia's small population, I maintained it was more like 2.6 degrees of separation. Schepisi's father actually even lived in my apartment block and we'd met during my renovation debacle. But this in-flight drama was more like a bad soap opera than a great movie.

With outward calm worthy of an Oscar, I refrained from revealing what a bastard he was until we were out of earshot in the car in Sydney. Then I let him have it. He had the gall to blame me for blowing things out of proportion, claiming his marriage was only a piece of paper and I was ignoring his feelings. His feelings! What about my feelings? Or his wife's? I felt badly for her. He pleaded with me not to call and cause her hurt although I knew he was only protecting himself. So why didn't I expose him? I'd probably be doing her a favour but I didn't want to be the bearer of bad news, nor get involved. I just wanted to get out.

He continued to call, telling me I was unreasonable and should listen to my own words of advice and look at the positive. Although there were indeed many positives in my life, I was now convinced beyond reasonable doubt that he wasn't one of them! I couldn't stand any more lies and made it quite clear that if he continued to call, I'd phone some of my mates in the police.

Strangely, he was not even the true love of my life, but it still seemed as though someone had shoved my heart through a shredder and asked me to pick up the pieces. I knew I could. I'd previously pieced my life back together. Still, I was down in the dumps and what's more, still being dumped in the surf.

Emotions, like surf are sometimes gentle, sometimes turbulent. Maybe I should choose waves and men more carefully so I don't get dumped. And hurt. Waves lost their wonder and I wonder if I've always battled stronger forces, not unlike Canadian salmon, swimming upstream, chasing a dream. Or

> maybe Mum was right about lots of fish in the sea. Maybe she
> was right about a lot of things. Am finally settled after the
> move and threw out canned food with use-by dates over ten
> years old. Guess I'd kept them, "just in case." I don't make the
> bed before my early morning surf. A voice from the past
> argues with that logic. I can't hear her voice – only the words.
> I miss her voice and so wish I'd taped it. She'd worry about
> what people would think if there was an accident. And would
> I be wearing clean knickers? Actually, none at all with a wetsuit!

I'd bought into the red-light man's fraudulent fantasy of a
happy-ever-after romance – the knight in shining armour to
protect the "helpless female," rather than the strong, independent woman who, by necessity, was quite able to take
care of myself. He was morally bankrupt, but like all effective
liars, his lies contained an element of truth. He had indeed
lost a testicle to cancer. Then again, maybe, just maybe, he
was sincere and we'd meet again.

My diary noted that my biological mother also seemed to
live in her own sort of fantasyland, without even knowing
it, according to her sisters.

> Why do these two individuals impact my heart when I so des-
> perately seek truth in the meaning of life? It's pointless to be
> part of the lies anyone else lives – which, in essence, is living a
> lie myself. After all, I only want what my mother wanted when
> she fell pregnant – to love and be loved. Is that too much to
> ask?

Hadn't Liz and I just witnessed the wisdom of the Dalai
Lama first-hand as he addressed ten thousand and we left
determined to live more in harmony with what he termed
our authentic self? Did I need someone special in my life?

Or was it simply enough to believe that my life, like every life, was special?

Well-meaning friends lined me up with eligible men, but I remained heavy-hearted because of the red-light man – or was it because of myself? "Don't worry about the happy-ever-after romantic scenario. Just go out and have fun," Liz encouraged. "Just be yourself."

"Oh sure! That hasn't worked in the past!"

After so many blind dates, I felt the Guide Dogs Association might give me a pup! Of course, my travelling lifestyle wouldn't be fair to a four-legged friend. As always, I threw myself into work, pausing only momentarily as Mother's Day approached again.

It's 1996 and twenty-three years later, the image of Mum cling-ing to so-called life support won't disappear. Surely she hasn't been dead most of my life while the euthanasia debate remains alive and kicking. I hope to die like cycling champion Sir Hubert Opperman who, after ninety-two active years, had a heart attack on his exercise bike at home.

32

HELP OTHERS HELP THEMSELVES

 Wheels still spinning, I was thrilled to learn that *Good Service is Good Business* had become the number one best-selling business book in Australia. Less enthusiasm greeted the twice-yearly royalty cheque that arrived in the same post as the quarterly phone bill. The latter exceeded the former. I reminded myself that I didn't write for the money but the book provided valuable credibility on the speaking circuit.

> I dream of being a writer who speaks, rather than a speaker who writes, but my mortgage provides a dose of economic reality. So glad I finally got a low-maintenance, short haircut as calculated I spent over five days a year blowing the bob! Filed my nails and tax return.

Even though I'd been unsure of my footing with the red-light man, at least I knew where I stood on stage and thankfully, my clients valued me more than he ever had. One invited me to the 1996 Atlanta Olympics, although I doubted it would be as exciting as my first Olympics in Barcelona. But when former boxing champion Muhammad Ali lit the flame in Atlanta, I wondered if any opening ceremony could be more moving. He trembled with

Parkinson's Disease, another poignant reminder that even world champions are mortal.

Although I once earned a living from sport, I could never equate the hero label with sports stars. Call them champions, winners or role models. But they've done nothing heroic. Heroism is about saving or improving lives. Without wishing to detract from their extraordinary dedication and hard work, I think it's fair to say that sports stars initially make their choices for personal gain. But full marks to those who leverage their moment of glory to go on to be champions for a cause greater than themselves.

Wandering around the Sweet Auburn district of Atlanta, it seemed to me unlikely that even the fastest athlete could ever compete with Martin Luther King's track record on human rights. That's the stuff heroes are made of! It still seemed incomprehensible he'd been jailed for "trespassing" in a white store in the 1960s before his assassination in 1968. Six years later, his mother was murdered while playing the organ in Ebenezer Baptist church, where both his father and grandfather had preached. I now sat in those pews, listened to black gospel singers and wondered if the world could ever live in harmony. This was not ancient history but during my lifetime – although it seemed a lifetime ago that, as a teenager in Canada, I'd written a letter to the editor, outraged about King's tragic death.

Next night, at the Atlanta closing ceremony, I had goose bumps when the mayor of Sydney accepted the Olympic flag. Later, I partied with the team and organizing committee at a nearby fire hall. As dawn approached, even the staunchest Sydney advocate wondered whether we'd be able to match the southern charm experienced in Atlanta. After all, we were only a country of 20 million people.

I met many people from all walks of life, as I returned

home to the speaking circuit. Australian audiences are less given than American to standing ovations, but I was warmly embraced by diverse gatherings, from plumbers, public servants, pharmacists and farmers to teachers, travel agents, high-tech specialists and sporting teams. Miners, medicos and the military also held their tribal gatherings, as did retailers and reinsurers. Whether speaking to construction builders or wealth builders, to twelve in a bank boardroom or 6000 in a stadium, I never took for granted the privilege of the platform and remained amazed at the response. In fact, my words were little more than common sense.

In the course of my work, strangers confided in me as I discovered that circumstances are never quite what they seem on the surface. A transvestite said I'd helped her regain self-esteem and another woman announced she'd gained confidence to leave her controlling husband. I'd thought the former had a firm handshake and the latter a happy marriage. I had certainly never addressed issues of gender or relationships.

One day, the CEO of a major corporation called.

"Good to hear from you. How's things?"

"Fine," he replied.

"You don't sound your normal, upbeat self," I ventured.

"No, I guess not." His voice cracked: "My, uh, my father died this morning and I wanted to thank you for helping me resolve some issues with him."

I remembered I'd spoken of interviews when journalists asked what was the biggest mistake I'd made and I'd replied: "Not telling my folks I loved them when I had the chance." I guessed that's what he referred to but I still found it strange he would call me and chat for an hour, as we'd only once met briefly. I then realized he was the head of a corporation, eldest son and head of his own and extended family. It could be lonely at the top – always being strong for others.

> Grief inhabits every continent and every heart, from tragedies on the front page to obituaries buried in the columns of the classifieds – words that mean almost nothing, until it's someone who meant everything to us. No grief is ever greater than our own. Never. It matters not whether we've lost a premature baby or elderly parents, we've lost part of our past. Depending on our culture, we wail openly in the marketplace or muffle sobs in a downy pillow. When tears dry in a deep well of silence, grief still grips the heart.
>
> Time passes. Yet loss, that visa of vulnerability, lingers on lost horizons of hope and clouds our view of opportunity. No passport can stamp out sorrow. Grief travels through time zones and time eternal. It knows no geographic boundaries although it borders perilously on pain that won't budge. No train, boat or plane can transfer that pain. It won't go away – even if we do. Loss is never lost luggage, but baggage we carry forever, whether we show it or not. Anyone with no baggage simply hasn't travelled.

Naturally, I never confided to any of my clients about the red-light man. They hired me because they thought I was smart! Yet how dumb I must have been to let him linger like a skeleton in my closet of intimacy, especially when life remained rich in experience. Riding a Harley along the Great Ocean Road, go-carting at Coffs Harbour, walking barefoot over 1100°Fahrenheit coals in the Blue Mountains and rafting rapids in Bali – a wealth of priceless memories, all courtesy of the world's leading organizations. I supposed I must be doing something right, although it was hard to put my finger on what that something could be.

I met charismatic colleagues on the speaking circuit, too many to mention – plus, it must be said, some charlatans who believe the exaggerated claims in their own glossy brochures. Some talk so much and say so little. I didn't want to turn into one of those who think they make the world go round and spend their time going around the world to convince others that they're right.

I learned much from the association of professional speakers and attended their annual conference in the United States. It's a wonder anyone got a word in edgewise! Was I in danger of becoming an applause junkie? Even introducers received standing ovations. On one particular stage, egos were bigger than Texas and the outback combined, so I jested that my specialty was "How nuclear physics improved your sex life." Sadly, some people believed it!

Like any respectable business of the 1990s, it seemed imperative to have a mission statement. Mine became "helping others help themselves." Unlike some speakers who claim they're in the business of changing lives, that's not my job. I have enough trouble managing change in my own life!

Today, I don't see myself so much as a professional speaker but as a catalyst for change. I'm not in the business of changing lives – just hopefully changing thinking through encouragement via the written and spoken word. All I can do is to provide a little hope and direction, as I tailor presentations for organizations to maximize their human potential.

I may even mix a business message with a more touchy-feely personal one – along the lines that we can't always control change, but we can always control our attitude towards change in both our personal and professional lives; that we're all faced with the choice of being victims of change or victors over change. I've also discovered, and willingly admit, that it's easier to talk about than do! So I simply try as best I can to make my life worth living as my own living is being made.

I never watch daytime television but admire the Oprah Winfreys of this world and have no patience with those who want to pull down tall poppies of personal empowerment. I readily concede that positive thinking doesn't fix everything – but negative thinking doesn't fix anything. And optimism costs nothing.

Being self-employed meant I no longer had my annual IBM performance evaluations as a litmus test of my effectiveness. Audience feedback is fabulous – and valuable – but too often, it is filtered. Few are likely to be openly critical to your face but will happily share their opinion with anyone within earshot. That's why I occasionally ask friends to anonymously infiltrate audiences. Call it spying or market research, it allows me to absorb less flattering and more candid comments, in order to improve my delivery.

One day, a friend called to say she'd been at a function where I was not present. A stranger spontaneously stood up and told the assembled gathering that I'd changed her life. A lovely sentiment, although conversely it was sobering to know someone else might just as easily claim I'd ruined his or her life. That's why I take no responsibility for anyone else's life. All we can do is take total responsibility for our own. Maybe that's why I'd always been bemused by the irony of self-help *groups*.

People often ask how I avoid stage fright. I don't. After all these years, I'm still nervous prior to each performance. A certain fear of failure always lurks somewhere in the wings and the day I relax is the day I'll quit. It would signal a dangerous complacency. Certainly, my nerves are no longer frayed and frazzled because I thoroughly prepare each presentation. Yet my pulse always races as I'm being introduced. As I once heard many years ago: "It's fine to have butterflies in your stomach before speaking. Just make sure they're flying in formation when you open your mouth."

That's not to say things can't go wrong . . . There were embarrassing moments – like forgetting to turn off my lapel microphone while in the loo with pre-presentation nerves, so every sound clearly transmitted back to the ballroom. Or the many times it didn't work at all. Or changing clothes behind a screen onstage, only to discover that backlighting silhouetted me to the entire audience. Or hurriedly packing only to discover a thousand miles later that I'd brought two left shoes. Fortunately they were the same style and colour, so I jammed my feet in and focused on the audience, not the pain. Hey, the show must go on and I was being paid big bucks to be clever!

Apart from this one incident, I was surely a contender for the international packers' hall of fame, as I methodically checked the list on the back of my wardrobe door and again wheeled the suitcase to the taxi. Well, the world's best packer may have slipped a notch or two as I left my speech and computer cable behind. I was doing too much. Liz, as usual, came to the rescue and couriered the missing items.

Intuition should have warned me to decline an after-dinner gig at the Gold Coast where I was expected to entertain two hundred men who'd been golfing and drinking on a hot summer afternoon. Most conferences are legitimate learning events but this was just a junket and for tax reasons, the organizer insisted I speak for an hour. By the time I got on, it was nearly 10 p.m. and I'd be lucky to hold their interest for ten minutes. This was one instance where the customer was not always right, but he insisted and I was too inexperienced to find a way to say no nicely. Fifteen minutes proved tough going but I held their attention by a thread. Before the hour was up, the rowdy crowd shouted: "Show us your tits, love." Little did they know how close I came to doing so, as the clasp on my jacket had broken moments before I went on stage and was held precariously in place by duct tape.

I'd also like to forget the dead body in the hallway out-side room 2208 as I left, freshly showered, to address 600 in the conference centre below. Perhaps only 599 were in attendance? Or the time smoke billowed into the ballroom and a fire alarm sounded in the midst of an amusing anec-dote, the punchline for which will forever remain a mystery to the audience. Or the loonies who stalked me and prompted the move from a comfortable home office to a more secure commercial one.

Another time, I was part of a panel seated on a platform that had been constructed by pushing together various components of building blocks to make one stage. While being introduced, I shifted my seat slightly, and the chair leg slipped through the gap in the floor. I toppled off the 3-foot-high stage, my own legs flailing skyward. Picking myself up, I was relieved that neither my stockings nor ten-dons were torn. I had only incurred bruising to my legs and ego. The emcee continued with my introduction: "She's cycled over the Andes but can't seem to balance on a chair!" Like previous embarrassments, I shrugged and smiled but wanted to run and hide, never to be seen in public again. However, two minutes into the presentation, my focus was fully on the audience and pain forgotten until I limped home that evening.

By far the worst presentation was the one I never gave. My client was to pick me up from the hotel at 6:30 a.m. for a breakfast meeting. My usual practice is to set my alarm, plus request a wake-up call for good measure. That night, I discovered my alarm had broken but figured that even if the hotel forgot the wake-up call, the worst-case scenario would see my client wait a few minutes in the morning while I dressed. Not only did the hotel forget the wake-up call but when the client arrived, the receptionist told her I had not checked in. My professional credibility was in tatters and the organizer went on stress leave after telling the mayor, local media and two hundred delegates that the customer service guru hadn't shown up!

When my grainy passport photo started to look positively flattering compared to the image in the mirror, it was a wake-up call of a different sort. It was time to refocus on physical activity because I couldn't look after my customers if I didn't look after myself. Liz and I trained for a short triathlon and believe it or not, I felt distinctly better after the 500-metre swim, 20-kilometre cycle and 5-kilometre run than when I started. I was thrilled when she won in her age group, while somewhere near the back of the field, I staggered across the line, glad to simply finish.

However, I was soon on an airplane again for my first speaking engagement in Britain. Would I be accepted or dismissed as someone from the colonies, whether Canadian or Australian? I'd had similar doubts if humour would translate when speaking to Asian audiences. Doubt so often lingers needlessly in the shadows of our self-esteem.

I immediately felt connected to Scotland because of stories heard on my grandfather's knee. It mattered not that I didn't have an ounce of Scottish blood in me. The Gaelic culture had been indelibly tattooed on my heart – the only history I'd known.

I strolled through Festival Square, up the hill towards the castle on a glorious summer's day, feeling almost like a local.

The essence of Edinburgh spread before me like the red tartan rugs dotting the green grass where hundreds of office workers welcomed the sun – some eating food from the McDonald's clan of fast food! Nearby, Alexander Graham Bell's home stood as it had last century when he'd invented the telephone to communicate with his deaf wife. Could he have imagined the Internet cafés now sprouting up around the corner?

Communicating to the mostly male audience proved no worry. Bagpipes preceded my introduction and we danced the night away to the 1960s sound of The Searchers while I diplomatically refused any offers of a fling – Highland or otherwise!

I drove around Scotland with one of Liz's high school chums and then met up with one of my own friends from that era, whom I hadn't seen since university. Her son was now graduating from Oxford and we caught up on a quarter-century – how our lives had diverged in distant lands when she headed across the Atlantic to marry a delightful Irishman and I across the Pacific.

Anne's directness and sense of humour had remained intact and talk quickly bypassed the superficial. We discovered our perceptions of the past were as different as the directions we had headed. Before meeting in high school, we had attended junior high schools on opposite sides of the track. The same principal who told my class we would never amount to anything because we lived in that neighbourhood told her classmates they could achieve anything. She likewise despised the principal I adored. He told us we could rise above our circumstance. Yet she remembered only that he called them spoiled rich brats when he had been posted to her junior high school.

At high school, Anne had seen me as the outgoing sports star and I thought of her as the wealthy, popular sorority girl. Neither was quite so. The only given was our underlying insecurity as young women, which, like most teenagers, we were both desperate to hide. We must have succeeded to some degree. We now saw each other just as we were: a happily married housewife and mother and a single "career girl," with great, but not perfect lives. We'd headed in opposite directions, made different choices and faced different challenges but we still shared the same silly sense of humour, along with values that spanned oceans and time.

> We can do most anything we want but not everything we want. Like the English sky overhead, Anne and I now acknowledged more grey areas in our lives. Some once-close friends, even bridesmaids, live in different cities, and birthdays or Christmas greetings are the only remaining bond of a shared past in a busy present, now that wrinkles have eclipsed pimples.

My next stop was a short vacation in Prague, where I met up with a relatively *new* friend from Sydney; Kim, a divorcee, was travelling with her teenage daughter. Mesmerized by the only Eastern European city not bombed during World War II, we explored narrow cobblestone streets that echoed with buskers' renditions of Vivaldi and Mozart. Surrounded by sound, baroque and Gothic architecture of the tenth century, each building seemed a relic in its own right, somewhat like imagining Sydney with fifty or five hundred opera houses! Since the 1989 Velvet Revolution against Communism, capitalism flourished and gold jewellery, crystal, blown glass and paintings sold for a song along the historic Charles Bridge. I, of course, paid Czech crown cash because my singing was less than worthless but as we single women explored this romantic city, our bond of friendship strengthened.

At dinner one evening, we debated Australian politics. Over the entrée, we couldn't reconcile why voting remained compulsory in Australia, as it didn't seem truly "democratic." But, as we settled back to a serenade by a string quartet, it was unanimously agreed that we were lucky to live in a country that allows free political debate. Yes, Australia can, at times, be sexist or racist but it's still God's own country – and to keep it that way, we agreed on the need for our nation to re-examine its prejudices and strive for a more compassionate alignment in a multicultural society.

Conversation became more frivolous as we finished our meal below Prague's romantic fairytale castle on the hill bathed in a gold spotlight at night. We mused if there might be a fine line between being a citizen of the world or a gypsy. We spoke of past travels and Kim and I joined her daughter in teenage speculation about mythical, enchanted, happy-ever-after endings with handsome princes. We doubted that would be the case at our age, but within months, Kim met a marvellous Brit living in Washington, DC. They married two years later in the New South Wales town of Terrigal, proving that in this wide world of both cynicism and wonder, fairytales can come true.

Horror stories also abound in this life of fickle fate. Another friend, Wendy, was buried alive in the Thredbo landslide while, miraculously, a ski instructor was found alive – a further reminder (as if we need them) that life is too short. I put some frequent-flyer points to good use to surprise my friend Lois at her sixtieth birthday in Melbourne. My tennis doubles partner had recovered from cancer (if one ever fully recovers?). She was in remission and, like Kim, had also married a marvellous man late in life.

I'd been around the world more times than I could count but still didn't have a man in my life who I could count on. Then I met a rather nice accountant at a charity ball. "Nice": the kiss of death according to one friend. We seemed perfect for each other because he certainly needed more excitement in his life and I could probably do with a bit less in mine! I was fond of him but where was the passion? Why couldn't I have chemistry and caring; romance and reliability; humour and honesty? Like the red-light man, he offered only part of the ideal mix.

I confided this frustration over dinner to a male friend I'd known platonically for ten years. He reached across the table and squeezed my hand: "Don't worry, Cath. Do you think we could live together?"

"It might get a little crowded with your wife and kids!" I laughed. I'd always found him incredibly attractive but had learned my lesson about married men and was stunned by the seriousness of his question.

"You're a good friend. Let's forget this conversation took place." Yet it took all my strength to pull away from his embrace. How fickle could I be if one kiss aroused me so? Was it a test for my feelings for the accountant, ironically of the same name?

When the accountant and I broke up months later, I felt simultaneously sad, relieved and confused. He was a nice guy but there had been no chemistry. Liz claims that even if an atomic bomb went off, I'd say there was no chemistry – only physics!

I actually quite liked my own company. After an offer

from a publisher, I closeted myself away in Byron Bay to housesit for a friend. It seemed an ideal time and place to again attempt the story of finding my family, as I'd found out more about myself. To supplement the discipline of transferring thoughts from my diaries to a laptop, I fasted for eight days – cleansing my body and mind of toxins. It may have seemed a strange way to spend Christmas but this catharsis was a most welcome gift, as grief and guilt spilled onto the page. That's where it could stay.

I knew I had an unusual story but could I write about it? Number one best-selling novelist Bryce Courtenay heard my tale from the stage we shared at a conference. Afterwards, we held a book-signing along with the inspirational founder of the Starlight Foundation, Ian Kennedy. It was my first such signing and to my surprise, people bought my customer service books.

Bryce urged: "Write your life. Write it as you speak it. But do it."

His comments were welcome but finding the time and mental space was proving difficult; a well-worn writer's excuse. Instead I procrastinated.

How can I find my own voice when I can no longer hear the voices of my grandfather or parents? Is it because I am indeed tone-deaf? Or because the past is subconsciously silenced? Still, a soundtrack of my essence echoes in every Dutch or Scottish accent of total strangers.

I hadn't sung much since Mum died, not even in the privacy of the car or shower, but nevertheless believed that music is one of the strongest means of communication. I felt certain that song would enhance my presentations. Never one to do anything in half-measure, I enrolled in summer school at the National Institute of Dramatic Art – the same school that had honed Mel Gibson's stage presence.

The teacher assured us that no-one was tone-deaf. Even when I confessed to miming a goldfish in the Sunday school choir, she remained outright dismissive: "Rubbish, everyone can sing in key."

After a number of ear-piercing eight-hour days, she conceded: "Well, Cath, I still maintain you can sing in key. It's just a different key to the rest of the world!"

What key? My jaws seemed musically locked. No matter how hard I tried, much like my early days in the surf, I still couldn't sing in tune but at least I developed a chord of compassion for those who fear public speaking almost as much as death.

Although "musically challenged" all my life, I was paid to perform at the Sydney Opera House, strutting my stuff on the polished inlaid wooden floor in front of the silvery organ pipes. As I waited in the dressing-room, surely, I thought, that was any performer's dream? Dad, who forced me to listen to the New York Met Opera from Carnegie Hall fame, would have been proud. Fortunately for the audience, I was only speaking, not singing, on the stage of the magnificent concert hall beneath Sydney Harbour Bridge. Applause was enthusiastic but I've yet to hear any narrator attain the cries of "Bravo, bravo"; those throaty accolades were reserved for divas.

I figuratively sang for my supper across the country and knew I was in danger of hitting a sour note with such a gruelling schedule. One day, I spoke at breakfast in Sydney, lunch in Brisbane and dinner in Melbourne. Three cities, three flights, thousands of kilometres. Running on empty, fuelled only by adrenaline, I was exhausted by dessert. Could I maintain this pace? At what price?

Time runs out the door as I might for the next flight and as others do for a bus in this time-poor but opportunity-rich reality. From a standing ovation to standing alone at a taxi rank. Maybe I've left my sense of adventure and libido on some luggage carousel, circling in infinity. Maybe I've been around the world far too often – and no longer carry with me quite that same sense of awe and wonder. Surely whoever invented those little wheels on suitcases deserves a medal and it's a sure sign that I'm travelling too much when airplane food tastes great.

Middle-of-the-night calls from the United States contributed to this exhaustion as I began receiving inquiries to speak over there. Like a grizzly woken from hibernation, I'm less than motivational at 3 a.m. so when one organizer offered me four times my normal fee, I sleepily replied that I only charged a quarter that amount.

"Y'all can't be as good as I heard, for that price."

I lost the booking but still felt guilty to earn more in one hour on stage than my father did in a year on his feet, slaving over a hot stove – even accounting for inflation. Never mind some inflated egos on the speaking circuit. I questioned if I was worth that much. I also knew that worth should never be simply defined by wealth.

Many see speaking as money for jam, without appreciating the overheads of office, staff and technology. It's not quite as easy as it looks. We're not just paid for the actual time on stage but "intellectual property" and countless hours of preparation that precede each paid performance. It's not as if we're paid two hundred days a year. Inevitably, weeks pass without income and suddenly, two or more inquiries fall on the same date. One day, I had six bookings and had to turn down five – then there was none for two months. It's a feast or famine scenario, so solid financial planning is essential to avoid cash-flow starvation. Yet, as my grandfather's favourite Scottish poet, Robert Burns, would say: "The best laid schemes o' mice and men gang aft agley."

Events beyond our control can still change our world, as I was about to discover.

33

CANCER SCARE

 March 5, 1998, should have been a straightforward day. I was booked to speak to a small group of thirty south of Melbourne and the limo wasn't scheduled to pick me up until 10:30 a.m. I went for a gentle jog around Albert Park Lake, aware of five stitches in my leg where an innocuous mole had been removed. Grand Prix crews revved their deafening engines as I mentally fine-tuned my presentation. Maybe I'd include the fact that electrocardiograph tests show that racing car drivers record the highest stress levels not while risking their lives at 300 kilometres per hour, but at a pit stop. There, the crew has control over their vehicle. Maybe I'd mention that we all feel greatest stress when we're "in the pits" and sense we have no control. Or is control only an illusion at the best of times?

I showered and ate breakfast – all part of the normal morning routine. My cell phone rang and I rummaged in my handbag. The driver was likely early and waiting downstairs. I recognized neither the number nor the voice. It was a doctor, acting as a locum for my normal GP.

"We have the biopsy report and I'm afraid the news isn't good. The mole was a malignant melanoma."

"You're kidding."

What a ridiculous response. Doctors don't kid about malignant biopsies, but surely there was an error? Not the same mole that two doctors had assured me was nothing to worry about? Three months earlier on my insistence, my GP agreed to remove it for cosmetic reasons. We also agreed to wait till after surfing season when I'd be on a tour of Victoria, where I now was. I calmly made an appointment to see her as soon as I returned to Sydney.

When I hung up, it suddenly hit me. My plans for that day, and every day, changed in a moment. Melanoma. Wasn't that what Mum died of? Or was it myeloma? It was a long time ago but I now clearly pictured myself in her hospital bed, like a bad movie, as frail and as pained as she had been in her last moments. Didn't doctors also tell her not to worry? Tears welled in my eyes, a tsunami of fear, as I told myself: "Be calm. Stay centred, Cath. Don't allow this melanoma to become a melodrama. You've got to motivate people in a couple of hours and don't need puffy eyes to match your red jacket."

No matter how much I talked to myself, my heart heard nothing and I burst into tears. This wasn't on my "to do" list – not on my game plan or life plan.

I couldn't allow this cancer to be a crutch; couldn't allow fear to be a sickly shadow that forever followed me. I knew negative thoughts and worry can multiply as quickly as deadly white cells, if you let them. I told myself what I'd often told others: "Stay positive." Like many things, it was easier said than done.

I dressed hastily. Will I ever be able to wear stockings again or will the scar be too unsightly? Will the speaker's bureau ever again receive a fax from Europe: "Great legs and great message."

It was a vain thought when faced with the most deadly

form of skin cancer but if I hadn't been somewhat vain in the first place, the killer mole would still be spreading below my left knee. My mind tracked through a maze of negative scenarios and possibilities. Maybe it had spread to my lymph nodes, as it did with Mum. Could this tiny little mole explain why I'd been so tired lately? Could my visits to the chiropractor be related to the excruciating back pain that Mum had experienced with her cancer?

I'd parachuted, bungee-jumped and dived with sharks. Only now did I face true fear. I was afraid. Yes, very afraid. Afraid of dying. Afraid of bursting into tears during my presentation. I'd received rave reviews from this client all week and suddenly I feared I would fail the audience because of preoccupation with myself.

These thoughts would have to wait as the driver could wait no longer if I was to arrive on time. It's bad form for a speaker on customer service to be late!

Ari and I shook hands in the lobby and soon the car was headed over the Westgate Bridge. During the ninety-minute drive to Deakin University near Geelong, I applied make-up at red lights. As if my eyes weren't red enough, I confused lipliner with eyeliner!

Somewhat bemused, in an accent I couldn't initially identify, Ari asked: "So, what you do today that you make yourself so beautiful?"

"I'm speaking at a conference."

"What you talk about?"

"Sometimes, about customer service, sometimes about coping with change and sometimes about personal motivation and positive thinking."

"You are professor?"

"No, I'm an author and motivational speaker."

"We need much motivation in my country today,"

responded my chauffeur from the Middle East. "You must be smart woman if businessmen pay you money to do nothing but to talk about the positive thinking."

Before I could reply, the locum called again to say she had arranged an appointment with a specialist as soon as I returned to Sydney. "The melanoma is well advanced. We really shouldn't wait."

I burst into tears. Ari told me not to worry.

"It is in the hands of Allah."

I appreciated his concern but didn't want to talk about it. I had to refocus on what I would talk about during my presentation. Recomposed, I took a deep breath, straightened my shoulders and strode through the heavy glass doors of the Deakin University Management School where sunbeams streamed onto a floral arrangement in the foyer. I promptly burst into tears again. The phrase, "Take time to smell the roses" had suddenly come into sharp focus for me. It mattered not that they were orange and yellow gerberas.

I ducked into the loo to reapply my make-up, which was beginning to resemble a thick layer of putty, and debated whether to tell the emcee that the motivational speaker was a bit of a basket case. In case I lost my composure, he shouldn't have any surprises.

"No worries, love," he laughed. That's what the doctors had said. "I had one of those melanomas myself a few years back. Then a double bypass. And look at me now. Right as rain."

He hardly looked it, grossly overweight and with eyes as red as mine, but he buoyed my spirits considerably!

I relaxed only after the audience laughed at my first anecdote. Until then I was convinced no-one would find anything I said funny that day. Surprisingly, although I'd told the story hundreds of times, that time I laughed myself. I then completely forgot about me and for the next hour went on "autopilot" for them. A couple of times, I lost my train of thought. It's a wonder I didn't lose an entire railroad! No-one would have guessed I felt like I'd been hit by the proverbial freight train.

I was surprised to receive many 10/10 evaluations although I knew I hadn't delivered my best performance. Still, I gave it my best shot. Maybe that's all we can ever ask for? We don't always have 10 out of 10 days but we need to make the most of those 2 out of 10 days.

As we drove back to Melbourne where I'd first met Frank Jansen all those years ago, again I reminded myself of his philosophy, the words on my business card since I left IBM: *Every day above the ground is a good one.*

I called the speakers' bureau to request an earlier flight home and immediately regretted conveying the reason. They'd simply see me as a product whose use-by date was approaching, along with the termination of their commission. There would be little point booking me for a conference in six months' time, if I was dead.

In fact, they were most understanding, as was Ari when I burst into tears again a few kilometres down the road. He simply shook his head sympathetically and muttered: "You motivational speakers are very strange people."

Fair comment. My thoughts changed from rational to irrational as quickly as the traffic lights. Cancer knows no speed limits and discriminates against no-one. What if I hadn't insisted on removing the mole? What if it had been detected earlier? What if it spread? What if I could no longer spread my message that life isn't about what if – but what is?

"Listen to your own words, Cath."

Was I a hypocrite? What lesson was I meant to learn from this? I told myself it was only a temporary setback and everything would be okay. Was it only three months ago I'd consoled my bookkeeper who was diagnosed with lung cancer? Affectionately known as Liz 2, she'd been with me since I started my business and we'd become good friends. I was the one who insisted she go to the doctor to investigate her persistent cough. We hypochondriacs have our uses! Her positive attitude was an inspiration. Until then, I had not known her father had committed suicide when she was twelve. Does early adversity make one more able to appear strong?

In my mind I replayed my words of encouragement to myself but somehow the fear of the big C kept chewing the tape up. I knew my advice to Liz 2 was sound but it fell on my own deaf ears. I had too many dreams left unfinished and death wasn't on my "to do" list.

All my priorities changed. Like a Grand Prix driver, I felt in the pits when I had no control of my vehicle – my body. Would the wheels fall off? The worst thing about the drive and flight home was the absence of any knowledge but once back in Sydney, hours on the Internet at least gave me a better idea of what questions to ask the doctor.

During that midnight stocktake of my life, I asked a string of questions and wondered a hundred thoughts – some rational and most not. Surely, there was a mistake in the biopsy? Mum shouldn't have died of melanoma because she was never out in the sun and even on picnics at Banff, Lake Louise and Moraine Lake wore stockings. Yet she had. I couldn't possibly have inherited it, because I was adopted. Yet we'd both had malignant moles below our left knees. What was the cause? Was the furniture polish toxic? Or, the desire to please everyone – whether bottling preserves or emotions? Those questions could never be answered but I had many for my doctor.

A nearby friend, Kristine, whom I'd met in Atlanta, drove me to the hospital. During the initial consultation with the surgeon, I learned he was visiting Tokyo in a few weeks so I had brought along a copy of my book on Japan, which happened to still be at the foot of my bed. As I was being wheeled to the operating theatre on the next floor, a male nurse in the lift commented: "Coming or going?"

"Going," I replied.

"First time?"

"Yes."

"You'll love it," was his rather odd reply. "I lived there for six months."

"In the operating theatre?"

"No, in Japan."

So preoccupied, I'd forgotten about the book. I awoke from the anesthetic with a crashing headache, nausea and a sore backside where the skin graft had been taken for the leg. The surgeon described the graft as like a thin slice of smoked salmon. I felt more emotionally raw than any sushi.

Eleven days later, I was back on a plane to Melbourne where one of my favourite clients welcomed me with a huge bouquet of flowers to lift my spirits. Awkwardly manoeuvring on crutches, I finished exhausted and in pain. I thought of cancelling my onward journey to Perth and by the time I arrived, I wished I had. The leg was weeping, red and hot all the way to the ankle. I took antibiotics for the infection and hobbled onto a makeshift stage at the Rockingham sports centre. The pain stopped as the applause started and I lost myself in the crowd – so much in fact, that I momentarily forgot I was on crutches. Reverting to my normal animated style, I waved my arms, gesticulating to make a point and promptly tumbled off the stage into the front row, a sort of middle-aged mosh pit of business suits.

The surgeon kindly saw me as soon as I got back to Sydney on Sunday. When I saw the gaping hole in my leg the size of a concave tennis ball, I nearly fainted. The red-dish-yellowish tissue looked like a cauliflower splattered with blood and egg yolk. He assured me no damage had been done and I could fly out Monday morning for Korea. The eleven-hour flight was bearable as I had two seats to myself, but marinated eel for breakfast was not my cup of tea. Nor was the interrogation by security officials who scrutinized the crutches as potential weapons.

This was a landmark presentation since it was to IBM's top sales staff from the Asian region. It was a sort of home-coming but because some of these people had been my colleagues, I was more nervous than normal. The manager of my manager, whose lack of faith had once forced me to don a blonde wig as disguise when I first spoke all those years ago, was in the front row. I couldn't help myself: "At one stage, many in management would have gladly paid me to shut up. Now they pay me to speak. It's a marvellous transition!"

I caught the next night flight home without the luxury of a spare seat next to me. Instead, my inebriated seatmate woke me with his hand on my breast. With the flight as full as he, there was nowhere to move and more time to think.

Where does time go? How will I know if I spend it wisely? How much more will I have to spend? My melanoma was level 4 on a scale of 1 to 5 – and 5 is deadly. My balance sheet is healthy enough but not nearly as important as my own health. What future moments will pay the greatest dividends professionally and personally? Am I touching lives or losing touch with mine? Am I really making a difference or just busy being busy?

Now was the time to slow down a little. With my schedule still on fast forward, I wasn't sure that was desirable, or even possible. I met all existing commitments but declined new bookings to give myself the best chance of a full recovery. Instead of power-dressing, I was power-sleeping and soon power-limping along the beach – boosting my body like a recharger does the cell phone. How wonderful to again wiggle my toes in the soft sand.

A routine pap smear tested negative; something I once took for granted was the highlight of my week. No doubt my mood was also enhanced by the all-clear on the mammogram and a radiographer who told me not to worry as she'd had a malignant melanoma sixteen years earlier. People were so kind as I exposed my own vulnerability, no longer under the illusion of total control.

After I'd spoken at a Red Cross charity function in Wollongong, the organizer gave me a hug: "You'll get your reward in heaven."

"Thanks, but I'm not nearly ready to accept it!" My cancer scare had made me realize that I largely led a life of heaven here on earth.

The surgeon and oncologist were wonderful and I felt confident that modern medicine had progressed substantially since Mum had died. But rather than rely solely on conventional medicine, I added more affirmations to my bathroom mirror and also incorporated more holistic, alternative therapies: acupuncture, meditation, Chinese herbs, organic foods.

I even abstained from chocolate – just in case. It was easy to see why sick and desperate people search out snake oil salesmen and women who promise a cure. I'd have stood naked in Times Square, balancing an organic pineapple on my nose, if I thought it would cure the curse of cancer. Instead, I visited a psychic closer to home, after a friend claimed that her deceased mother would visit and sit on the edge of her bed and chat. "Just be open to it," she urged. I tried but found I was only talking to myself.

I also attended a group workshop. Within two hours of arrival, I was admittedly judgmental as others revealed horror stories of their past. Whether abused or adored as a child, an executive or an ex-con, married or divorced, seventeen or seventy, male or female, gay or straight, a drug junkie or success addict, it initially seemed we had nothing in common. Yet, we had everything in common – similar inner fears, doubts and hopes, expressed and repressed differently.

Over the weekend, the leader suggested that just as some people hide behind drugs, alcohol or abusive relationships, maybe I hid behind achievement. Maybe I was addicted to it? Maybe, but if his theory about hiding behind achievement was valid, so be it. He added that perhaps I should have obtained professional help earlier.

Perhaps. After refusing any counselling when my folks died, I sought marriage guidance in Melbourne when our marriage was on the rocks. When Tim refused to attend the second visit, I found the next three or four sessions quite therapeutic and surprised myself by talking about my parents more than my husband. The psychologist reaffirmed that I wasn't experiencing anything unusual, given the circumstances. When I was transferred to Sydney months later, doubts reappeared and I made a visit to another psychologist. He said the same. Much relieved, I called Liz: "Thank goodness, I'm normal."

"We want a second opinion," she laughed.

"That *was* a second opinion!"

Only a handful of close friends can see through us – and see us through tough times. Still kindness is of many kinds, from kin, near-kin or the kindred spirit of total strangers.

There must be a softer, more socially acceptable word than addict but I can't think of it. Might I have an addictive personality? When I start something, I'm reluctant to stop. There's a fine line between persistence and stubbornness and I'm sometimes on the wrong side of it. We all have our demons and fortuitously, mine are more socially acceptable than most.

Life is too short to eat carob. I didn't sign up for subsequent workshops. I did, however, resume eating chocolate, become somewhat more tolerant and mellow, but constantly have to remind myself to stress less and keep things more in perspective.

Sure, I'd still stress out when the computer crashed, the photocopier jammed or the Internet connection was down. Constantly confronted by a tyranny of technology, my increasing dependence on machines made me apprehensive. During hospitalization, I'd become addicted to computer games – which have since been permanently deleted from my PC. Life is far too short to waste time that way.

As two, noisy, bickering expat brats kicked the back of my seat halfway across the Pacific on the way to another speaking engagement, I practised meditation but after three hours, it became apparent that we'd reach our distant destination long before I arrived at inner peace!

By the time we approached Vancouver in a thunderstorm, the entire plane had joined me in meditation (or was it prayer?) when the pilot announced that there was a problem with the landing gear and that we would need to dump fuel at sea.

34

COUNTRIES OF CONTRAST

I'd been invited to speak in Canada for the first time. As I filled in the date on the customs declaration form, it struck me like a bolt of lightning – maybe the same one that narrowly missed the plane. It was 7 May 1998, exactly twenty-five years to the day since Mum died. Back then, I had slept on a yellow lounge in a bleak sterile hospital room, as low and frightened as I could remember. A quarter of a century later, a stretch limo dropped me at a five-star waterfront hotel with a king-sized bed as wide as it was long. Was this the same country I had run away from? I'd just been in hospital with what killed Mum. Where would I be in another twenty-five years? It's hard to imagine what life will hold as we have such a tentative hold on life itself.

On this late spring day, snow sparkled atop surrounding mountain peaks and any lingering melancholy melted in a moment as a helicopter prepared to lift off the pontoon and head towards nearby Whistler Mountain. Along with the organizers of the International Year of the Oceans Conference and Jean-Michel Cousteau, I nervously buckled my safety belt, and remarked jovially to the pilot: "It's great to see a woman in control. What prompted you to pursue such an unusual career choice for a female?"

"My eyesight was too bad for the air force," she replied without a hint of a smile.

As we awaited clearance for take-off, the air traffic controller's voice came over the radio. "How many passengers aboard?"

Her reply engendered even less confidence.

"About five."

About five? I would have preferred a bit more precision. Undoubtedly a competent pilot, but somewhat lacking in social graces, she asked Cousteau if he was interested in marine life. "A leetle," he dryly replied in his French accent. Apart from the pilot, everyone laughed. Oblivious, she pointed out the aquarium below, as Cousteau guffawed: "Nothing but jails for whales." He was right, but by the same token, few people in the world had experienced the privilege to see marine animals in their natural habitat, as he had done with his world-famous father. As advisory board members of Oceans Blue, an organization committed to cleaning up the harbours of the world's major cities, we debated the merits of zoos and aquariums. Surely they helped educate millions to the wonders of nature?

It was the second anniversary of Rob Hall's tragic death on Everest, and as I lay awake, jet-lagged in bed, I thought of Sir Edmund Hillary and Jacques Cousteau, both international legends. How hard it must be for their sons to follow in their footsteps, to live up to the expectations of others. The only expectations placed on me were of my own making.

Over those few days I experienced a different Vancouver than when I first married and lived there eighteen years earlier. Had the city changed or only my observations of it? In my room, I read the morning edition of the *Globe and Mail*, not quite sure why a Toronto paper was delivered to a

Vancouver hotel. It made little difference because I hardly recognized any of the players in the political, social or ice hockey arena. I was a foreigner in my country of birth – but strangely, no longer a stranger to difference.

> Only mountain peaks remain the same. Even the national anthem has changed. No longer my "true north strong and free" I rejoice in "nature's gifts of beauty rich and rare," the lyrics of Australia's anthem equally true to Canada. Like night and day, these two Commonwealths of contrast are ironically alike; built on rural pioneering foundations, romanticized by we urban-dwellers. Large empty land masses and small populations, wealthy in natural resources and racked by natural disaster. Opposite but similar landscapes in the terrain, temperature and temperament of those who dwell within. Fans of the sports we excel at and champions of the underdog, we receive relatively little media coverage beyond our own borders.
>
> We don't really know much about each other, but we like each other. Maybe that's because we've emerged from the parental shadows of the UK and US that have dominated our export of goods and talent. We now share an optimistic outlook for more independent futures, growing up on the global stage.

A cruise ship took delegates from Vancouver to Alaska. Tough work but someone has to do it! And why shouldn't it be me? In Skagway, far from the tourist trail, I came across a little library. I've always found buildings with books to be barometers of a cultural climate. The librarian proudly produced a volume of local Eskimo artists and the image on the jacket cover was almost indistinguishable from one I had seen most days of my life. A lone ice fisherman and sled dog team were likewise etched on a piece of sealskin the size of a mouse pad that my father had acquired when stationed in Alaska during the war. I had no inkling that George A. Angupuk was one of the first Eskimo artists to gain international acclaim, somewhat akin to Aboriginal artist, Albert Namatjira.

That primitive, yet haunting, black, white and grey landscape of the Eskimo hunter in a harsh environment hangs in my climate-controlled living room today. I value it no more or less than before I learned its commercial worth, because its monetary value is irrelevant to me. What is important is the connection it holds: to my own past and to my father. I wonder if Dad knew much about the Eskimo artist or, like most of us untrained in art appreciation, just knew what he liked? If only I'd spoken to him about his time in Alaska.

I was apprehensive about my first presentation in the United States the next week. To me, it was the Everest of speaking engagements and I feared I could take a tumble but thankfully, employees of the information technology company in Colorado were wonderful and welcoming.

So, too, were my hosts in India a few weeks later where warmth took on a different dimension. The thermometer topped over 47°Celsius and frequent electricity blackouts rendered air-conditioning useless. The extra generators in the hotel provided relative comfort and only partial power losses, affectionately termed "brownouts." One seminar attendee philosophized: "You can't experience the light without the blackouts."

Neighbouring Pakistan had recently exploded a nuclear bomb and I'd been advised not to visit its arch-enemy, India. Although apprehensive, I would be nowhere near the border and easily explored Bombay, now Mumbai, with New Zealand cricket captain Mark Greatbatch, who I'd met when we changed planes in Singapore.

Maybe it was his presence in a country where cricket is as sacred as the cows that roam the streets, but I felt less confronted than on my previous visit to the subcontinent. India is a country of contrasts. The largest democracy in the world, it is home to both abject poverty and more millionaires than the entire population of Australia.

Some of them sat in my audience – men in dark Armani suits and women in bright saris interwoven with gold thread. In a nation where captains of industry employ yogis and swamis to inspire their management team, it was rather remarkable to be treated as an Australian management guru. My most able agent also obtained a contract for me to become a columnist with *The Hindu* newspaper.

There were non-stop media interviews and splendid dining in high-security compounds in Chennai (Madras) and Bangalore, although the Delhi tour was cancelled because of the heat, which had now killed thousands.

I left India with a book written by a swami and signed by the entire audience. Most Australian audiences were still somewhat wary of any symposium of a remotely "touchy-feely" nature but in India, spirituality sat easily with other contributors to the success of a business. People couldn't have been kinder in sharing their different perspectives. While we in Western society look up to those with more material possessions and feel somewhat lacking or envious of wealth or status, Hindus look down to those less fortunate and feel grateful for what they do indeed have, rather than wish for more. Behind a group of dilapidated tin-roofed shacks, a billboard for a bank blazed: *Find purpose – the means will follow.*

I arrived back just in time for Liz's birthday celebrations in the crisp, cool, clean air of the Blue Mountains. As ten of us swapped travel stories over a sumptuous Christmas in July dinner, my room was ransacked and everything stolen – phone, wallet, keys, camera, even my undies. I was only upset about losing the ring that Granddad gave me before he died. The rest of the gold and diamond jewellery were only bits of metal and rocks as far as I was concerned.

The next day, I got the all-clear from my cancer checkup. Some twelve months after the operation I was free from the disease. To h . . . with the burglary! With a clean bill of health, little else matters! I treated myself to a large chocolate milkshake and on the long drive home from the hospital decided to be more excessive and sell some shares to buy a Mercedes sports car. The sick people in the waiting room were a reminder that you couldn't take it with you.

My parents never even owned a car and I felt this was somewhat "beyond my station in life," as Mum would say. Then again, I felt it could be justified – not that I needed to justify it to anyone but myself. Besides, I saw many more Mercs in Mumbai than in Manly!

Why does guilt cling like Gladwrap to us women? Was that why when asked what sort of car I drove, I'd initially reply "a black one"? And then steer conversation away from the prestigious brand I'd coveted by adding: "It's a nuisance to keep clean."

A few weeks later, straight from the car wash, my shiny black car with the tinted windows, low-profile racing wheels and dual exhaust conveyed my friend Kristine's son, Iain, and his date to their first prom. I was their make-believe chauffeur – although someone commented that I looked more like a misguided drug dealer.

Since I'd met Iain's mother, Kristine, in Atlanta, not only was a friendship evolving between us, but I'd also become extremely fond of her only child. He was growing into a fine young man who somehow managed to converse easily with adults and bypass the monosyllabic grunting stage of most males that age. I occasionally hired him to do some database entry or join the group of seventy-year-old neighbours around my dining-room table, as we manually wrote, addressed, stuffed and stamped thousands of Christmas cards in assembly-line fashion. In spite of the age difference, our unlikely bunch shared a similar sense of humour and lively debate on topical issues.

Iain's youthful insight impressed me and gently helped open my eyes to issues and ideas of another generation. He was far wiser and worldlier than I was at his age, but at times just as foolish and reckless and we had a couple of conversations about youthful misdemeanours. I gradually realized that my self-centred youth had been pretty normal, but I just never reached the stage where I could make amends and become friends with my parents. It was something that I had silently punished myself for all these years, since Mum and Dad were no longer around to fulfil that role. Now, it seemed the melanoma and long-lingering guilt had been removed around the same time, both somewhat belatedly.

I'd just arrived at a Melbourne Cup client breakfast, thinking how much Mum disliked horses but would have loved any excuse to wear one of her feathered hats, when Iain's grandmother phoned to say he'd had a skateboard accident and was in a coma.

Sensing that Kristine, a single mum, needed support, I didn't hesitate to tell the intensive care staff that I was next of kin; didn't have time to feel guilty about an outright lie; didn't even think that the last time I saw anyone on life support was when Mum died. I couldn't begin to imagine how my friend, as a mother, must feel. I'd never been a parent and, apart from my folks, couldn't remember feeling so helpless about a possible loss of life – willing Iain to live with every ounce of stubborn strength I possessed. I'd always felt a strong connection with Iain, maybe because I knew what it was like to be an only child in a world of adults.

He lay unconscious with a punctured lung, broken arm and unknown head injuries. A nurse at each end of the bed monitored his heart rate and other vital signs. His mother and grandmother reluctantly left for a quick cup of coffee after their all-night vigil. Carefully avoiding the intravenous drip, I tentatively held his hand, an action that would have undoubtedly horrified him had he been conscious.

I'd read somewhere that people in a coma may be able to hear, even if they show no visible signs of response. I had my doubts but felt totally useless just sitting there so figured it couldn't do any harm. Even if this subliminal stuff worked, I wasn't quite sure what to say to a sixteen-year-old in a coma. This wasn't my normal gig.

I'd never talked down to him as some adults once had to me and wasn't about to start now. I whispered how much I valued him as a person in his own right – not just as my friend's son, nor an employee. I probably babbled on about what we'd do when he woke; how much I needed him to finish the mail-out; that I'd give him a raise. Or maybe I mentioned that he was as musically gifted as I was challenged and I appreciated his introducing me to the songs of

Savage Garden and the technology of PowerPoint. This was well and truly outside my scope of motivational presentations but possibly, just possibly, the most important one I'd ever deliver.

The nurse at the bottom of the bed glanced up at the ECG monitor and quickly moved to take his pulse.

"I have no idea what you just said but this is the first time there's been a change in his heartbeat."

Frankly, I had no idea either. His mother came back in, still as white as the sheets and I promised to return in the morning.

On my way to the hospital the next day, I met a delegate from the previous week's conference and was unnerved to learn her younger brother had been killed in a skateboard accident in South Africa many years earlier. I hadn't meant to re-open her pain but she openly shared what had been of comfort to her parents at that time.

The thoughtfulness of total strangers can be strangely reassuring at times. I was touched, like I had been three months earlier when an overzealous New Zealand ski patrol suspected I'd incurred a spinal injury and insisted I be flown off the peak by helicopter. My friend returned in the bus that had driven us there and the driver visited me in hospital on his day off. That was my last time in Emergency and as I continued to the hospital, I had a calm sense that Iain would be okay.

By the time I arrived, he'd been transferred from intensive care to pediatrics. His loving but extremely straitlaced grandmother greeted me accusingly: "You'll be pleased to know that when he came out of the coma, his first word was 'shit.'"

Apparently, that's what I'd said when she first called me. Profanity is quite common after regaining consciousness but since she'd never heard him swear before, she remained convinced that I was surely the bad influence. My Presbyterian grandfather and parents likewise would have been appalled. Their life was one of struggle but also of grace and dignity and I never once heard a blasphemy in our home. I, on the other hand, have used some words that would make my mother blush – and hopefully more that would make her proud.

35

DIFFERENT TRACKS
AND TRUTHS

 Although I'd resumed writing my story, its telling revealed more gaps in knowledge of my new-found family. Another speaking engagement in California provided a chance to head north to Canada once again.

I first visited our old next-door neighbour and as we chatted in the garden, the current owner of my childhood home invited us in. Although much the same from the out-side, it was little more than a run-down shell of a building. My folks would turn in their graves if they knew it had housed a brothel in recent years. No nostalgia lingered. Not only was my childhood home empty of anything and any-one important to me but also it seemed to have shrunk over the years, as we do with age.

South another 200 kilometres, silos dotted the flat prairie and the bright yellow line in the centre of the highway was as vivid as the alfalfa fields either side. Two hours later, I pulled into the gravel driveway of my biological father's bun-galow. It was great to see Harold and Pearl with fewer visible signs of ageing than those of my childhood home. But my visit had another purpose. I wanted to ask my birth mother to clarify the circumstances of my adoption. I admittedly pre-ferred her first rather romantic version of snowflakes on my cradle but didn't mind if her sisters' more austere account of being left in a Montana motel room was closer to the truth. It made no difference to who I am today.

Who was telling the truth? My mother or her sisters? Frankly, I doubted the sisters would know anyway. I was likewise uncertain how to broach the subject with Trudy. Still uncomfortable together, mother and daughter sat awkwardly on the well-worn brown velour sofa and flicked through old scrapbooks. As photographs helped break the ice that had again settled since our first meeting over ten years earlier, I pieced together a picture of her past. Rather than a crisp, clear snapshot of the woman who had given me life, it was still somewhat blurry.

"You were very pretty," I commented as she showed me a grainy image taken by one of the many photographers that positioned themselves on Calgary street corners in the early 1950s. After the war years, many families still did not own a household camera.

"You think so? Uh, well, uh, thanks . . . ." Her voice drifted off. "That was before I had any children and troubles."

I waited silently, thinking she might open up to tell me of the specifics of those children and those troubles.

"It was taken outside the Hillhurst coffee shop, where I used to work as a waitress."

The Hillhurst coffee shop? It couldn't be the same one I thought it was – just over the Louise Bridge on the other side of the Bow River. "My Dad used to own one near there!" I exclaimed. "Was it next door to a barber shop run by Joe and Addie Ireland?"

In another coincidence I still can't comprehend, she replied: "Yes, there was a barber next door but I don't recall their name. They were English, I think."

For a split second, I wondered: had I met my birth mother as a child? I hadn't thought of Mr. and Mrs. Ireland for years but I remember my four-year-old curiosity had led to laughter when I'd once asked why they, like my grandparents, talked about coming from "The Old Country" but they didn't speak the same way. Of course, Cockneys sound nothing like Scots – and more adult mirth followed when I asked why they weren't called Mr. and Mrs. England – instead of Ireland. Strange, how this all came back.

"I used to get in trouble for spinning around on the bar stools." They encircled the old-fashioned soda fountain-like counter, while half a dozen dining booths sat off to the right.

As if we both sat in a time warp there, Trudy replied, "They were bright red leather."

"Yes, yes they were!"

They were more likely red vinyl. And, of course, there was no link between my adoptive parents and my birth mother because Dad bought the coffee shop about a decade after Trudy had worked there.

"Well, what a small world," she sighed. "Isn't it funny we both remembered the red stools? I hadn't thought about them for years."

"Me neither." I gathered the courage to ask her what she remembered about the first few months of my life. I didn't want to confront her with her sisters' version of events.

"It's bizarre that we clearly recollect an ordinary coffee shop layout over forty years ago but I couldn't tell you where I ate last week. You know, I'm writing a book about finding you all. But it was such a surprise to me at the time that I'm not sure I correctly recall everything you told me when we first met."

"Yes, it was a surprise to me too when we met! But, you know, all those years, I never stopped wondering what had happened to you."

I had no doubt that much was true. But had we been parted due to snowflakes on the cradle or the thin walls of a Montana motel room? It wasn't important which version was true but being truthful was important. I sat stunned like a coyote or a kangaroo caught in the headlights of a car, as she drifted into yet another account: "In those days, it was very hard for an unwed mother, especially in a small town."

I was certain that, too, was true and could only imagine and empathize how tough it must have been for her.

"There was no welfare back then and my sisters had sort of disowned me so I went up to Calgary to find work. During the day, I left you and your [half] sister with two women in daycare. They boiled the diapers in a big copper pot and scrubbed them on an old-fashioned wooden scrub board, so I knew you were well looked after. One day I went to pick you both up after work and you were gone. Just gone . . . Someone from the government came and took you away . . . No-one would tell me where you were. They just kind of stole my baby."

Trying to hide my amazement and sound non-judgmental, I asked: "How did 'they' know where we were?" After some hesitation, she replied: "Oh, they tricked me in hospital a few months earlier and must have come looking for me. Your father wanted to marry me but didn't want your sister. They didn't take her."

I didn't have the heart to challenge her further but knew in my heart she was kidding herself and likely didn't even realize it.

"In those days, no-one cared about a single mother and wouldn't give me any information. Yeah, they just stole you away."

I could hardly believe my ears. Had she forgotten what

she had first told me about the snowflakes on the cradle? Now, was I part of the stolen generation – a debate raging about Indigenous people an ocean away.

I was relieved when we arrived at Trudy's youngest daughter's for dinner. I had liked Debbie from the day we met, in spite of the friction surrounding the fact that our mother hadn't told her and my other siblings that the stranger at dinner all those years ago was a long-lost sister.

This was the first time we'd been together since then, and we were joined by two of Trudy's sisters. The atmosphere was markedly more relaxed than that first dinner and I wasn't about to say a word about this latest revelation. Observing lots of laughter amongst an obviously close-knit family, I wondered if they knew the sadder truth about Trudy's past. Did I want to tell them? And others? That's what I'd be doing if I finished the book. I'd done my best to search for the truth but maybe I'd never find it. I didn't want to write anything to hurt anyone but I would harm my own integrity if I altered the truth about my life – as I know it.

My biological father claims he never proposed to Trudy but was about to be engaged to his now wife by the time he heard about my existence. Who knows? Who cares? I guess I'll never know the truth. God knows, I've tried to discover it but it seems that different people with different memories reveal different truths. It doesn't much matter now, as long as I tell my own truth. Whatever I write, someone will challenge. I can only write, as best I can, what I believe to be the most true. That, itself, is enough of a challenge. My memory may not be the best but the reliability of my diary and family correspondence has helped sift fact from fiction.

I mulled this over and, before finally sedated by sleep, scrawled in my diary:

I feel more at home in a foreign hotel room than under the roof of my family. With now over ninety nights on the road, no wonder friends tease me about "sleeping around." Unfairly, I might add, in the colloquial sense.

Before I left, a friend admitted feeling jealous of my lifestyle: "You're lucky to be able to flit off when you want, without having to answer to anyone. I'm stuck at home with two teenagers."

We'd made quite different choices and yet, I often looked forward to heading home more than most people relish the thought of a trip.

36

MID-LIFE OPPORTUNITIES

 I was gradually being booked to speak overseas, purely through word of mouth. The stretch limo whisked me to the Washington Hilton, where a bellboy showed me into a palatial four-room suite big enough for the entourage I've never had! He proudly proclaimed that President Ronald Reagan had been shot on the very spot where I'd just alighted. This was more information than I needed, especially since it seemed I'd lost nearly as much blood in the last twenty-four hours. After no menstrual period since my operation, I was almost hemorrhaging. It was probably nothing more sinister than the beginnings of the menopause but fear of cancer still lingered in the wings while I did a hurried sound check amid a sea of Stars and Stripes and red, white and blue balloons before George W. Bush's security team invaded the ballroom to prepare for his presidential campaign speech.

Retreating to my room, I spent most of the night in the bathroom, afraid my highest-profile and highest-paid presentation to date would be a bloody disaster, so to speak. Thankfully, I felt better before I took to the stage with George Stephanopoulos, President Bill Clinton's former adviser. After the book-signing I was still writing – in my diary:

> Write your own destiny and autograph your dreams. I don't
> have time for menopause . . . and precious little time to even
> pause. Nor can I comprehend contemporaries who worry
> about a mid-life crisis. This must be my mid-life opportunity.
> There's still many on the horizon so why lament those lost
> along the way? If born in some undeveloped countries, with an
> average life expectancy of thirty-seven, we baby boomers
> wouldn't be around to give a second thought to the so-called
> mid-life crisis.

Next stop was Kansas City where I was warmly greeted by the team of a prominent speaking bureau, who acted for a short time as my exclusive agent in the United States. Although I never did get any work from them, this visit to the Midwest hometown of President Harry Truman was a pleasant surprise. I attended my first poetry reading by Pulitzer Prize nominee, James Regan, and a writers' week-end hosted by the impressive and time-generous staff at the intimate university setting.

It was humbling to be amid talented, but mostly commercially unrecognized, writers. I was one of the few who had been published and paradoxically, as the only non-fiction writer, I was proud of my books but not necessarily of my writing. A few of us chewed the fat and spare ribs at Arthur Bryan's café on the corner of 18th and Vine. It finally seemed I was heading down the path of a writer who speaks rather than a speaker who writes.

It was a contrast – not better or worse – just a complete contrast to the first writers' conference I'd attended at a luxurious resort in Maui the year before. There, best-selling authors spoke to hundreds of spellbound writers and "wannabe" writers in the audience, and we paid a fee for each fifteen-minute appointment to pitch our book proposals to literary agents and publishers.

The day before the conference commenced, a group playing volleyball in the pool was missing a player on one side, so I joined in. I had no idea who my teammates were until they were introduced on stage next day as Mitch Albom (*Tuesdays with Morrie*), Jeff Arch (*Sleepless in Seattle*), Ridley Pearson (thriller writer) and Dave Barry (humourist).

Bryce Courtenay also introduced me to *Chicken Soup for the Soul* author, Jack Canfield, who generously endorsed my next book. I shared a room, perspectives and much-needed laughter with fellow Australian author Kris Cole. I also met novelist Julie Harris and literary agent Margaret Gee, who acted as invaluable sounding boards in Maui and have since become trusted friends back home.

Agents seemed to like my "pitch" and asked for proposals. One even asked for the movie rights but it was hard to separate the hope from the hype in this Hawaiian paradise. Why did I still doubt my ability to write the story of finding my biological family? Somewhat buoyed to hear even Pulitzer Prize–winner Tad Bartimus speak of her self-doubt, I wondered if such doubt was a prerequisite for writing success. Or is persistence more important? I returned home, sent the requested proposals, waited for the million-dollar offers and visualized adoptive mother Nicole Kidman starring in the movie as my mother. I received nothing but rejection letters, so shelved the notion of the family saga yet again, to write a preamble for the Australian Constitution, horrified by the divisiveness in our country over refugees. My preamble was likewise rejected. Certain that politicians and publishers have the same template of rejection letters, I resumed writing another self-help book.

The following year, I completed the manuscript for *Hot Lemon and Honey: Reflections for Success in Times of Change*, noting in my diary:

> Relieved to finally finish at 3 a.m. But it's never really finished – there's always something to add.

Many months later, I never expected to add a flattering jacket comment from Sir Edmund Hillary. After speaking to him, I hung up the phone covered in goose bumps, not quite believing I'd been casually chatting to my childhood hero.

> The only stars that impress me are in the night sky. It's been disappointing to meet some celebrities in real life – possibly because their egos have them so far removed from it. But Sir Edmund redefines the distinguished difference between hero and celebrity. He reached fame with the first footprint on the summit of Everest but attained greatness when he went on to build over 26 schools and hospitals in Nepal, leaving a lasting legacy for humanity.

Humbled to be even remotely associated with Sir Edmund, my feelings upon being appointed an "Ambassador of Dreams" to celebrate Barbie's fortieth birthday were a little more ambiguous. Maybe it's because I'd never played with dolls as a little girl. Admittedly, there was some sense of pride in being seen as a role model in such company as Qantas chair Margaret Jackson and world surfing champion Layne Beachley (also adopted) but it was somewhat surreal to stand beneath a 40-foot-high statue of a pink doll on the banks of Melbourne's Yarra River.

The young taxi driver taking two of us to the airport

overheard our conversation of the evening's celebrations and politely interjected: "Excuse me, but what does it feel like to be honoured?"

How unexpected – and thought-provoking – a question. I'd never really thought about it. It felt good.

"No-one's ever said anything nice about me," he lamented and I was surprised to hear he'd been on the streets of Melbourne since he was twelve but pulled himself through. "Times weren't tough on me. I was tough on myself." So true for so many. He received a handsome tip to match his smile and a heartfelt thank you for his safe driving.

How sad that many people go through an entire lifetime of work with no sense of recognition for a job well done. Yet, others take accolades – or others – for granted.

A few days before I left for a European speaking tour, the red-light man had called out of the blue, after all these years. He'd left his wife and pleaded with me to visit him in the Philippines, where he was working offshore to clear his debts. Tempted to do so, surely I had more sense?

"Honey, please just give me one more chance."

Like guilt, he'd be best left forgotten. Then again, I could stop over in Manila on my way back from Europe, where I'd joined a group of Norwegians, Germans and Swiss to cycle from Vienna to Budapest.

When we're the same, we want to be different – to break out of the mould and dampness of routine; to see new sights; meet new people; taste different food; think different thoughts. Yet after a time of being different, we yearn to be the same. Travelling afar, we long for home. Initial excitement wears off when it's time to do the laundry. We seek similarities amid a landscape dotted with new experiences. We might commence a cycling trip with a common interest but is that enough? Sometimes we long for a commonality of language or gender. We talk to people we'd otherwise have nothing in common with except they speak our language and hear our hearts reach out for home.

Pedalling through sunflower fields along the back roads and bike paths adjacent to the Danube, my only disenchantment was to discover that the river, so romanticized by Strauss, was far from blue. An incurable romantic, would I regret changing my flight to include a stopover in the Philippines?

At the hotel lobby in Manila, orchids taller than the concierge – and a soothing waterfall to counter street chaos beyond the plate-glass walls – greeted me. But, after pleas of undying devotion, Mr. Red Light was nowhere to be seen. Why was I not surprised?

He arrived, late as usual, with his normal array of excuses. Like in a clichéd scene from a Mills and Boon novel, I melted into his arms in the elevator, dreamily looking forward to his caresses.

Do leopards ever change their spots? Or do they just become more careless in their predatory ways? He'd forgotten to tidy his room and I immediately noticed a woman's swimsuit in the bathroom and a fax to his wife: "Honey, can you check the bank balance?" He was still married and the size 6 swimsuit did not belong to his wife! I was out of there, with no doubt in my mind that my invitation to Manila was reminiscent of coals to Newcastle. After lunch with a former IBM colleague, I was on the next available flight to Sydney.

I was tempted to call Mr. Red Light's wife to tell her what was happening in Manila. She, like me, deserved better. But like me, she probably believed what she wanted to and I didn't want to risk being involved in this messy drama for another nanosecond.

> No-one, including me, can understand why I put up with him for so long. Was it only chemistry? Or does Stupidity have a friend named Gullibility? We'd met at the red light – at a junction in my life. He appeared to give all the right signals and I took the wrong turn; a dead end journey of the heart.

Back home, I ploughed through the pile of paperwork that awaited my return. Amid the bills, brochures and bank statements, was a bright invitation to a fortieth birthday party the following night. Donning my sexiest sparkly dress and high heels, I tried to pick myself up and at least pretend to have a good time at the gala function in the Blue Mountains.

I didn't need to pretend to forget the blues. It was a wonderful evening with old friends and new acquaintances, plus the flirtations of the man seated next to me gave the old ego a well-needed boost.

I didn't expect to hear from him again, but two days later he was in my neighbourhood and called to ask if we could catch up for coffee. Since I'd returned earlier than planned from Manila and my schedule was unusually free, I thought, why not?

Why not indeed? During his speech, the birthday host had mentioned something about my flying in from the Philippines for the party. Making small talk, the man now opposite asked: "What's Manila like? I have a friend who's been working up there for a few months and think I might go and visit."

Before the cappuccino had cooled enough to drink, I discovered he was best friends with the red-light man in primary school. Surely not! What's more, he was best man at his wedding.

Now, what were the odds of that? Whereas I'd debated whether to tell his wife, I had no such qualms with his best friend. Maybe I was unwise to tell the whole truth? Maybe I gave more gory details than he needed? So what! I was tired of feeling my love-life was like a B-grade soap opera. Mateship stopped him from saying much about Mr. Red Light but even his silence confirmed my worst suspicions. It felt good to get it off my chest and I was quite sure that after I lambasted his best friend, I'd never see either of them again.

To my surprise, he called and I agreed to meet him a few weeks later when I attended a conference in the Blue Mountains. He'd been divorced (a fact confirmed by my friends) and although he'd been dating a woman, that had apparently ended months earlier.

"I can't get rid of her. She's still harassing me and I'm thinking of taking out an AVO [Apprehended Violence Order]."

He seemed a nice enough guy but again, there was no chemistry whatsoever. We chatted about nothing in particular. A few days later, an angry message was left on my voice mail: "What the hell do you think you're doing with my boyfriend?"

Fortunately, absolutely nothing!

I called his home and to my surprise, this same woman answered the phone. How could he claim she "harassed" him if she was sleeping there? What was in the water – or the ceiling – at that primary school that produced such deceitful men? He came on the line and muttered something about "trying to find" himself.

Why is it that losers always need to find themselves? I thought the next morning. Sitting in the hospital waiting room surrounded by terminally ill patients always had a way of putting things in perspective. My six-monthly checkup was all clear, as surely the consciences of Mr. Red Light and friend could never be.

> I used to get impatient to be kept waiting in the aptly named waiting room but no longer see these checkups as a waste of time – more like taking time out. Some patients have little time left. I remind myself that I'd rather be kept waiting for two hours because of unforeseen circumstances with another cancer patient, than be the one with the unforeseen circumstance. Medical treatment is much more advanced than when Mum was sick. Thank God for under-recognized researchers and scientists. As Einstein once said, with uncharacteristic sentiment for a scientific mind: "There are two ways to live your life. One as if nothing is a miracle and the other as if every day is a miracle."

I chose the latter.

That night, Liz, Alan and I went to the movies to see some implausible romantic comedy. They suggested I write a script about the saga of the red-light man but we agreed the most imaginative Hollywood producer would claim it was too farfetched even for that genre. (Although Alan teased that my love-life might be akin to Bridget Jones's auntie's!)

My lifestyle seemed equally unbelievable. At a conference in Phuket, Thailand, Jana Stanfield and I sea-kayaked under stalagmite arches and returned to breakfast, savouring mango, papaya, lychees and pineapple. The talented Nashville singer's jaw dropped as a baby elephant ambled past our wicker table: "Sure beats the Holiday Inn in Cincinnati," echoed her Southern drawl.

It was nearly six years since I'd first taken the plunge and backed myself in my own business venture, which was now accumulating a rare combination of money and memories. Other highlights had included two hundred rural women in Stanthorpe singing "Happy Birthday" around the biggest birthday cake I've ever seen, launching a truck on Father's Day with Australian Wallaby rugby great Peter FitzSimons and another gig with rival captain of New Zealand All Blacks, Sean Fitzpatrick.

Addressing a division of the Royal Australian Navy the day the ground war broke in the Gulf, I doubt anyone heard a word about leadership theory, as they were so eager to see action.

"Aren't you worried about the danger of combat?" I asked.

"A little," one officer conceded briefly before enthusing, "We've trained all our life to be ready and this is the chance to prove our mettle. Can you imagine being a surgeon and never operating on a patient?"

I respected but didn't envy their role. The only battles I'd fought in the course of duty were verbal. The only military toes I trod on were those of Fijian coup leader and subsequent prime minister, Major-General Rabuka, while we danced on the sand at another conference. Australian, New Zealand and Thai political leaders had also been among my audiences. So too, CEOs of major corporations and some hatchet men of industry. At one event, the managing director retrenched 50 percent of staff on the spot, the operations manager burst into tears and the conference organizer expected me to motivate the remaining delegates after morning tea!

Such a contrast to the setting of Freycinet National Park with a gathering of all-male transport executives. I gasped at the beauty of the view from my room. Was I really being paid for this?

Unlike the fracas with an earlier macho group, these were thorough gentlemen. In fact, I was so impressed by them and their product that I bought shares in the company. Far from insider trading, I always research an organization prior to making a presentation and if I like the product and the people, it seems as good a reason as any to invest my fees back into their business. Apart from one time (where I'm still holding onto sinking shares) this strategy has proved profitable, much to the surprise of my broker who employs more sophisticated financial techniques.

Following a five-hour hike, I toasted my own more modest business with a swig of crystal-clear water from Wineglass Bay in Tasmania's soul-renewing wilderness. My job offered these peak experiences on an almost-weekly basis and peer recognition was icing on the cake when in November 1999, I accepted the National Speaker Association's Speaker of the Year award at the Sydney chapter.

A few conferences later, chatting with New Zealand golfing champion, Phil Tataurangi, we concluded that the international golf and speaking tours were on somewhat of a par. Both of us were in envied but often lonely occupations. And even though only a few reach the top, it didn't matter because we loved what we did every day.

Sitting in the frequent-flyer lounge at the airport, I glanced up and noticed a replay of a pre-recorded television interview. Two businessmen sitting opposite stared and whispered until one asked: "Is that you?"

Rather chuffed, I responded: "Yes, it is."

"So you're an author, eh? Well, I hope the book sells well so you can afford a new jacket!"

Don't you love the way Aussies take the wind out of your sails? Sure enough, I was wearing the same red jacket.

Fortunately I have other jackets and only a few skeletons left lurking in the closet. So why did my skin tingle with goose bumps when a couple approached me after a luncheon in Brisbane?

"Remember us?"

Their faces bordered the margins of my memory but I'm a bit short-sighted and have stopped feigning familiarity when someone approaches me at the supermarket and says, "Hi, remember me? I was in the first row at the XYZ conference."

Long before my speaking days, this was my old housemate and her now husband from Weipa and I hadn't seen them in over a quarter of a century. "We couldn't believe that was you! You used to be so shy. And why didn't you tell us your parents had died? We can't believe you kept it all to yourself, silly girl."

Silly indeed. It was great to see them, admittedly looking quite different in business suits instead of our Weipa wear of shorts and thongs.

One of the few things I don't love about my job is the annual Christmas mail-out. Each year I swear I won't do it and each year, the list grows larger. How can it be that I personally sign greetings to over four thousand people and still receive cards from some I didn't send to?

I felt equally superficial that year dishing out Christmas meals for the homeless, as I'd done for many years. There now seemed to be more once-a-year "do-gooders" than destitute homeless. Shouldn't we make more of an effort every day to make a difference to less fortunate lives? My former neighbour and honorary Mum, June, had done so, and she was recognized with a senior citizens award for thirty-four years of continuous service to Meals on Wheels and Girl Guides.

I was proud to be her honorary daughter and her real daughters had even printed an "adoption" certificate. Having been adopted before and knowing the ropes, I promised to be less trouble this time round! Seated next to ninety-four-year-old Jack "Snowy" Pearce, the last Rat of Tobruk, I watched a generation of givers accept their awards with humble grace. Maybe they no longer wore stylish high heels, but as unsteady legs shuffled to the stage in stable flat sandals or assisted by walking frames, they seemed no less attractive than Katharine Hepburn in her prime. I hoped I'd look, and be, half as good at their age. Yes, I'd rather be eighty years young than thirty years old! I was nearly fifty but still felt twenty-seven most days. June, in her mid-seventies, claimed she felt likewise as she walked along the beach every morning while another sage of the surf, eighty-four-year-old Hazel, danced in the water because her arthritis restricted her to barely walking on land. So too, I was buoyed by seventy-year-plus male mates who boasted of their "junior geriatric" status at the golf and surf clubs. And my ninety-year-old friends in Montana who said they might take up golf when they got older!

Yes, many mid-life opportunities await and maybe the second phase of my life will be more settled – more contented.

37

MY ADOPTED COUNTRY

January 1, 2000. Is it or isn't it a new millennium? Who cares if it's this year or next? What does a new millennium mean any more than a new day? We can only live one day at a time. Why be pedantic when there is little argument that it symbolizes the start of an exciting era?

Fireworks over Sydney Harbour couldn't help but ignite awe in all but the staunchest cynic. Far from Scotchman's Hill in Calgary, life has moved from somewhat tragic to mostly magic – that same timeless magic when the sky explodes, but for a moment, in a blaze of colour and sound, to the oohs and aahs of more than a million people lining the foreshore. At midnight the Harbour Bridge momentarily mirrors Niagara Falls. Streams of sparkling white light cascade like rivers from steel rivets that have stood stationary since construction commenced in 1929. The word "Eternity" emerges as luminous handwriting on the arch that spans not just a quay – but also a century. Was it really half a century ago that I was conceived – born nine months later on September 29?

A sole soprano, precariously perched on the tip of the once-maligned Opera House, greeted dawn at 5:30 a.m. as onlookers waded through calf-high garbage. By 7:20 a.m., thanks to the hardworking sanitation staff of Sydney, it was all cleared away.

Privileged to eyewitness the six-million-dollar fireworks extravaganza from a close friend's nearby balcony, I questioned such expenditure. Midnight had not yet struck other parts of the planet where the garbage from this city alone would have fed a village for a week. Was it morally right? I pondered this only briefly. It simply "was." As the ferry arrived back in Manly thirty minutes later, I was selfishly relieved that my own bread and butter was intact and my computer free from the predicted Y2K virus. I tidied files in the computer and office, organized for the year ahead.

Around that time, *Hot Lemon and Honey* was launched and billed as the first motivational book of the new millennium. I was exhausted after the launch with a strange sense of excitement, relief and nervous expectation. It was not unlike the birth of a baby; those thoughts had gestated, alone, inside my being, albeit for substantially more than nine months. Eventually the book had popped out with a minimum of pain. All that remained was anxious anticipation, hoping no unsightly birthmarks or typos had gone unnoticed and that it would be accepted and welcomed to the world of bookshops, to stand alone and make its own way on the shelves.

I enthusiastically signed copies, and a friend's young daughter commented: "Mum, now I know why they type books. No-one can read her writing."

After the nervous energy of the launch, late that night I was about to collapse into bed but first had a quick flick through the snail mail over a cup of herbal tea. Most correspondence was now electronic and I seldom received any good news in a window envelope – only bills, junk, cheques, advertising, bills, statements, junk, junk, junk. Another window envelope was about to be tossed in the bin until I took a second glance:

> . . . we inform you of selection as a Community Torchbearer for the Sydney 2000 Olympic Torch Relay. You have been chosen as a representative for your community values, spirit and national pride. As an ambassador of Australia, you will assist the Olympic flame as it travels from coast to coast.

Excitedly reaching for the phone, I realized it was too late to call anyone; just as well – further reading insisted on confidentiality until the official announcement a few weeks later. A few weeks? Imagine how difficult it is for a professional speaker to keep silent that long! Especially one known to talk in her sleep!

On 26 January at the Australia Day ceremony under the Moreton Bay fig tree outside Manly Town Hall, the local torchbearers were announced and names of all published in the national media. I sang with gusto (nevertheless, still out of tune) the national anthem. Tears filled my eyes as strains of "Advance, Australia Fair" wafted across the crowd, then trickled down my cheek as a children's choir gave a more melodious rendition of Bruce Woodley's "I Am Australian."

> "We are one but we are many; and from all the lands on earth we come.
> We share a dream and sing in one voice
> I am. You are. We are Australian."

The magnitude of the honour hit me like a wave pounding the nearby beach. The Chamber of Commerce president handed me his handkerchief before I went on stage sniffling like some silly beauty pageant queen. Surely this wasn't the same person who never shed a tear in public when my folks died years earlier?

> I wished they were here. But if so, I wouldn't be. Nor would I have met songwriter Bruce Woodley a few months earlier. He was a pretty good cook, but I had no idea he was a member of The Seekers. What was I seeking? I wasn't sure but maybe, just maybe, I've found it here under the Moreton Bay fig tree in Manly. Maybe it's a sense of belonging? Or at least as close as I've ever felt to belonging.

Philosophy evaporated in the midst of another move. Although remaining in Manly, changing phone lines still created chaos and I was again annoyed with myself for getting stressed and assured my more patient PA it had nothing to do with her. We were both frazzled when she answered the cell phone and an attendee at one of my presentations commented: "Catherine had us in stitches the entire hour. It must be such fun to work with her."

Ever loyal, my PA replied: "Oh yes, a laugh a minute," and we both convulsed in fits of it, as soon as she hung up.

People would likewise laugh when I'd joke: "My boss is such a bitch" – but I knew I'd been driving myself far too hard when a trip to the dentist was welcome relief to sit down for what seemed the first time in weeks! Travelling at the speed of light, I rushed to a book-signing in the city and missed the ferry. Impatiently awaiting the next, another enforced rest found me sharing a wooden bench with two middle-aged transport workers in blue uniform. A deep baritone voice read out loud. Curious, I edged a little closer to better hear. Sure enough, the tall man, a recovering addict, shared written words of encouragement with his illiterate colleague. It was touching to witness him translate the print on the page.

I left a copy of my book and gained insight and friendship.

Weeks later, I spotted the familiar yellow cover, shared by two other workers and for the first time, I felt like a writer. I might have missed the ferry that day but arrived at a premise that maybe, just maybe, I was a fully fledged author.

Strangely, that moment seemed greater validation than that of the many TV and radio chat hosts who generously commended the book to listeners as I did interviews across the country. Don't get me wrong – of course, I was thrilled and appreciative of the media support, without which books have little chance of success these days. The response still seemed somewhat surreal and over a three-hour lunch interview for the Bulletin, I confessed to multi-talented ABC journalist Maxine McKew how awkward it was to talk about myself for so long.

"Don't worry. Just call it therapy . . . and Kerry Packer's paying," she laughed.

Therapy indeed. It may have been a good idea but I dumped in my diary, instead:

The laptop broke. Wonder if my spirit will be next? I feel as fragile as a microchip on an eight-lane freeway. Sometimes feel I'm losing my grip. Other times, I wonder if I ever had one. Am I finding success or losing myself?

Onstage, I was more vibrant and connected than ever, but offstage somewhat lacking in passion. I enjoyed each conference but returned to the office overwhelmed with the paperwork, introduction of GST and packing for the next trip no sooner than I'd unpacked from the last. Oftentimes, the suitcase lay sprawled by the washing machine. Occasionally, I'd have two packed, walk through the door with one, go to bed and walk out next morning with the other. Wollongong, Washington and Wellington. Hobart, Honolulu and Harare. It's little wonder I'd lost my sense of wonder and felt burned out.

A flame of a more optimistic nature was about to spread across Australia, to ignite a sense of national pride on the international stage.

On 8 June 2000, the Olympic flame reached the Red Centre of Australia. I'd arrived the day before, as a co-author of the official report for the International Olympic Committee. The night before, on the edge of the desert amid the glow of campfires and candles, dignitaries, officials, sponsors, traditional owners and past Olympian torchbearers sipped champagne and sat at tables covered in crisp white linen to partake of a sumptuous silver-service meal.

Around one of the campfires strategically placed between tables, two young Aboriginals stood shivering. Both were about to be among the first to carry the torch in the morning and I overheard their conversation.

"How'd you feel when you were selected?"

"Mate, I gotta say I cried."

"Yeah, me too."

"How do you feel now?"

"Nervous. What if I drop it or trip?"

Intrigued, I prodded them for more and learned that both were champion footballers and role models to their own people and countless others.

"You won't drop it," I assured them. "You've got sure hands. Why would professional athletes, like you, be nervous about such a short run?"

"Ah, this is different. The other is a team sport. This is an incredible individual honour for our country," replied Australian Rules footballer and Brownlow medallist nominee Andrew McLeod.

Governor-General Sir William Deane joined the campfire camaraderie, with no visible security and nothing but desert as far as the eye could see, which wasn't very far in the pitch-black night. Buses soon departed for the hotel, many passengers thinking about the role they'd play on the international stage in a few hours.

Early next morning, the torch relay started in the spiritual heart of a land older than the Olympics, about to create its own unique imprint on the archives of the Antipodes.

Nova Peris-Kneebone, the first Aboriginal to win gold at an Olympic Games, nervously accepted the flame.

As the rest of the crowd was bundled up in the cold chill of the morning sub-zero temperatures, before the sun had a chance to warm the red earth, she stood barefoot and proud out of respect for her people, the traditional landowners.

The absence of any prominent logo on running shoes was no protest about sponsorship or land rights. It was a dignified gesture, above argument, regardless of where one stood on reconciliation. Today, there seemed no need to say sorry, as black and white showed unity of spirit for the biggest event ever staged in the shadow of the world's largest monolith. Ayers Rock would now undoubtedly be known throughout the world by its Aboriginal name, Uluru. A quarter of a century earlier, I'd climbed to the top but would not do so today because it is now generally recognized as a sacred site. It's unthinkable that until granted citizenship in 1967, Aboriginal people were classed as "flora and fauna" – unable to vote or hold public office. Yes, times do change, as do our views of those times. Controversy remains timeless. Only issues change – like the colour of the rock at dusk. Public debate that surrounded Australia's hosting the Olympics now also seems on the wane.

Nova patiently flashed her winning smile for a gold-medal media performance. She radiated warmth that belied the near-freezing temperature of the early morning. That same warmth had been evident when we casually chatted the day before, surrounded only by green bush, grey spinifex and blue sky, awaiting arrival of the international media.

"Normally I try to run as fast as possible but carrying the torch, I'll run slowly to savour the moment."

Nova was the first to carry the torch on the red earth of her ancestors, that same soil as my adopted country. Canadian by birth but Australian by choice, how would I feel when my turn arrived in a hundred days' time?

After a late breakfast next morning, I bumped into Andrew McLeod and asked if he'd recovered from his pre-torch nerves.

"Yes, it was great . . . right up there with winning a grand final championship!"

The next day I followed the flame to Alice Springs, where the banks of the Todd River were as dry as the desert dust. It was impossible to imagine the uncharacteristic flooding that had stranded my flight on the tarmac all those years ago and led to my becoming an Australian. The bulk of twenty-seven thousand residents created the first ever traffic jam in a town like Alice, as they turned up to witness the "relaying of the fire stick," known in the Pitjantjatjara language as *waru tjango para ungkularintankunytja*.

Storytelling is an integral part of life for Indigenous Australians; tales of the history and culture of the people handed down since the beginning of time – the Dreaming. Along the Olympic torch journey were many stories of dreams.

For each runner this was their "fifteen minutes of flame," whether the heroes of yesterday, the heroes of today or the unsung heroes of everyday life. Some were nominated for their work with the disadvantaged or for overcoming their own adversities. There were the macho sportsmen and war veterans who held back tears, and the many tales of courage and contribution by others who had fought disease or emotional trauma.

One man lost his battle with cancer only six hours before his scheduled torch run and some others sadly passed away before the flame was passed to them. A luckier heart transplant recipient pinned a photo of his donor to his shirt. Others claimed the experience was better than winning the lottery and on a par with the birth of their first child. There were countless heart-warming stories from young and old. Whether tackling their task at a sprint or a sprightly shuffle, all made a lasting footprint on the memories of a nation.

I next saw the flame in the Melbourne Cricket Ground, home of the 1956 Olympics, where Ron Clarke lit the cauldron as he had done forty-four years earlier. Now, nearly halfway through its journey, even the harshest cynics began to admit that, from the time the flame first touched down on Australian soil, it touched the lives of all those who carried it and the millions more who watched it pass by.

I found myself counting the days like a little kid looking forward to Christmas, as I once did a long, long time ago. Only 101 more sleeps, 50, 36, 14, 6 . . . As the flame reached the outskirts of Sydney, crowds grew – and grew – igniting an Olympic fever and fervour of national pride unprecedented in this nation. The Land Down Under was now getting top billing on the world stage. Australians were no longer reluctant to parade their patriotism. But what if no-one, apart from friends, showed up on my leg of the run?

After all, I wasn't an Olympic champion or Olivia Newton-John. Or Greg Norman, who was the first to carry it on the day of the opening ceremonies, only a few hours before it would be in my grasp. It would pass through only 27 more hands before Cathy Freeman lit the cauldron at the Sydney 2000 Olympics opening ceremony a few hours later. Coincidentally, I shared a name with this Aboriginal athletic icon; and not just Catherine. The English translation of the Dutch DeVrye is "Freeman."

My hairdresser thankfully talked me out of having the Olympic rings shaved into my hair and instead, opted for a more sensible statement of colouring my hair, fingernails and toenails in the red, green, blue, yellow and black Olympic colours. I'd seriously considered running barefoot, as Nova Peris-Kneebone had done at Uluru. She had done so out of respect for her people. The ancient Greeks also ran barefoot. Then again, they ran naked!

That was one track I wouldn't be heading down, even if I hadn't been suffering from a cold and chest infection. The previous week, I'd been bedridden with a bad case of bronchitis and wondered if I'd be well enough to run. Wild horses couldn't drag me away – but then again there weren't many wild horses in a city of four million! Amid the controversial drug testing of athletes, if torchbearers were dope-tested, I'd have surely been disqualified for the amount of medication I was on (medically prescribed antibiotics, I might add).

On the day, adrenaline seemed a potent enough perform-ance enhancer. Never known for arriving early, I didn't want to get caught in a traffic jam like one earlier runner who couldn't get to the start of his relay leg amid all the hype. So my PA and honorary Mum made sure I arrived early at the starting point where all torchbearers were briefed before boarding a bus to be dropped at our respective points along the way.

As determined as I'd been to heed Nova's advice to savour the moment, it passed all too quickly as I sprinted along the street, which was lined four or five deep. With security guards, the escort runner and motorcycle convoy hot on my heels, whatever possessed me to attempt a cartwheel and tumble to the bitumen? Thankfully, the TV cameras broad-casting to 3.2 billion missed that graceless moment.

More gratefully, media and friends provided subsequent footage and photos because I was so overwhelmed with emotion, I would not have recalled the incredible sea of young and old faces and hands reaching out to touch the torch. Pacific Islanders, Caucasians, Asians, Africans, Brazilians were readily identifiable, as a larger cross-section of the United Nations all waved Australian flags. I was swamped like the Pied Piper; people shoved babies and cameras in my face, tugged at my uniform and tried to grab the torch. Later I joined a more sedate, but no less enthusi-astic, gathering of the mayor and members of parliament from both political parties, as Australia's first winter Olympic medallist, Zali Steggall, boarded the Manly ferry and a flotilla of crafts accompanied us to Circular Quay. There, I'd planned to alight and watch the opening ceremo-ny with friends, but security guards advised they couldn't guarantee my safety if I left the ferry to the mob surround-ing the Opera House and harbour area. I retreated to Liz and Alan's, where I promptly fell asleep on the sofa like a child who'd eagerly awaited Christmas and then faced too much festivity to absorb it all.

Restless dreams of the crowd mob scenes woke me. Was it a dream? No, it had been one of the best days of my life. The worst were far, far behind me. I'd been burned by old flames, but now basked in the warm glow of the Olympic one. I'd done nothing but carry a torch but it was a torch that touched the heart of a nation. With immense pride and greater humility, it touched me at another level. I was still an only child; still single. But, with every single step along the torch relay, I became a small part of something much bigger than myself – embraced by my adopted country – a continent and country of contrast.

I had little time to reflect further, as I rose early next morning to cover the first event of the Sydney 2000 Olympics. It was also the first time that the triathlon had been an Olympic event and a sense of history surrounded the Opera House steps where competitors emerged like seals from the harbour swim, jumped on their bikes and eventually ran across the finish line, followed by international cameras showcasing Sydney. As top athletes performed at their peak, I struggled to merely write about their athletic feats in water polo, mountain biking and cycling. The bronchitis was so bad that I gave away prized tickets to athletic events, as I needed to conserve every ounce of energy to cover the events I'd been assigned.

There were many stories of winning gold and of the dedication to overcome obstacles along an athlete's Olympic journey. Just as few Australians would forget Cathy Freeman's 400-metre run, there was also celebration of "Eric the Eel," an African swimmer who had never before swum in a 50-metre pool and struggled to finish his race. There was steely determination on the face of Lance Armstrong, two times Tour de France winner, at the cycling events press conference. Although he finished third, he received more media attention than the winner, since he had recently been cleared of cancer. So too, efforts of Paralympians a few weeks later would prove inspiring.

The city was alive with revellers who watched live telecasts on big outdoor screens. I had not celebrated my twenty-first in the year Dad died of cancer but now, as I turned fifty during the Games, in a strange way, carrying the torch was a coming of age. Dad would have been 100. Born in 1900, he lived the first half of the twentieth century and was fifty when I was born to live the last half.

On 29 September 2000, my birthday, former Canadian prime minister Pierre Trudeau, who was my teenage political pinup, died aged eighty. Earlier, a newspaper interviewer had asked me who I would most like to sit next to on an overseas flight. "No-one! But, if there wasn't an empty seat, I'd choose Nelson Mandela, in the hope that some of his incredible compassion might osmotically rub off on me at 30,000 feet." Liz saw the article and as a birthday gift, took me to a corporate dinner in the Hilton ballroom in honour of this former "terrorist" who, although about the same age as Trudeau, did not make his mark on the world political stage until many years later and subsequently united a nation with his forgiveness.

Mandela received a standing ovation when he entered the room, another when he was introduced, another after he spoke, another when he was thanked and yet another when he left the room. He shook our hands, and those of some of the waiters on his exit, ignoring many of the high-flyers present.

Now, three of the most memorable nights of my life had been spent at that hotel – the other two being the night I hosted a Young Achievement dinner with the prime minister and chairman of the Business Council at my table and the night I first learned of my biological family.

As others at the Mandela dinner sipped champagne, I discreetly swigged cough syrup hidden in my handbag. By the time I'd beaten the bronchitis, I seemed to have more wheels spinning than a peloton as I tried to catch up on work that had fallen behind during the Games. That, in itself, would be a marathon effort.

I frantically packed for a speaking engagement in California. Like most kids, I had dreamed of going to Disneyland but knew we could never afford it. I *never* dreamed someone would one day actually pay me to speak at a conference there. I looked out over the Magic Kingdom from my room. "Wow." My parents had never even stayed in a hotel and I thought back to those happy times when we first got television and together watched *Disneyland* on a Sunday night. I danced around the hotel room, singing the Jiminy Cricket theme song:

> "When you wish upon a star,
> makes no difference who you are.
> When you wish upon a star,
> your dreams come true."

Indeed they can if we dare to dream – then act accordingly.

> I still can't sing in tune but march to my own. If it's a different key to the rest of the world, so be it. I may be tone-deaf but now listen more closely to a little inner voice of hope and happiness. I'm tired of the song that sorrow sang.

Each sunset takes with it the horizon. It disappears in the darkness of night. On an all-night flight back from Los Angeles, dawn eventually greets the plane on its approach to Sydney. Gazing idly out the window at 30,000 feet, I look down on light radiating through fluffy white clouds. As a child I'd look up to their cumulus cousins; puffy cotton balls floating in a fair-weather sky, fuelled by buoyant bubbles of air that rise upward from the earth's surface. I'd imagine formations of ships or horses but never imagined events would precipitate as they did and rainbows emerge from stormy times on life's choppy seas.

Surf on the eastern edge of the Pacific gently laps the shore or pounds the rocks. It's hard to tell from this height. Regardless, it reminds me of a past an ocean away from life today. Waves of wonder have washed over those of woe.

My next conference was in Hong Kong and after boarding the plane, was delighted that a former neighbour was the flight attendant.

"What a small world," exclaimed my seat companion.

Where had I heard that before? Not nearly small enough, I soon discovered.

After a walk and brunch with a friends, I completed early Christmas shopping at Hong Kong's Stanley markets and, laden with gifts, strolled past groups of Philippine *amahs* (nannies and maids), gathered together on their day off near the ferry terminal, merrily chatting on a sunny Sunday afternoon. It had been a marvellous day and I was about to board the Star ferry for a twilight ride across the harbour to my hotel in Kowloon.

Coming straight towards me was the one man I never wanted to meet again. By the time I realized it was no optical illusion, it was impossible to avoid Mr. Red Light. Clasping the hand of a Filipino woman young enough to be his daughter, he smiled and disingenuously asked, "Hi. How ya doing?"

I felt I'd seen a ghost.

"I'm fine. How's your wife, you lying, cheating bastard!" Without waiting for a reply, I turned to the young woman. "Please be careful. He is a very bad man."

Shaking, with a tightness in my chest definitely not caused by bronchitis, I did the only sensible thing a woman could do and stormed into Mrs. Field's for two large double-chocolate fudge brownies!

By the time I boarded the ferry a few minutes later, I was relaxed and relieved that he was no longer a part of my life. I hoped he'd take a long walk on a short pier! Still, I pondered, what are the odds of that happening? What lesson am I meant to learn? And was there an easier way to learn it? As I don't believe in coincidence, and I'd had so many with this man, I wondered why. It would be a wonderful tale if only it had a happy ending, I thought. Then again, having him out of my life was indeed a happy conclusion.

We all have those "isn't it a small world" stories of coincidence. Mine seemed more miniature than most when it came to this jerk; sitting next to his wife's best friend on the plane from Perth, his best friend at a birthday party in the Blue Mountains, finding evidence of at least one girlfriend in Manila and now this . . . surely, this would be the last time?

38

MEMORIES OF TOMORROW

Over the last half of the twentieth century, there have been many marvellous men in my life but no one "Mister Wonderful." (A friend suggests there is no such creature and I should settle for "Mister Not Too Many Bad Habits.") At risk of shattering the myth of the independent career woman, there are times when I long for a strong arm around my shoulder, a deep voice to console. Then again, it's tempting to be cynical and a diary entry reads:

> The Mounties that I played with as a kid always got their man, so why can't I? Can passion really last a lifetime or, like ink in this ballpoint pen, does it eventually dry up on the pages of our heart?

Plus, I have indeed witnessed a handful of loving lifetime partnerships that have defied growing divorce statistics, not counting those who simply stay married for the sake of the children or economic dependence.

I'd like one of those partnerships for the rest of my life. But I don't think I "need" a man and am surprised that many men have told me that they feel the need to be needed. I jest that the two most essential men in my life are my chiropractor and IT expert who keep my lumbar disc and hard disk in working order.

A friend finds this disconcerting. Too often individuals, especially women, point at singles and say: "Oh, I couldn't cope without my partner." Of course they could. They do. We cope because we have to. We come into the world alone and leave alone. So it's not the end of the world to spend chunks of time without a partner. I don't mind my own company, nor being the odd-one-out at dinner parties. So it was no surprise when a management personality profile classified me as an introvert. With the extroverted nature of my job, others were amazed at the result but the fact is that I quickly get "all peopled out" and need to retreat to the bliss of solitude. Just as some schedule alcohol- or caffeine-free days, I'll mark my calendar for days free of computers, phones and company. The sporadic chaos of coping on one's own is balanced by the serenity of self-sufficiency.

Far from the speaker's rostrum, sitting quietly on an ocean's edge or mountain peak, I applaud the marvels of Mother Nature. Like the Desiderata poster my roommate gave me for my twenty-first birthday, I've come to treasure what peace there may be in silence.

> You are a child of the universe no less than the trees and the stars; you have a right to be here. And whether or not it is clear to you, no doubt the universe is unfolding as it should.

As it should indeed . . .

One of my surfing buddies once queried, "I can't understand why you don't have a bloke in your life. You're a catch – no kids, no mortgage, no in-laws. Although I guess you probably scare a few of 'em?"

This wasn't the first time I'd been told I intimidate men,

even though I'm as mushy as a roasted marshmallow underneath that tough corporate persona. As the eastern morning sun cast our shadows on the beach (and at fifty, our shadows looked pretty damn good, with wetsuits holding in the wobbly bits!) I knew one of the answers to his question. I didn't want to walk in anyone's shadow or have anyone walk in mine. True partners together leave footprints on the landscape of life.

"So why haven't you remarried? Too fussy? Too set in your ways? Too busy?"

"Probably, all of the above," I admitted.

"When was the last time someone asked you out?"

"Lately, I've had more advances from publishers than eligible men."

"No, seriously – I'm curious," he persisted.

"Well, if you don't count the drunk astronaut in Thailand last month or the fat dotcom executive who invited me to Mexico next week . . ."

"Take a chance. Go. There's great surf there."

"No way. The proviso was that I'd have to have sex with him on the fourth night. So, I said I'd leave after three!"

He laughed: "If I was five years younger I'd chase you myself!"

"And if I were ten years younger I'd let you catch me!"

I'd learned my lesson about choosing waves and men more carefully. I've been dumped by big surf and small men, but never completely drowned in despair. Still, I remain an incurable romantic. Even without a man in my life, I have a wonderful one. Admittedly, the times I've been in love (or serious lust) the sky seemed a bit bluer, the grass a bit greener, the air a bit crisper and the surf a bit more forgiving.

I may spend long periods alone but am seldom lonely. I value my male mentors and mates. Platonic relationships stick like Velcro over the years, while amorous ones assume the qualities of Teflon. So, today, I'm content with the wonderful array of friends in my wardrobe of womanhood. Male and female, they come in all shapes, sizes and styles. Name brands and no-frills. All distinctly unique designer people. At present, there's no one "special person" but many special people with whom I can share meals, concerns or confidences. We may exercise our bodies or stretch our minds. We might discuss politics, books, movies or the meaning of life.

Some friends make us think and others make us laugh. Some are more reliable, logical and help keep us grounded. Others are more nurturing, ideological and help us dream. One size does not fit all – but a handful remain ready to wear and weather, on any occasion, firmly stitched in trust through time. With age, we're more comfortable in our own skin – and with that give-and-take lycra of acceptance. We're connected because we're open enough with each other to say when we sometimes feel disconnected from life. There's no need to pretend.

There's a tiny tinge of pointless regret that I haven't had lifelong friends who have shared a simultaneous and parallel past, present and future. Still, we have shared similar concerns from a distance and from different perspectives. Friends are sometimes stressed or sad because of family issues. Yet, if I'm sad, it's because I lack that sense of security I once took for granted in my own family home.

Sure, I'm delighted to have discovered my biological family scattered on the other side of the world and would like to get to know some of them better because there's potential for friendship. But, realistically, in many ways, most of us remain oceans apart.

Maybe fitting into a family is a learning curve for me, where it's as natural as breathing to others?

Is there such a thing as a "normal" family, anyway? I was tempted to title this book "My family's more dysfunctional than yours." Curious readers may have bought the book to see if indeed, someone else's family drama compared with their own! Not that I think my biological or adoptive family is, or was, dysfunctional. All families have those moments of being so.

One of my long-lost cousins and her husband visited Australia, and later I mused in my diary.

What great people but their talk of a large and extensive family tree was unfamiliar to me. Maybe my Utopia would be the snow-capped Rockies rising majestically on the edge of Sydney's sunny shores; a twenty-minute ferry ride, not a twenty-hour flight spanning the distance from past to present.

A New Zealand client surprised me with his observation: "Your family reaches far wider than most." I was puzzled: how did he know about the far-flung relatives in North America and Europe? He didn't. "You have a family of friends throughout the world."

Months later in Indonesia, a taxi driver discovered I was an author. He heaved a heavy suitcase of books into the boot and proudly declared in broken English: "Oh my friend, I have read Mr. Hemingway's *Goodbye to Weapons*." Amused by his translation of *A Farewell to Arms*, I didn't bother to correct him, although we concurred that any ideology of farewell to weapons would likely remain only that, as innocent civilians die daily in the name of peace.

What a refreshing contrast to the driver in Sydney with his non-stop monologue of what's wrong with the world and his personal woes. He didn't even pause when I mentioned a news report that World Bank figures estimate 800 million go to bed hungry each night.

Indonesia is a mainly Muslim nation and in the hotel, a compass on the fire alarm in my room pointed to Mecca. Morning calls to prayer sounded outside as I prepared to speak to four hundred delegates of an international financial firm about the need to connect head and heart, to be of service to our clients, communities and planet. The managing partner later told me it was the first time any speaker had received a standing ovation and I was deeply moved. Audience members gathered round.

One asked: "Are you Christian?"

Before I had a chance to reply, another interrupted: "No, she is Hindu I think."

"A Buddhist?"

A heavily veiled woman, alongside her Chanel-suited colleague, whispered, "Maybe you are Muslim, but your religion does not matter. You spoke to me like a sister today."

Although Islamic Sharia law bans adoption to prevent confusion of bloodlines, she could easily have been a sister, as we shared similar views of life over lunch. After all those years in Sunday school, heaven knows what the Presbyterians would say.

Pressed on the question of faith, which I'd tried unsuccessfully to deflect, I could only reply that I believed in a God more than a specific religion. Our table of mixed beliefs unanimously agreed on one aspect of Buddhist philosophy, along the following lines: *If we threw all our individual problems into a big bucket, and then drew them out at random, most would wish we'd picked our own problems.*

The more we're different, the more we're the same if we take time to explore. Time is so often the common enemy. I may never find the answers I seek but will continue asking the questions. As for the meaning of life, I have no idea what it is. I know some of what it is not. It is not a fast car or a big house. It is not a healthy bank account or even a healthy newborn baby. It is not an overseas trip. It is a journey. At times, my own seemed more of an oddity than an odyssey. We have to go somewhere to get anywhere – even if we never leave our hometown.

Was there merit in my New Zealand client's comment? Did I really have a family of friends – a family of choice – around the world? Did I have a strange family or family of strangers?

Family, after all, is about sharing common ground and memories. It's about sharing a past, present and future. It's about sharing good, bad and mostly mundane times. It's not only about sharing genes.

A family is all things familiar – some things a little too familiar. Whether a painful or pleasant past, and most likely a bit of both, only shared memories make a family – or even a family of friends.

There's a marked difference between enduring friends and fleeting acquaintances. Both are welcome additions to life's rich tapestry but true friends are found forever embroidered on your sleeve, where you may have once worn your heart. In the final wash-up, I'd rather have the love of a few people for a lifetime, than the adoration of many for a moment.

I've received standing ovations, polite applause and

some heckling, but always gave my best. Success isn't about thunderous acclaim from thousands. It's about sitting alone to quietly applaud that you've done your best – and knowing your best is good enough for you.

As for the red-light man, I'd like to report a classical, happy-ever-after ending to this story, similar to the romantic comedy genre I so enjoy.

Or, that he vanished into thin air. That's what I'd like to report. Two facts prevent me from doing so:

1. I left my last cancer checkup with a sense of relief, as always. Stopped at traffic lights opposite the hospital, I sensed someone watching and glanced in the rear-vision mirror. Forty kilometres from home, in a city of nearly 4 million people, there he was. I could only guess the woman in the passenger seat was his wife. Sadly, she looked ill. I accelerated with a similar sense of reprieve to that I'd felt minutes earlier, after the all-clear from the oncologist. Any symbolism eludes me. I'm content to trust the mystery.

2. There is no "happy-ever-after ending" because happily, my life is not yet ended. Hopefully, there remain pages to turn, chapters to live. I'm mostly happy today. That's enough.

One could say a lot about my life, but never that it has been boring. Parts have seemed a combination of sitcom, soap opera, adventure and fantasy. Thankfully not reality TV but reality all the same. Never, in my wildest imagination, could I have scripted this improbable plot.

Maybe one day I'll find myself reminiscing in the proverbial rocking chair. Possibly arthritic, short of breath and hearing, but still of sound mind (well, at least as sane as I've ever been, some might argue!). Nurses may smile, nod sagely and surmise, "Poor old dear, delusional again. We'd better increase her medication."

But that's far on the distant horizon. Now it's nearly time to turn off this keyboard of consciousness, to stop writing about my life and start living it again.

This placement of words upon the page has given me a more complete picture of who I am today. Although I don't always like the portrait, I have a clearer view of the subject and I more readily understand and accept the elements of its composition.

Sometimes I pinch myself (and although I'm the same dress size as I was in high school, admittedly there's a bit more to pinch these days!). Surely, all my experiences thus far couldn't possibly happen in one person's lifetime? At least, not to one single person? Yet, single I am in every sense of the word. When I feel a little too single and alone, I remind myself that such an array of adventure would have been unlikely had I been typically married, with 2.2 children. I need not seek permission, nor explain my actions to anyone but myself. Responsible for no-one but myself, I take total responsibility for that self – to create my own tomorrows with my thoughts and actions today.

Certainly, I view things differently at fifty than I did at twenty, thirty, or forty – and no doubt will at sixty. No longer do I bottle up past pain. If only I could bottle a solution for others. Such is impossible. I only hope these words may at least help others learn from my mistakes, help a little to better cope with their own doubt and despair during loss. No-one can help a lot.

Yes, grief is global but so too is joy. I've travelled miles with both on the serendipity road and the load has lightened with thoughts of brighter tomorrows. Along the way, we meet those who ease our burden while others simply drive us round the bend! We discover a richness of life paved with potholes, speed bumps, U-turns and even dead ends because if we travel a path with no obstacles, it likely doesn't lead anywhere. Sometimes at a crossroads, faced with a choice of direction, we miss – or misread – signs that seem so obvious to others. We may occasionally choose the wrong path and inevitably get lost from time to time, simply because there is no universal road map or satellite navigation for our individual journeys. Therefore, we need to be open to new directions when dreams take detours. And it's only the truly wise person who can enjoy the view on those detours.

Everyone dies but not everyone lives life to the full. It's not what we've done, but what we'll do with what we've done to date. It's not where we go, but how we make the journey. It's not who we know, if we don't know who we are. Closer to knowing who I am, and appreciative of glimpsed perspectives, from Cousteau's ocean beds to Hillary's mountain peaks, I've lived life from top to bottom – but mostly in between.

As an adult . . . I've dined with royalty and doted on my dog. I've renovated a house and built a career but life remains a work in progress. I've tasted luxury but thankfully prefer simple pleasures.

As an adolescent . . . a teacher prophetically wrote in my autograph book: *Smiles are passports through deserts and visas to all alien countries.*

As a little girl . . . I dreamed of a bright red bicycle with big wide handlebars, white tassels and a shiny silver bell, but I never dreamed of cycling over the Andes. I've since skinned my elbows, knees and heart.

Growing up in the land-locked prairie of Canada I dreamed of one day walking on warm Hawaiian sand but never imagined waking up each morning to one of the best beaches in the world. Somewhere along the way, the tide turned.

Since I first boarded that plane in Canada after my mother's funeral, I've lost count of the times I've been around the world but know my days are numbered. In generally excellent health, I still get bronchitis but seldom get homesick for that land where Mum first smothered my chest with Vicks, that evocative menthol-and-eucalyptus scent. My home and heart are now firmly embedded among the gum trees of Australia.

I don't miss four distinct seasonal changes but in rare bouts of nostalgia, might hanker for spring skiing, autumn's pumpkin pie and a white Christmas – or occasionally crave cold root beer, fresh donuts and old friends. I regularly call Canada to speak to those friends and relatives but no longer call that country home, because it no longer calls to me. Did I go to Australia or from Canada? It's a moot point on which I am silent, only because I honestly don't know the answer. Maybe I ran away from Canada or maybe I ran forward to a new life in Australia. I never consciously thought of doing either.

I've lived the daydreams of many and the nightmares of some. During sleepless nights, I don't count sheep, but blessings, and remain grateful to whoever is in charge of bestowing them. I've rented stuff, owned stuff, lost stuff but mostly, done stuff. I've done a lot and believe that life is about doing things, not about having things. Easy to say, as I have so much in abundance.

I once wondered if I had a snowball's hope in hell of survival – until that snowball gathered momentum, ironically under a hot Australian sun. A three-month working holiday rolled into nearly thirty years, seemingly overnight.

Myself and my life are far from perfect, but I'm closer to accepting that they never will be. I've worked hard to move from working-class to business-class, and learned that money can never buy true class. I've been fortunate to set foot on every continent but now know one need not venture to the ends of the earth to explore new territory. Approaching the homeland of the heart can be just around the corner, in the heartland of home.

Be where you are – otherwise you will miss your life. So true, that Buddhist saying. Relaxing at home for a record seventy-eight airplane-free days, I eventually settled down to read the biography of David Livingstone that my grandfather received as a school prize in Scotland over a hundred years earlier. Stanley, the great explorer, was also an orphan, and took the name of the philanthropist from Wales who adopted him.

Yes, I was technically orphaned twice. But adopted more than once. The first and foremost time was by the most loving parents I could ever have asked for – they will always be Mum and Dad. The second time was by surrogate families and friends. And now I have again been embraced by my adopted country. I adopted Australia and it adopted me. Over a quarter of a century since I first set foot on its golden soil, I have moved from longing to belonging.

Whether Canada's child or Australia's adult, my sense of space and place as a woman in today's world is not confined to neat national borders. From the shoreline of my consciousness to the coastline of my heart, I've found home.

My maternal grandmother, Frida, has no need to fret: "I wonder whatever happened to that baby Trudy gave away?"

That little baby has been blessed to already pack one hundred years into fifty with a suitcase of dreams still open . . . to be filled with memories for tomorrow.

THE END
THE BEGINNING

ACKNOWLEDGEMENTS

Memories and emotions (mine and others') undoubtedly fade and are unconsciously blurred through the inevitable passage of time and re-telling. There may not be such a thing as universal truth to the post-modernists, and certainly my story may seem somewhat unbelievable at times, but the overall essence and integrity of events in this book are nonetheless intact, as far as research and diary entries permit. However, during the course of the storyline, some dates may be slightly out of sequence and the dialogue less precise than Hansard would allow.

In sleepless nights before the final edit, I typed, wondered and worried. Would I forget someone in the "Acknowledgements" – the kindness of a friend or a stranger? Would I look back with embarrassment on what I have written? Would I question the words now indelibly on paper? My values and views formed from 1950–2000 are as clear as the print on the page today, but will they hold true over the test of time? Memories marinate over the years and hopefully become more tender than tough. Just as my view of the world has, thankfully, changed since my teenage diary entries, hopefully I'll continue to mature and see life's ever-unfolding events with increasing clarity.

In telling my story, honesty has been paramount, and sometimes painful for me. By omitting some individuals and ensuring others are included I have tried not to hurt anyone, and I offer my sincere apologies if I've inadvertently done so. The first draft contained many more names and detail but it read a little like a Russian novel.

I am sorry that I can't mention all the special people who've contributed to my life. For editorial purposes, many things seen as important to me were not seen as central to the overall narrative, which was judiciously reduced thanks to the expert editorial skills of Karen Ward and Catherine Hill. I am extremely grateful for their invaluable guidance in helping me to better tell my tale and sometimes in saving me from being seen in public with the literary equivalent of spinach on my teeth!

Also, to the entire teams at Random House Australia and McArthur & Company in Canada. My appreciation goes out to the unsung talents behind the scenes in production, design, sales, marketing, publicity and distribution. And of course to the booksellers . . . and readers.

Thanks to my agent, Sheila Drummond, for believing in the story, and to fellow writers who never wavered in their belief, even when I did – especially Kris Cole, Julie Harris, Margaret Gee, Mark Victor-Hansen and of course Bryce Courtenay. Words are inadequate to express my heartfelt gratitude. They understood more than most that writing a memoir was no gentle jog down memory lane, but rather an endurance marathon; a seemingly never-ending carousel of composition – going round and round, up and down and sometimes seeming to go nowhere fast, despite revision after revision . . .

My love and thanks to all Bachman, DeVrye, Mandeville and Smart extended families; to Trudy for the gift of life; to Harold for the seed; to Mum and Dad (Marg and Henk DeVrye) for the only life I'd known; to Frank, Kay, June,

Jansens, Keddies, Schwanks and Whittles for making me part of their lives and enriching mine.

Thanks to countless other friends, colleagues and clients who have shared my life, but especially to those who were actively involved in this book. To Louise Christiansen, Alice Colwill, Dick and Rie Schipper and Pat Smith for providing family histories; to Val Ball, Joan Bennet, Rosemary Cottrell, Ellie Marx, Fiona Stuart and, of course, Liz Burrows for your feedback and support on the original manuscript. I have valued your candidness and support almost as much as I value your ongoing friendships!

To my extended family of friends throughout the world: *merci, muchas gracias, danke schön, domo arigato, xie xie ni, asante sana* . . . In any language, thank you for your contribution to the mosaic of memoir and here's to sharing future chapters in life's journey of discovery.

Agli-Allan-Amiss-Antonopolous-Antonsen-Appleby-Arends-Baker-Barker-Barnes-Barry-Barton-Bassat-Bath-Baylor-Beal-Beausoleil-Bedal-Bell-Belvin-Benoist-Lucy-Blue-Boezman-Bouris-Brand-Bridge-Broadbent-Brown-Bryant-Burroughs-Butcher-Butler-Cahill-Caldwell-Canfield-Carlisle-Cerezo-Christiansen-Christie-Claxton-Cole-Cool-Coolidge-Corbett-Crosswhite-Crotty-Cudmore-Cullen-McMechan-D'Indy-Darrah-David-Davidson-Day-Delroy-Dixon-Dowse-Doyle-Dreiberg-Drobot-Dunne-Durante-Ebstein-Ebsworth-Edwards-Evans-Farrow-Fitzsimmons-Fletcher-Friedman-Fries-Frieze-Fukushima-Fuller-Fynmore-Galbraith-Gallagher-Gammon-Gett-Gibbons-Gibson-Giles-Gladding-Gold-Goodrich-Goodwin-Gore-Graham-Gray-Greatbatch-Greenwich-Gribble-Gwozdecky-Haddock-Hall-Hallett-Harrison-Hay-Heath-Henderson-Highton-Hillary-Hinch-Hindle-Hodgkinson-Horscroft-Howell-IBM-Idnani-Inglis-Ingrey-Ireland-JacksonJames-Jansen-Johnston-Jones-Katz-Kefford-

Kennedy-King-Kirkwood-Koch-Kolenc-Kooyong Tennis Club-
Kozicki-Lacy-Larsen-Lauterbach-Lawrence-Lawson-Lea-
Leaphart-Lee-Leishman-Lochead-Lothian-Lukianchuk-Lynn-
MacKay-Mackie-Maher-Malone-Malouf-Mangos-Manly Surf Club-
Marbut-Markoff-Markovic-Marks-Martin-Matthews-Matsuzaka-
Mazzatelli-McAuley-McGinnis-McGovern-McKew-McKillop-
McKindley-Mclauchlan-McLean-McLeod-Hill-McRitchie-
Menzies-Merchant-Miles-Miller-Mis-Mitchell-Moss-Moyes-Myer-
Naher-Nayda-Neilson-Neville-Newinger-New South Wales Golf
Club-Newton-Nichols-Ninnes-Noble-Norris-O'Connell-
O'Donahue-O'Neill-O'Regan-Oldcorn-Oldham-Ozaki-Park-
Pearce-Pederson-Pemberton-Pena-Penny-Percy-Perez-Physick-
Potter-Powney-Pressley-Preston-Pringle-Provest-Rallings-Raut-
Reed-Reichenbach-Richards-Richardson-Robertson-Ross-
Routley-Ruzic-Saunders-Scaduto-Schipper-Sheedy-Shrimpton-
Silva-Silverthorne-Simpson-Singleton-Skuse-Smallwood-Smart-
Smith-Spittler-Stanfield-Stewart-Story-Switzwer-Styles-Tacchi-
Tawse-Thomas-Thompson-Thorpe-Toohey-Ueno-Tostevin-
Tritter-Tymson-Ushiyama-VanHeytheyson-Walker-Wares-Watt-
Webb-Webster-Weisner-Weyl-Willet-Williams-Whitehead-
Whitney-Whyte-Wilson-Wood-Wrublewski-Yabsley-Yanik-Yates-
Yellowlees-Zoi

And also, my deep admiration goes out to the caring
individuals within The Salvation Army. A percentage of all
sales from this book will be donated towards helping
those who, on a daily basis, help others who have been
less fortunate than me. Donations can be made to
www.salvationarmy.org.au

LIST OF ILLUSTRATIONS

Photographs follow page 192.